SERIES DIRECTOR

Jayme Adelson-Goldstein

Jenni Currie Santamaria

OXFORD
UNIVERSITY PRESS

OXFORD
UNIVERSITY PRESS

198 Madison Avenue
New York, NY 10016 USA

Great Clarendon Street, Oxford OX2 6DP UK

Oxford University Press is a department of the University of Oxford. It furthers the University's objective of excellence in research, scholarship, and education by publishing worldwide in

Oxford New York

Auckland Cape Town Dar es Salaam Hong Kong Karachi Kuala Lumpur Madrid Melbourne Mexico City Nairobi New Delhi Shanghai Taipei Toronto

With offices in

Argentina Austria Brazil Chile Czech Republic France Greece Guatemala Hungary Italy Japan Poland Portugal Singapore South Korea Switzerland Thailand Turkey Ukraine Vietnam

OXFORD and OXFORD ENGLISH are registered trademarks of Oxford University Press

Library of Congress Cataloging-in-Publication Data
Adelson-Goldstein, Jayme.
Step Forward : language for everyday life / series director: Jayme Adelson-Goldstein; intro.: Jenni Currie Santamaria
p. cm.
Includes index.
ISBN 978-0-19-439843-5 (pbk. : student bk : introductory level) 1. English language–Textbooks for foreign speakers. 2. Adult education. I. Santamaria, Jenni Currie. II. Title.
PE1128.A34 2007.
428.2'4–dc22
2007016227

Editorial Director: Sally Yagan
Senior Publishing Manager: Stephanie Karras
Head of Project and Development Editors: Karen Horton
Managing Editor: Sharon Sargent
Associate Editors: Meredith Stoll, Olga Christopoulos
Design Project Manager: Maj-Britt Hagsted
Project Manager: Allison Harm
Production Layout Artist: Julie Armstrong
Production Manager: Shanta Persaud
Manufacturing Coordinator: Faye Wang
Packager: Bill Smith Studio

Student Book:
ISBN: 978 0 19 439843 5

Student Book with CD-ROM:
ISBN: 978 0 19 439652 3

Student Book as pack component:
ISBN: 978 0 19 439657 8

Audio CD-ROM as pack component:
ISBN: 978 0 19 439662 2

Printed in China

20 19 18 17 16

This book is printed on paper from certified and well-managed sources.

ACKNOWLEDGMENTS

Cover photograph: Corbis/Punchstock
Back cover photograph: Brian Rose

Illustrations by: Shawn Banner, p. 21, p. 49, p. 60, p. 84, p. 97, p. 112, p. 124 (bottom), p. 125 (top), p. 144; Barbara Bastian, p. 44, p. 118; Kenneth Batelman, p. 29, p. 38, p. 65, p. 89, p. 110, p. 131; John Batten, p. 23, p. 34, p. 54, p. 70, p. 102, p. 109, p. 114, p. 138; Kathy Baxendale, p. 32, p. 36, p. 100, p. 105, p. 111, p.128; Bill Smith Studio, p. 4; Annie Bissett, p. 123 (bottom); Arlene Boehm, p. 2, p. 10, p. 45, p. 66, p. 89, p. 101, p. 148; Kevin Brown, p. 7, p. 37, p. 42, p. 88, p. 90, p. 124 (top and middle), p. 130, p. 135; Gary Bullock, p. 9, p. 33, p. 57; Richard Carbajal, p. 22, p. 41, p. 49, p. 63, p. 100, p. 111, p. 135; Laurie A. Conley, p. 30, p. 78, p. 141, p. 150; Mona Daly, p. 61; Bill Dickson, p. 24, p. 58, p. 82, p. 85, p. 112, p. 121, p. 142; Jody Emery, p. 40, p. 62, p. 75, p. 98, p. 113, p. 123 (top), p. 137; Colin Hayes, p. 4, p. 26, p. 41, p. 86, p. 101, p. 134; Kevin Hopgood, p. 14, p. 31, p. 62, p. 91, p. 127, p. 146; Jay Mazhar, p. 6, p. 86, p. 106, p. 110, p. 134; Karen Minot, p. 125 (middle); Marc Mones, p. 11, p. 25, p. 35, p. 76, p. 107, p. 136; Jay Montgomery, p. 116; Terry Paczko, p. 56, p. 63, p. 80, p. 104, p. 177, p. 138; Pamorama.com, p. 5, p. 7, p. 12, p. 13, p. 39, p. 71, p. 132, p. 136; Geo Parkin, p. 20, p. 21, p. 38, p. 55, p. 79, p. 115, p. 122, p. 139; Roger Penwill, p. 19, p. 43, p. 67, p. 103, p. 151; Pixelation Digital Imagery, p. 2, p. 5, p. 7, p. 17, p. 28, p. 29, p. 41, p. 53, p. 64, p. 65, p. 77, p. 89, p. 95, p. 99, p. 111, p. 137, p. 143, p. 147, p. 149; Karen Pritchett, p. 8, p. 68, p. 92, p. 93; Marthe Roberts, p. 48, p. 52, p. 87, p. 113; Don Stewart, p. 69; William Waitzman, p. 16, p. 18, p. 46, p. 64, p. 94, p. 112, p. 120, p. 135; Graham White, p. 126; Simon Williams, p. 60, p. 81, p. 129, p. 132, p. 140; Ron Zalme, p. 26, p. 50, p. 52, p. 72, p. 74, p. 88, p. 93, p. 98, p. 108.

Photographs: Tony Anderson/Getty Images, p. 73; Christine Balderas/iStockphoto, p. 12 (center right), p. 17 (center left), (top right), p. 30; Big House Productions/Getty Images, p. 144; Blend Images/Alamy, p. 12 (bottom left), p. 73; Bloomimage/Corbis, p. 30; ©Brand X Pictures/Alamy, p. 64 (bottom right); Keith Brofsky/Getty Images, p. 148; Bubbles Photolibrary/Alamy, p. 96 (bottom right); Ron Chapple/Jupiter Images, p. 83; Comstock Images/Jupiter Images, p. 95; Kitt Cooper-Smith/Alamy, p. 40; Corbis/Jupiter Images, p. 3 (center left); Dennis Kitchen Photography, p. 3 (top right), (center right), (bottom center), p. 17 (bottom left), p. 96, p. 145; Mary Kate Denny/ PhotoEdit, p. 148; Kevin Dodge/Corbis, p. 76; Mark Downey/Getty Images, p. 144; Dynamic Graphics, Inc./Jupiter Images, p. 3 (bottom left); Christoph Ermel/ iStockphoto, p. 40; FredS/iStockphoto, p. 12 (top right); Getty Images/Blend Images, p. 12 (bottom right), p. 75; Jaume Gual/age footstock, p. 30; Hill Street Studios/ age footstock, p. 144; Jack Hollingsworth/Getty Images, p. 47; Zigy Kaluzny/Getty Images, p. 148; Bonnie Kamin/PhotoEdit, p. 40; I and I/ Masterfile, p. 75; Jupiter Images, p. 143; Jutta Klee/Corbis, p. 73; Ruediger Knoblock/A. B./zefa/Corbis, p. 133; Mark Leibowitz/Masterfile. p. 73; Robert Manella/Comstock/Corbis, p. 76; Felicia Martinez/ PhotoEdit, p. 17 (top left); Gib Martinez/Alamy, p. 40; Masterfile/Royalty Free, p. 76; ©Neil McAllister/Alamy, p. 64 (bottom left); Ryan McVay/Getty Images, p. 23, p. 35, p. 119; Amos Morgan/Getty Images, p. 10; Paul Morley/Shutterstock, p. 3 (top left); Gala Narezo/Getty Images, p. 75; Richard T. Nowitz/Corbis, p. 76; Gabe Palmer/Alamy, p. 12 (top left); Michael N. Paras/age footstock, p. 75; Jose Luis Pelaez Inc./Jupiter Images, p. 75; Barbara Penoyar/Getty Images, p. 59, p. 131; Michael Poehlman/Getty Images, p. 96 (bottom left); Mike Powell, p. 30; Lorne Resnick/age footstock, p. 144; Royalty-Free/Corbis, p. 75; Bob Thomas/Getty Images, p. 12 (center left); T Stock Free/Jupiter Images, p. 107; Pierre Tremblay/Masterfile, p. 148; David Young-Wolff/ PhotoEdit, p. 3 (bottom right).

We gratefully acknowledge the collaborative spirit, dedication and skill of the *Step Forward Intro* editorial and design team: Stephanie Karras, Sharon Sargent, Ellen Northcutt, Meredith Stoll, Meg Araneo, Maj-Britt Hagsted and Bill Smith Studio. We also want to express our deep appreciation to our students and colleagues who inspire us on a daily basis.

Jenni Currie Santamaria

Jayme Adelson-Goldstein

Oceans of gratitude to Sharon Sargent, whose dedication to "getting it right" can be seen on every page of this book, and to Jayme Adelson-Goldstein for her insightful leadership.

For Tony and Amaya, my bedrock.

–Jenni Currie Santamaria

My heartfelt thanks to the wondrous Jennie Currie Santamaria whose commitment to the learner never falters. I also thank Kathy Santopietro Weddel for her many insights and "level vigilance."

–Jayme

ACKNOWLEDGMENTS

Curriculum Consultant
Kathleen Santopietro Weddel

Northern Colorado Professional Development Center, Longmont, CO

The Publisher and Series Director would like to acknowledge the following individuals for their invaluable input during the development of this series:

Robert Anzelde Triton College, River Grove, IL

Patricia Bell Lake Technical Center, Eustis, FL

Curtis Bonney North Seattle Community College, Seattle, WA

Ana Patricia Castro Harvest English Institute, Newark, NJ

Edwidge Bryant University of North Florida, Jacksonville, FL

Julie Caspersen Old Marshall Adult Education Center, Sacramento, CA

Bart Chaney Dallas Independent School District, Dallas, TX

Kathleen Fallon Clackamas Community College, Oregon City, OR

Cheryl L. Fuentes ESOL Consultant, Alexandria, VA

Carol Garcia College of DuPage, Glen Ellyn, IL

Ann Jackson Mid Florida Tech, Orlando, FL

Gaye Kendall Harris County Department of Education, Houston, TX

Jennifer Martin Baldwin Park Adult and Community Education, Baldwin Park, CA

Suzi Monti Community College of Baltimore County, Baltimore, MD

Rob Patton Communities in Schools—Central Texas, Austin, TX

Linda A. Pelc New York City Department of Education, New York, NY

Marvina Pérez Hooper Lake Technical Center, Eustis, FL

David L. Red Fairfax County Public Schools, Falls Church, VA

Barbara Sample Spring Institute for Intercultural Learning, Denver, CO

Denise Selleck City College of San Francisco—Alemany, San Francisco, CA

Esther Shupe Brookdale Community College, Lincroft, NJ

Margaret B. Silver English Language and Literacy Center, Clayton, MO

Melissa Singler Cape Fear Community College, Wilmington, NC

Betty Stone Somerville Center for Adult Learning Experiences, Somerville, MA

Maliheh Vafai Overfelt Adult Center, San Jose, CA

Cynthia Wiseman Borough of Manhattan Community College, New York, NY

We would also like to thank the following students in the Fall 2006 Beginning Literacy Class at ABC Adult School in Cerritos, CA.

Emelia Alvarez
Virej Benyamin
Liang-Ming Chen
Li Yu Chen
Yang Ja Choi
Soon Hee Chong
Chi-Yu Chou Chiu
Lotai Chung
Somath Oeurn Dell
Adulfo Garcia
Kyung Soon Han
Shu-yeh Hsu
Hee Sik Im
Jin Taek Jung
Jung Soon Jung
Jin Shik Kim
Kil Su Kim
Soon Hi Kim
Soon Yi Kim
In Taek Lee
Jung So Lee
Myung Yong Lee
Ok Ja Lee
Tae Soo Lee
Wan Chen Lee
Phourngmalay Long
Vanny Long
David Lopez
Maria Luisa Lopez
Kai Pang Ng
Ga Young Oh
Oknyu Park
Sun Soon Park
Sung Ja Park
Young Sun Park
Norma Talavera Riviera
Zaihong Shen
Angelica Torres
Min Chen Wang
Tzu Tseng Wang
Keum Soon Woo
Young Ja Yoo

TABLE OF CONTENTS

Listening & Speaking	CASAS Life Skills Competencies	Standardized Student Syllabi/LCPs	SCANS Competencies	EFF Content Standards
• Listen to basic classroom directions • Say and spell names • Listen and say telephone numbers • Listen for plurals • Introduce yourself • Talk about the classroom	**L1:** 0.1.2 **L2:** 0.12, 0.1.5, 6.0.1 **L3:** 0.1.2, 0.1.4, 0.1.5	• **L1:** 1.15.07, 1.17.01, 1.17.02 • **L2:** 1.06.01 • **L3:** 1.05.01, 1.15.02	Most SCANS are incorporated into this unit, with an emphasis on: • Participating as a Member of a Team • Acquiring and Evaluating Information • Interpreting and Communicating Information • Reading • Seeing Things in the Mind's Eye • Speaking	Most EFFs are incorporated into this unit, with an emphasis on: • Listen actively • Observing critically • Cooperate with others • Speaking so others can understand • Reading with understanding
• Listen to classroom directions • Talk about the classroom • Give personal information • Practice social conversations • Listen for *a* or *an* **Pronunciation:** • Differentiate between *i* and *e*	**L1:** 0.1.2, 0.1.5, 7.4.5 **L2:** 0.1.2, 0.1.4, 0.2.1 **L3:** 0.1.2, 7.4.7 **L4:** 0.1.2, 0.1.4, 0.2.1, 7.4.7 **L5:** 0.1.2 **RE:** 0.1.2, 0.1.5, 7.4.5, 7.4.7	**L1:** 1.15.07, 1.15.08 **L2:** 1.15.02 **L3:** 1.15.06, 1.15.08, 1.16.01 **L4:** 1.05.01, 1.15.02, 1.15.08, 1.17.02 **L5:** 1.15.07, 1.15.08, 1.16.09 **RE:** 1.15.07, 1.16.01	Most SCANS are incorporated into this unit, with an emphasis on: • Participating as a member of a team • Interpreting and communicating information • Seeing things in the mind's eye • Knowing how to learn • Problem solving • Listening • Reading	Most EFFs are incorporated into this unit, with an emphasis on: • Listening actively • Speaking so others can understand • Cooperating with others • Reading with understanding • Solving problems and making decisions • Observing critically
• Talk about feelings • Listen for personal information • Respond to personal information questions • Express regret **Pronunciation:** • Listen for syllables	**L1:** 0.1.2, 0.1.5, 7.4.5 **L2:** 0.1.2, 0.1.4, 0.2.1 **L3:** 0.1.2, 7.4.7 **L4:** 0.1.2, 0.1.4, 0.2.1, 7.4.7 **L5:** 0.1.2, 0.2.2, 7.4.7 **RE:** 0.1.2, 0.1.5, 7.3.1, 7.3.2, 7.4.5	**L1:** 1.15.02 **L2:** 1.15.02 **L3:** 1.15.06, 1.15.08, 1.16.11 **L4:** 1.05.03, 1.15.08 **L5:** 1.05.02, 1.15.05, 1.15.08 **RE:** 1.16.11	Most SCANS are incorporated into this unit, with an emphasis on: • Participating as a member of a team • Interpreting and communicating information • Seeing things in the mind's eye • Knowing how to learn • Problem solving • Listening • Reading	Most EFFs are incorporated into this unit, with an emphasis on: • Listening actively • Speaking so others can understand • Cooperating with others • Reading with understanding • Solving problems and making decisions • Reflecting and evaluating • Learning through research • Observing critically
• Listen for *a.m.* and *p.m.* • Listen for and ask about the time • Ask for information about places in the community **Pronunciation:** • *Yes/No* question intonation	**L1:** 0.1.2, 0.1.5, 2.3.1, 7.4.5 **L2:** 0.1.2, 0.2.1, 7.4.7 **L3:** 0.1.2, 0.1.4, 7.4.7 **L4:** 0.1.2, 0.1.4, 0.2.1, 7.4.7 **L5:** 0 .1.2, 0.1.5, 2.2.4, 7.4.7 **RE:** 0.1.2, 0.1.5, 7.3.1, 7.3.2, 7.4.5, 7.4.7	**L1:** 1.08.02, 1.15.07 **L2:** 1.15.02 **L3:** 1.15.08 **L4:** 1.05.01, 1.15.08 **L5:** 1.15.08 **RE:** 1.15.08	Most SCANS are incorporated into this unit, with an emphasis on: • Participating as a member of a team • Interpreting and communicating information • Knowing how to learn • Problem solving • Time • Seeing things in the mind's eye • Listening • Reading	Most EFFs are incorporated into this unit, with an emphasis on: • Listening actively • Speaking so others can understand • Cooperating with others • Reading with understanding • Solving problems and making decisions • Convey ideas in writing • Learning through research

Unit	Life Skills & Civics Competencies	Vocabulary	Grammar	Critical Thinking & Math Concepts	Reading & Writing
Unit 4 **What day is it?** **page 44**	• Identify days, months, years, and dates • Recognize abbreviations for days of the week • Respond to information questions • Say goodbye appropriately • Read a calendar	• Days, months, years, and dates • Ordinal numbers	• *On* with days • *At* with times • Information questions with *when, what time,* and *where*	• Interpret a calendar **Problem solving:** • Determine what to do when late	• Read and write about the months • Read a birthday invitation • Interpret a school calendar
Unit 5 **How much is it?** **page 56**	• Talk about prices • Interpret price tags • Identify methods of payment • Read a simple bill • Read and complete a check	• Money • Clothes • Methods of payment	• *This* and *that* • *These* and *those*	• Interpret price tags **Real-life math:** • Compute 50% off **Problem solving:** • Decide what to do when short on cash	• Read and write about shopping • Write sentences using *this, that, these,* and *those* • Read a simple bill • Read and complete a check
Unit 6 **That's My Son** **page 68**	• Identify family members • Describe family members and marital status • Identify school requirements • Interpret a note from a teacher	• Family members • Marital titles • The U.S. school system	• Possessive adjectives • Simple present statements with *live*	• Interpret a chart **Real-life math:** • Convert inches to feet **Problem solving:** • Decide how a parent should respond to a child who receives a failing grade	• Read and write about family members and friends • Write statements in the simple present • Read about schools in the U.S. • Interpret a note from a teacher

Listening & Speaking	CASAS Life Skills Competencies	Standardized Student Syllabi/LCPs	SCANS Competencies	EFF Content Standards
• Listen for days, months, years, and dates • Talk about the days of the week • Respond to information questions • Say goodbye appropriately **Pronunciation:** • Differentiate between *t* and *th*	**L1:** 0.1.2, 0.1.5, 7.4.5 **L2:** 0.1.2, 7.4.7 **L3:** 0.1.2, 0.2.3, 7.4.7 **L4:** 0.1.2, 0.1.4, 0.1.5, 7.4.7 **L5:** 0.1.2, 0.1.5, 7.4.7 **RE:** 0.1.2, 0.1.5, 7.3.1, 7.3.2, 7.4.5, 7.4.7	• **L1:** 1.05.01, 1.15.07 • **L2:** 1.05.02, 1.15.08 • **L3:** 1.15.08, 1.16.08 • **L4:** 1.05.01, 1.15.08, 1.17.02 • **L5:** 1.08.01, 1.15.08 • **RE:** 1.15.08, 1.16.08	Most SCANS are incorporated into this unit, with an emphasis on: • Participating as a member of a team • Interpreting and communicating information • Seeing things in the mind's eye • Knowing how to learn • Problem solving • Listening • Reading	Most EFFs are incorporated into this unit, with an emphasis on: • Listening actively • Speaking so others can understand • Cooperating with others • Reading with understanding • Solving problems and making decisions • Observing critically • Reflecting and evaluating • Conveying ideas in writing • Learning through research
• Listen for and talk about prices • Listen for change amounts	**L1:** 0.1.2, 0.1.5, 7.4.5, 7.4.7 **L2:** 0.1.2 **L3:** 0.1.2, 7.4.7 **L4:** 0.1.2, 6.2.3, 7.4.7 **L5:** 0.1.2, 7.4.7 **RE:** 0.1.2, 0.1.5, 7.3.1, 7.3.2, 7.4.5, 7.4.7	**L1:** 1.08.05, 1.15.08 **L2:** 1.08.05, 1.11.01 **L3:** 1.15.06, 1.15.08 **L4:** 1.08.05, 1.11.01, 1.11.03, 1.15.08 **L5:** 1.08.07, 1.15.08 **RE:** 1.15.08	Most SCANS are incorporated into this unit, with an emphasis on: • Participating as a member of a team • Interpreting and communicating information • Arithmetic/Mathematics • Problem solving • Money • Listening • Seeing things in the mind's eye • Reading	Most EFFs are incorporated into this unit, with an emphasis on: • Listening actively • Using math to solve problems and communicate • Cooperating with others • Reading with understanding • Solving problems and making decisions • Observing critically • Conveying ideas in writing • Reflecting and evaluating
• Talk about family members and friends • Listen for marital status and titles	**L1:** 0.1.2, 0.1.5, 0.1.6, 7.4.5 **L2:** 0.1.2, 7.4.7 **L3:** 0.1.2, 7.4.7 **L4:** 0.1.2, 0.1.4, 6.6.4, 7.4.7 **L5:** 7.4.7 **RE:** 0.1.2, 0.1.5, 7.3.1, 7.3.2, 7.4.5, 7.4.7	**L1:** 1.14.01, 1.15.07 **L2:** 1.14.01, 1.15.08 **L3:** 1.15.06, 1.15.08, 1.16.10 **L4:** 1.15.08 **L5:** 1.15.08 **RE:** 1.15.08	Most SCANS are incorporated into this unit, with an emphasis on: • Participating as a member of a team • Interpreting and communicating information • Knowing how to learn • Problem solving • Arithmetic/Mathematics • Listening • Seeing things in the mind's eye • Reading	Most EFFs are incorporated into this unit, with an emphasis on: • Listening actively • Cooperating with others • Reading with understanding • Solving problems and making decisions • Using math to solve problems and communicate • Conveying ideas in writing • Reflecting and evaluating

Listening & Speaking	CASAS Life Skills Competencies	Standardized Student Syllabi/LCPs	SCANS Competencies	EFF Content Standards
• Describe food preferences • Ask for help in a store • Listen for prices	**L1:** 0.1.2, 0.1.5, 7.4.5 **L2:** 0.1.2, 7.4.7 **L3:** 0.1.2, 7.4.7 **L4:** 0.1.2, 0.1.4, 0.1.5, 6.1.3 **L5:** 7.4.7 **RE:** 0.1.2, 0.1.5, 7.3.1, 7.3.2, 7.4.5, 7.4.7	**L1:** 1.07.06 **L2:** 1.15.08 **L3:** 1.15.06, 1.15.08, 1.16.02 **L4:** 1.05.01 **L5:** 1.15.08 **RE:** 1.15.08	Most SCANS are incorporated into this unit, with an emphasis on: • Participating as a member of a team • Interpreting and communicating information • Seeing things in the mind's eye • Arithmetic/Mathematics • Problem solving • Listening • Reading	Most EFFs are incorporated into this unit, with an emphasis on: • Listening actively • Speaking so others can understand • Using math to solve problems and communicate • Reading with understanding • Solving problems and making decisions • Conveying ideas in writing • Learning through research • Reflecting and evaluating
• Talk about parts of the body • Listen for and check problems on a medical history form • Make medical appointments • Listen for medical appointment information **Pronunciation:** • Differentiate between *a* sounds	**L1:** 0.1.2, 0.1.5, 7.4.5 **L2:** 0.1.2, 3.1.1, 3.2.1 **L3:** 0.1.2 **L4:** 0.1.2, 0.1.4 **L5:** 3.3.1, 7.4.7 **RE:** 0.1.2, 0.1.5, 7.3.1, 7.3.2, 7.4.5, 7.4.7	**L1:** 1.07.01, 1.15.07 **L2:** 1.07.02 **L3:** 1.07.02, 1.15.06 **L4:** 1.17.01 **L5:** 1.07.04, 1.15.08 **RE:** 1.15.08	Most SCANS are incorporated into this unit, with an emphasis on: • Participating as a member of a team • Interpreting and communicating information • Seeing things in the mind's eye • Knowing how to learn • Problem solving • Listening • Arithmetic/Mathematics • Reading	Most EFFs are incorporated into this unit, with an emphasis on: • Listening actively • Speaking so others can understand • Cooperating with others • Reading with understanding • Solving problems and making decisions • Conveying ideas in writing • Learning through research • Reflecting and evaluating
• Talk about colors • Listen for clothing sizes and prices • State weather conditions	**L1:** 0.1.2, 0.1.5, 7.4.5 **L2:** 0.1.2, 7.4.7 **L3:** 0.1.2, 7.4.7 **L4:** 0.1.2, 1.2.1, 6.2.1, 7.4.7 **L5:** 2.3.3, 7.4.7 **RE:** 0.1.2, 0.1.5, 7.3.1, 7.3.2, 7.4.5, 7.4.7	**L1:** 1.15.07 **L2:** 1.15.08 **L3:** 1.15.06, 1.15.08, 1.16.02 **L4:** 1.11.03, 1.11.04, 1.15.08 **L5:** 1.15.06, 1.15.08 **RE:** 1.15.08	Most SCANS are incorporated into this unit, with an emphasis on: • Participating as a member of a team • Interpreting and communicating information • Applying technology to task • Arithmetic/Mathematics • Problem solving • Seeing things in the mind's eye • Listening • Reading	Most EFFs are incorporated into this unit, with an emphasis on: • Listening actively • Using math to solve problems and communicate • Cooperating with others • Using information and communication technology • Solving problems and making decisions • Conveying ideas in writing • Learning through research • Reflecting and evaluating

Listening & Speaking	CASAS Life Skills Competencies	Standardized Student Syllabi/LCPs	SCANS Competencies	EFF Content Standards
• Talk about places in a community • Listen for locations • Ask for and give locations	**L1:** 0.1.2, 0.1.5, 7.4.5 **L2:** 0.1.2, 1.1.3 **L3:** 7.4.7 **L4:** 0.1.2, 0.1.4, 1.1.3, 6.1.1 **L5:** 0.1.5, 2.1.2, 7.4.7 **RE:** 0.1.2, 0.1.5, 7.3.1, 7.3.2, 7.4.5, 7.4.7	**L1:** 1.15.07 **L2:** 1.09.03 **L3:** 1.15.06, 1.15.08 **L4:** 1.09.03 **L5:** 1.12.02, 1.15.08 **RE:** 1.15.08	Most SCANS are incorporated into this unit, with an emphasis on: • Participating as a member of a team • Interpreting and communicating information • Seeing things in the mind's eye • Knowing how to learn • Problem solving • Listening • Arithmetic/Mathematics • Reading	Most EFFs are incorporated into this unit, with an emphasis on: • Listening actively • Speaking so others can understand • Cooperating with others • Reading with understanding • Solving problems and making decisions • Conveying ideas in writing • Learning through research • Using math to solve problems and communicate • Reflecting and evaluating
• Talk about objects in the home • Listen for information about things in the home • Ask about a home for rent • Listen for housing information	**L1:** 0.1.2, 0.1.5, 7.4.5 **L2:** 0.1.2 **L3:** 0.1.2, 7.4.7 **L4:** 0.1.2, 0.1.4, 1.4.2, 6.1.1 **L5:** 1.4.2, 7.4.7 **RE:** 0.1.2, 0.1.5, 7.3.1, 7.3.2, 7.4.5, 7.4.7	**L1:** 1.15.07 **L2:** 1.05.02 **L3:** 1.15.06, 1.15.08, 1.16.10 **L4:** 1.11.08 **L5:** 1.11.08, 1.15.08 **RE:** 1.15.08	Most SCANS are incorporated into this unit, with an emphasis on: • Participating as a member of a team • Interpreting and communicating information • Seeing things in the mind's eye • Knowing how to learn • Problem solving • Listening • Arithmetic/Mathematics • Reading	Most EFFs are incorporated into this unit, with an emphasis on: • Listening actively • Speaking so others can understand • Cooperating with others • Reading with understanding • Solving problems and making decisions • Conveying ideas in writing • Learning through research • Using math to solve problems and communicate • Reflecting and evaluating
• Talk about jobs • Listen for information about job skills • Respond to basic job-interview questions • Listen to a work schedule **Pronunciation:** • Differentiate between *can* and *can't*	**L1:** 0.1.2, 0.1.5, 7.4.5 **L2:** 0.1.2, 4.1.8 **L3:** 0.1.2 **L4:** 0.1.2, 0.2.1 **L5:** 4.1.3, 4.1.8, 7.4.7 **RE:** 0.1.2, 0.1.5, 7.3.1, 7.3.2, 7.4.5, 7.4.7	**L1:** 1.15.07 **L2:** 1.05.02 **L3:** 1.15.06 **L4:** 1.15.02, 1.17.02 **L5:** 1.01.07, 1.15.08 **RE:** 1.15.08	Most SCANS are incorporated into this unit, with an emphasis on: • Participating as a member of a team • Interpreting and communicating information • Seeing things in the mind's eye • Knowing how to learn • Problem solving • Listening	Most EFFs are incorporated into this unit, with an emphasis on: • Listening actively • Speaking so others can understand • Cooperating with others • Reading with understanding • Solving problems and making decisions • Conveying ideas in writing • Learning through research • Reflecting and evaluating

A Word or Two About Reading Introductions to Textbooks

Teaching professionals rarely read a book's introduction. Instead, we flip through the book's pages, using the pictures, topics, and exercises to determine whether the book matches our learners' needs and our teaching style. We scan the reading passages, conversations, writing tasks, and grammar charts to judge the authenticity and accuracy of the text. At a glance, we assess how easy it would be to manage the pair work, group activities, evaluations, and application tasks.

This Introduction, however, also offers valuable information for the teacher. Because you've read this far, I encourage you to read a little further to learn how *Step Forward's* key concepts, components, and multilevel applications will help you help your learners.

Step Forward's Key Concepts

Step Forward is...

- the instructional backbone for single-level and multilevel classrooms.
- a standards-based, performance-based, and topic-based series for low-beginning through high-intermediate learners.
- a source for ready-made, four-skill lesson plans that address the skills our learners need in their workplace, civic, personal, and academic lives.
- a collection of learner-centered, communicative English-language practice activities.

The classroom is a remarkable place. *Step Forward* respects the depth of experience and knowledge that learners bring to the learning process. At the same time, *Step Forward* recognizes that learners' varied proficiencies, goals, interests, and educational backgrounds create instructional challenges for teachers.

To ensure that our learners leave each class having made progress toward their language and life goals, *Step Forward* works from these key concepts:

- **The wide spectrum of learners' needs makes using materials that support multilevel instruction essential.** *Step Forward* works with single-level and multilevel classes.
- **Learners' prior knowledge is a valuable teaching tool.** Prior knowledge questions appear in every *Step Forward* lesson.
- **Learning objectives are the cornerstone of instruction.** Each *Step Forward* lesson focuses on an objective that derives from identified learner needs, correlates to state and federal standards, and connects to a meaningful communication task. Progress toward the objective is evaluated at the end of the lesson.
- **Vocabulary, grammar and pronunciation skills play an essential role in language learning. They provide learners with the tools needed to achieve life skill, civics, workplace, and academic competencies.** *Step Forward* includes strong vocabulary and grammar strands and features pronunciation and math lesson extensions in each unit.
- **Effective instruction requires a variety of instructional techniques and strategies to engage learners.** Techniques such as Early Production Questioning, Focused Listening, Total Physical Response (TPR), Cooperative Learning, and Problem Solving are embedded in the *Step Forward* series, along with grouping and classroom management strategies.

The *Step Forward* Program

The *Step Forward* program has five levels:

- Intro: pre-beginning
- Book 1: low-beginning
- Book 2: high-beginning
- Book 3: low-intermediate
- Book 4: intermediate to high-intermediate

Each level of *Step Forward* correlates to *The Oxford Picture Dictionary*. For pre-literacy learners, *The Basic Oxford Picture Dictionary Literacy Program* provides a flexible, needs-based approach to literacy instruction. Once learners develop literacy skills, they will be able to transition seamlessly into *Step Forward Student Book Introductory Level.*

Each *Step Forward* level includes the following components:

Step Forward Student Book

A collection of clear, engaging, four-skill lessons based on meaningful learning objectives.

Step Forward Audio Program

The recorded vocabulary, focused listening, conversations, pronunciation, and reading materials from the *Step Forward Student Book.*

Step Forward Step-By-Step Lesson Plans with Multilevel Grammar and Literacy Exercises CD-ROM

An instructional planning resource with interleaved *Step Forward Student Book* pages, featuring multilevel teaching strategies and teaching tips, and a CD-ROM of printable multilevel grammar and literacy practice.

Step Forward Workbook

Practice exercises for independent work in the classroom or as homework.

Step Forward Multilevel Activity Book

Photocopiable communicative practice activities and over 300 picture cards; lesson materials that work equally well in single-level or multilevel settings.

Step Forward Test Generator CD-ROM with ExamView® Assessment Suite

Hundreds of multiple choice and life-skill oriented test items for each *Step Forward Student Book*.

Step Forward Introductory Level also includes:

Step Forward Literacy Reproducible Book

Photocopiable fundamental skills practice for literacy-level students placed in the beginning classroom.

Multilevel Applications of *Step Forward*

All the *Step Forward* program components support multilevel instruction.

Step Forward is so named because it helps learners "step forward" toward their language and life goals, no matter where they start.

Regardless of level, all learners need materials that bolster comprehension with an appropriate amount of challenge. This makes multilevel materials an instructional necessity in most classrooms.

Each *Step Forward* lesson provides the following multilevel elements:

- **a general topic or competency area** that works across levels. This supports the concept that members of the class community need to feel connected, despite their differing abilities.
- **clear, colorful visuals and realia** that provide pre-level and on-level support during introduction, presentation and practice exercises, as well as prompts for higher-level questions and exercises. In addition, *Step Forward* correlates to *The Oxford Picture Dictionary* so that teachers can use the visuals and vocabulary from *The Oxford Picture Dictionary* to support and expand upon each lesson.
- **learner-centered practice exercises** that can be used with same-level or mixed-level pairs or small groups. *Step Forward* exercises are broken down to their simplest steps. Once the exercise has been modeled, learners can usually conduct the exercises themselves.
- **pre-level, on-level, and higher-level objectives for each lesson and the multilevel strategies** necessary to carry out the lesson. These objectives are featured in the *Step-By-Step Lesson Plans*.
- **the *Step Forward Workbook* and *Multilevel Grammar and Literacy Exercises CD-ROM* provide excellent "wait time" activities** for learners who complete an exercise early, thus solving a real issue in the multilevel class.
- **a variety of pair, whole class, and small group activities** in the *Step Forward Multilevel Activity Book*. These activities are perfect for same-level and mixed-level grouping.
- **customizable evaluation exercises** in the *Step Forward Test Generator CD-ROM with ExamView® Assessment Suite*. These exercises make it possible to create evaluations specific to each level in the class.

Professional Development

As instructors, we need to reflect on second language acquisition in order to build a repertoire of effective instructional strategies. The *Step Forward Professional Development Program* provides research-based teaching strategies, tasks, and activities for single- and multilevel classes.

About Writing an ESL Series

It's collaborative! *Step Forward* is the product of dialogs with hundreds of teachers and learners. The dynamic quality of language instruction makes it important to keep this dialog alive. As you use this book in your classes, I invite you to contact me or any member of the *Step Forward* authorial team with your questions or comments.

Jayme Adelson-Goldstein

Jayme Adelson-Goldstein, Series Director
Stepforwardteam.us@oup.com

Step Forward: All you need to ensure your learners' success. All the *Step Forward Student Books* follow this format.

LESSON 1: VOCABULARY teaches key words and phrases relevant to the unit topic, and provides conversation practice using the target vocabulary.

New vocabulary is introduced through vibrant art and listening texts.

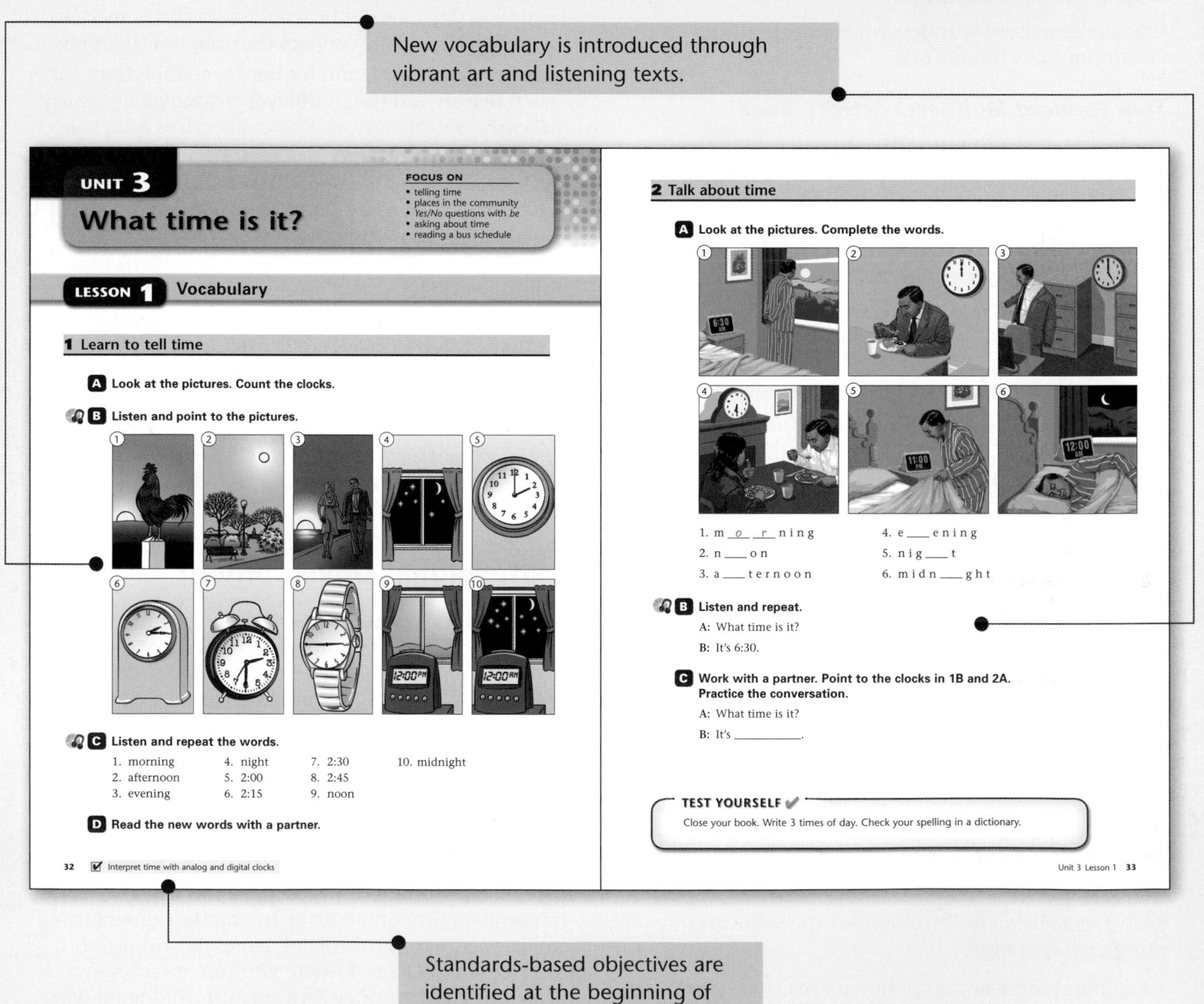

UNIT 3

What time is it?

FOCUS ON
- telling time
- places in the community
- *Yes/No* questions with *be*
- asking about time
- reading a bus schedule

LESSON 1 Vocabulary

1 Learn to tell time

A Look at the pictures. Count the clocks.

B Listen and point to the pictures.

C Listen and repeat the words.

1. morning
2. afternoon
3. evening
4. night
5. 2:00
6. 2:15
7. 2:30
8. 2:45
9. noon
10. midnight

D Read the new words with a partner.

32 Interpret time with analog and digital clocks

2 Talk about time

A Look at the pictures. Complete the words.

1. m _o_ _r_ n i n g
2. n ___ o n
3. a ___ t e r n o o n
4. e ___ e n i n g
5. n i g ___ t
6. m i d n ___ g h t

B Listen and repeat.

A: What time is it?
B: It's 6:30.

C Work with a partner. Point to the clocks in 1B and 2A. Practice the conversation.

A: What time is it?
B: It's ___________.

TEST YOURSELF ✓
Close your book. Write 3 times of day. Check your spelling in a dictionary.

Unit 3 Lesson 1 33

Standards-based objectives are identified at the beginning of every lesson for quick reference.

LESSON 2: LIFE STORIES expands on vocabulary learned in Lesson 1 and furthers learners' understanding through reading and writing about a life skills topic.

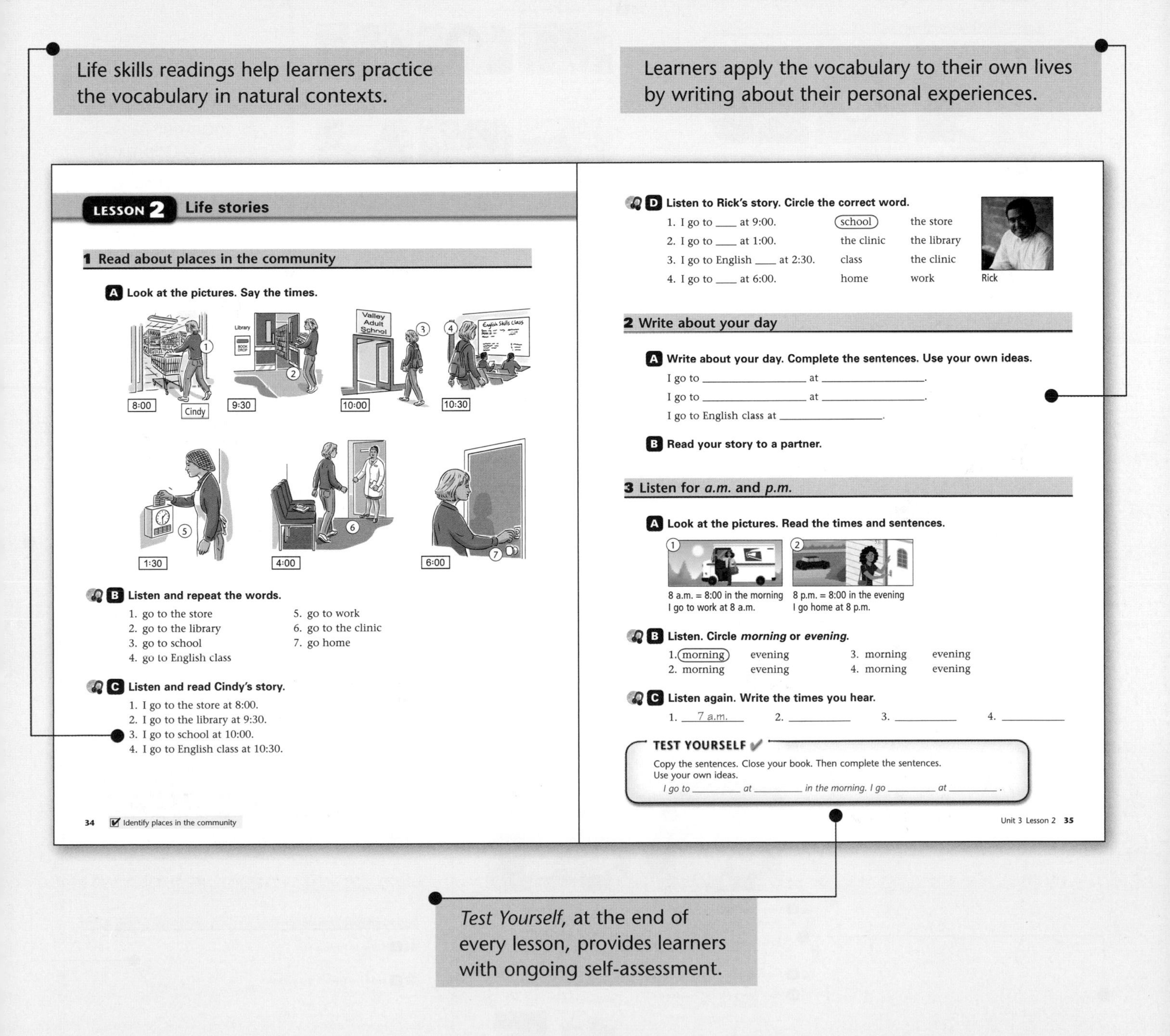
Life skills readings help learners practice the vocabulary in natural contexts.
Learners apply the vocabulary to their own lives by writing about their personal experiences.
Test Yourself, at the end of every lesson, provides learners with ongoing self-assessment.

LESSON 2 Life stories

1 Read about places in the community

A Look at the pictures. Say the times.

Library
Valley Adult School
English Skills Class
8:00
Cindy
9:30
10:00
10:30
1:30
4:00
6:00

B Listen and repeat the words.

1. go to the store
2. go to the library
3. go to school
4. go to English class
5. go to work
6. go to the clinic
7. go home

C Listen and read Cindy's story.

1. I go to the store at 8:00.
2. I go to the library at 9:30.
3. I go to school at 10:00.
4. I go to English class at 10:30.

34 Identify places in the community

D Listen to Rick's story. Circle the correct word.

1. I go to ___ at 9:00.	(school)	the store
2. I go to ___ at 1:00.	the clinic	the library
3. I go to English ___ at 2:30.	class	the clinic
4. I go to ___ at 6:00.	home	work

Rick

2 Write about your day

A Write about your day. Complete the sentences. Use your own ideas.

I go to __________ at __________.
I go to __________ at __________.
I go to English class at __________.

B Read your story to a partner.

3 Listen for *a.m.* and *p.m.*

A Look at the pictures. Read the times and sentences.

1. 8 a.m. = 8:00 in the morning
I go to work at 8 a.m.

2. 8 p.m. = 8:00 in the evening
I go home at 8 p.m.

B Listen. Circle *morning* or *evening*.

1. (morning) evening
2. morning evening
3. morning evening
4. morning evening

C Listen again. Write the times you hear.

1. 7 a.m. 2. ______ 3. ______ 4. ______

TEST YOURSELF ✓

Copy the sentences. Close your book. Then complete the sentences. Use your own ideas.

I go to ______ at ______ in the morning. I go ______ at ______.

Unit 3 Lesson 2 35

LESSON 3: GRAMMAR provides clear, simple presentation of the target structure followed by thorough, meaningful practice of it.

Clear grammar presentation and exercises help learners develop language confidence and accuracy.

Learners work together to increase fluency and accuracy, using the grammar point to talk about themselves.

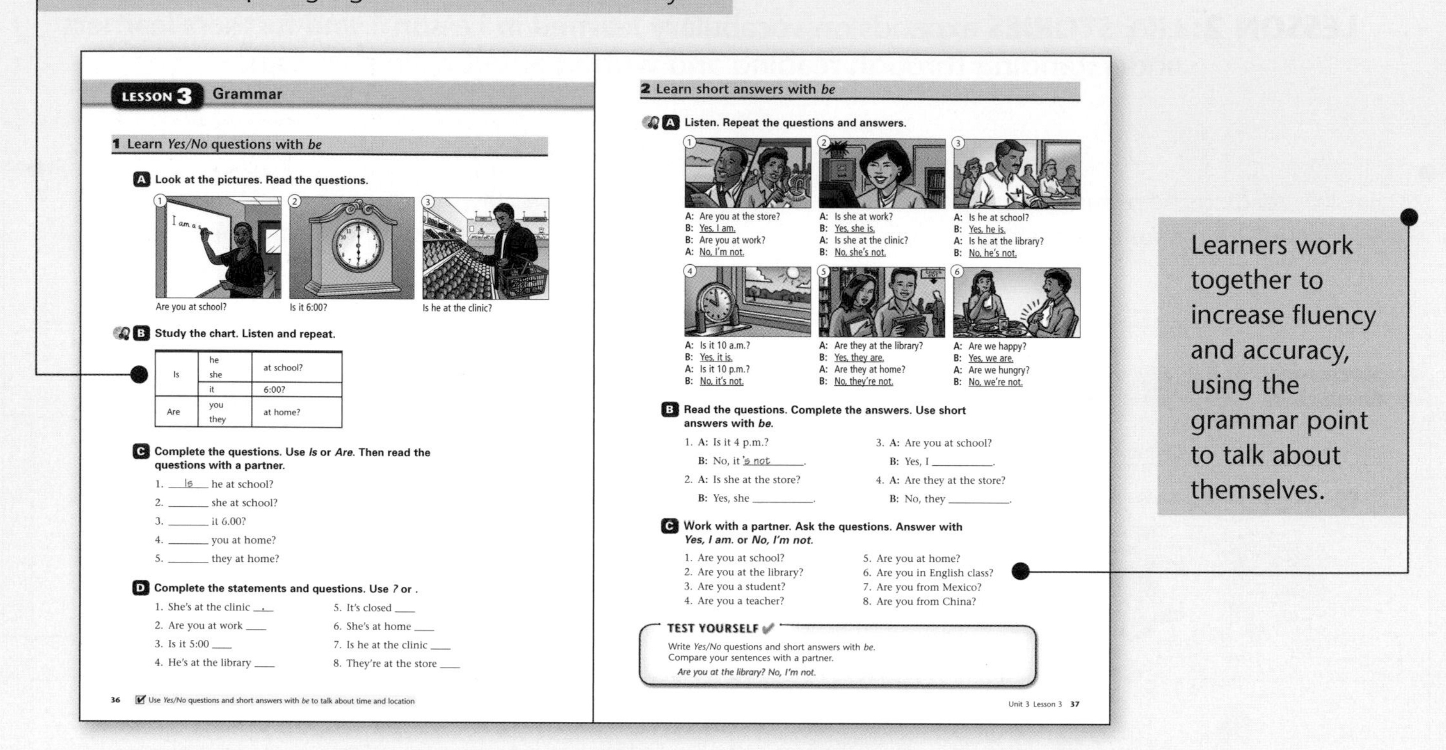

LESSON 3 Grammar

1 Learn *Yes/No* questions with *be*

A Look at the pictures. Read the questions.

Are you at school? Is it 6:00? Is he at the clinic?

B Study the chart. Listen and repeat.

Is	he she	at school?
	it	6:00?
Are	you they	at home?

C Complete the questions. Use *Is* or *Are*. Then read the questions with a partner.

1. __Is__ he at school?
2. ______ she at school?
3. ______ it 6:00?
4. ______ you at home?
5. ______ they at home?

D Complete the statements and questions. Use *?* or *.*

1. She's at the clinic __.__
2. Are you at work ____
3. Is it 5:00 ____
4. He's at the library ____
5. It's closed ____
6. She's at home ____
7. Is he at the clinic ____
8. They're at the store ____

36 Use *Yes/No* questions and short answers with *be* to talk about time and location

2 Learn short answers with *be*

A Listen. Repeat the questions and answers.

1. A: Are you at the store? B: Yes, I am. B: Are you at work? A: No, I'm not.
2. A: Is she at work? B: Yes, she is. A: Is she at the clinic? B: No, she's not.
3. A: Is he at school? B: Yes, he is. A: Is he at the library? B: No, he's not.
4. A: Is it 10 a.m.? B: Yes, it is. A: Is it 10 p.m.? B: No, it's not.
5. A: Are they at the library? B: Yes, they are. A: Are they at home? B: No, they're not.
6. A: Are we happy? B: Yes, we are. A: Are we hungry? B: No, we're not.

B Read the questions. Complete the answers. Use short answers with *be*.

1. A: Is it 4 p.m.? B: No, it 's not.
2. A: Is she at the store? B: Yes, she ______.
3. A: Are you at school? B: Yes, I ______.
4. A: Are they at the store? B: No, they ______.

C Work with a partner. Ask the questions. Answer with *Yes, I am.* or *No, I'm not.*

1. Are you at school?
2. Are you at the library?
3. Are you a student?
4. Are you a teacher?
5. Are you at home?
6. Are you in English class?
7. Are you from Mexico?
8. Are you from China?

TEST YOURSELF
Write *Yes/No* questions and short answers with *be*.
Compare your sentences with a partner.
Are you at the library? No, I'm not.

Unit 3 Lesson 3 37

LESSON 4: EVERYDAY CONVERSATION provides learners with fluent, authentic conversations to increase familiarity with natural English.

Pronunciation activities focus on common areas of difficulty.

Listening activities build listening skills.

Model dialogs feature authentic examples of everyday conversation.

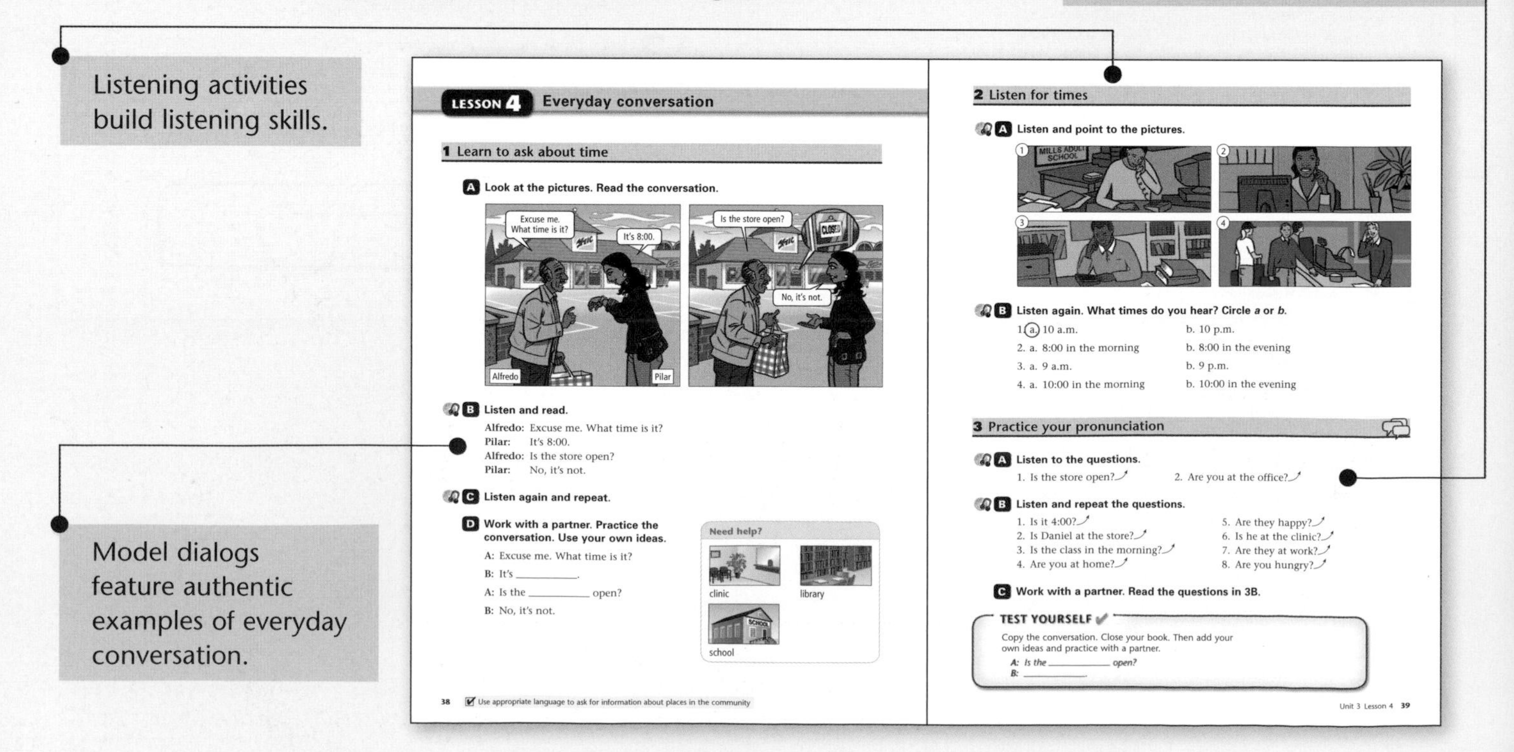

LESSON 4 Everyday conversation

1 Learn to ask about time

A Look at the pictures. Read the conversation.

B Listen and read.

Alfredo: Excuse me. What time is it?
Pilar: It's 8:00.
Alfredo: Is the store open?
Pilar: No, it's not.

C Listen again and repeat.

D Work with a partner. Practice the conversation. Use your own ideas.

A: Excuse me. What time is it?
B: It's ______.
A: Is the ______ open?
B: No, it's not.

Need help?
clinic
library
school

38 Use appropriate language to ask for information about places in the community

2 Listen for times

A Listen and point to the pictures.

B Listen again. What times do you hear? Circle *a* or *b*.

1. (a.) 10 a.m. — b. 10 p.m.
2. a. 8:00 in the morning — b. 8:00 in the evening
3. a. 9 a.m. — b. 9 p.m.
4. a. 10:00 in the morning — b. 10:00 in the evening

3 Practice your pronunciation

A Listen to the questions.

1. Is the store open?
2. Are you at the office?

B Listen and repeat the questions.

1. Is it 4:00?
2. Is Daniel at the store?
3. Is the class in the morning?
4. Are you at home?
5. Are they happy?
6. Is he at the clinic?
7. Are they at work?
8. Are you hungry?

C Work with a partner. Read the questions in 3B.

TEST YOURSELF
Copy the conversation. Close your book. Then add your own ideas and practice with a partner.
A: Is the ______ open?
B: ______.

Unit 3 Lesson 4 39

LESSON 5: REAL-LIFE READING develops essential reading skills and offers life skill reading materials.

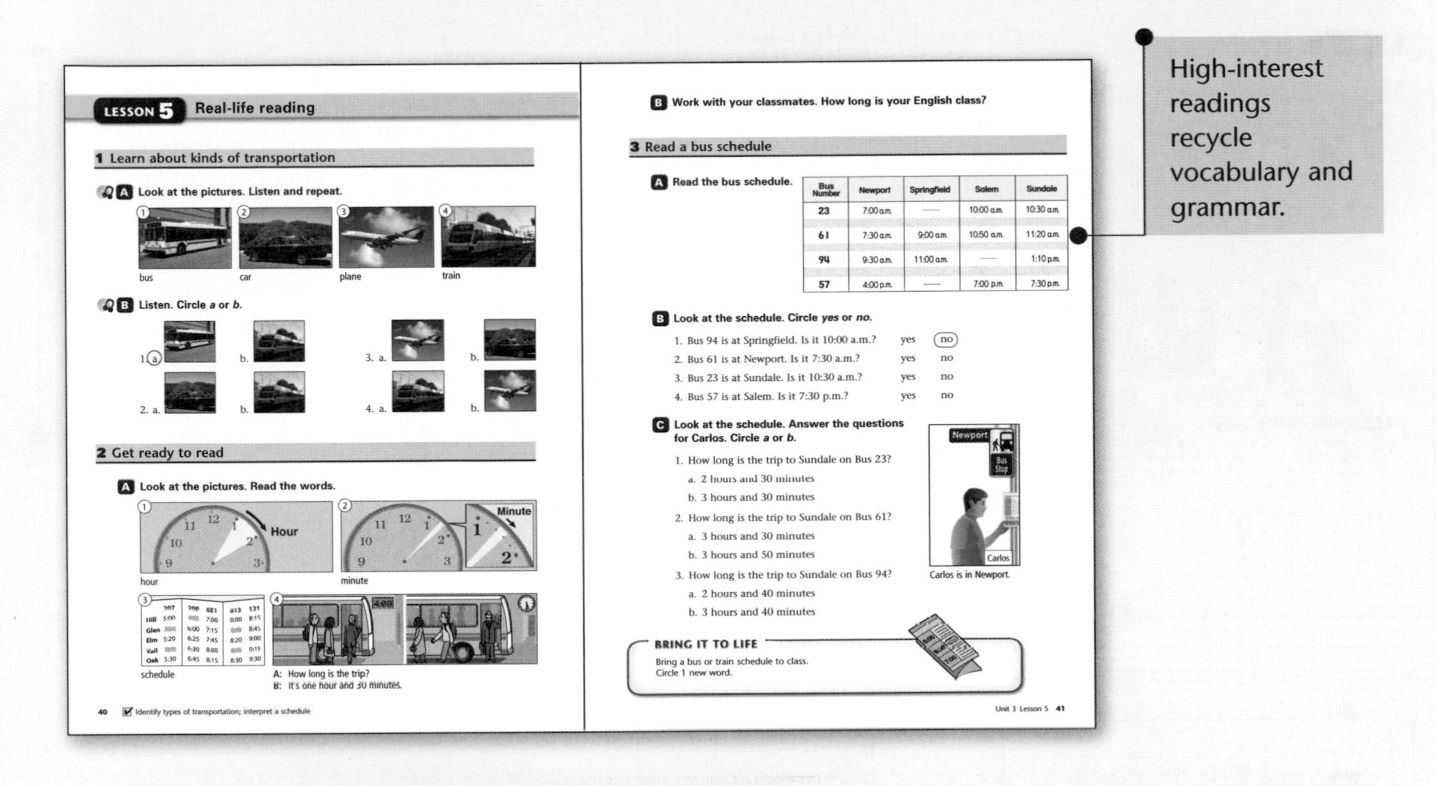

LESSON 5 Real-life reading

1 Learn about kinds of transportation

A Look at the pictures. Listen and repeat.

1 bus 2 car 3 plane 4 train

B Listen. Circle *a* or *b*.

1. a. b. 2. a. b. 3. a. b. 4. a. b.

2 Get ready to read

A Look at the pictures. Read the words.

1 hour 2 minute 3 schedule 4

A: How long is the trip?
B: It's one hour and 30 minutes.

40 Identify types of transportation; interpret a schedule

B Work with your classmates. How long is your English class?

3 Read a bus schedule

A Read the bus schedule.

Bus Number	Newport	Springfield	Salem	Sundale
23	7:00 a.m.	—	10:00 a.m.	10:30 a.m.
61	7:30 a.m.	9:00 a.m.	10:50 a.m.	11:20 a.m.
94	9:30 a.m.	11:00 a.m.	—	1:10 p.m.
57	4:00 p.m.	—	7:00 p.m.	7:30 p.m.

B Look at the schedule. Circle *yes* or *no*.

1. Bus 94 is at Springfield. Is it 10:00 a.m.? yes no
2. Bus 61 is at Newport. Is it 7:30 a.m.? yes no
3. Bus 23 is at Sundale. Is it 10:30 a.m.? yes no
4. Bus 57 is at Salem. Is it 7:30 p.m.? yes no

C Look at the schedule. Answer the questions for Carlos. Circle *a* or *b*.

1. How long is the trip to Sundale on Bus 23?
   a. 2 hours and 30 minutes
   b. 3 hours and 30 minutes
2. How long is the trip to Sundale on Bus 61?
   a. 3 hours and 30 minutes
   b. 3 hours and 50 minutes
3. How long is the trip to Sundale on Bus 94?
   a. 2 hours and 40 minutes
   b. 3 hours and 40 minutes

Carlos is in Newport.

BRING IT TO LIFE
Bring a bus or train schedule to class. Circle 1 new word.

Unit 3 Lesson 5 41

High-interest readings recycle vocabulary and grammar.

REVIEW AND EXPAND includes additional grammar practice and communicative group tasks to ensure your learners' progress.

UNIT 3 Review and expand

1 Grammar

A Read the questions. Complete the answers.

1. A: Is Deenah at the store?
   B: No, she's not.
2. A: Is Monica at the clinic?
   B: Yes, ______.
3. A: Is Bob at home?
   B: Yes, ______.
4. A: Are the students at the library?
   B: Yes, ______.
5. A: Is it 11:00?
   B: No, ______.
6. A: Is he at work?
   B: No, ______.
7. A: Is she at home?
   B: No, ______.

2 Group work

A Work with 2–3 classmates. Look at the pictures. Say what you see.

42 Review and expand

B Work with your group. Look at the pictures in 2A again. Write what you see. Check your spelling in a dictionary.

1. clinic
2. ______
3. ______
4. ______
5. ______
6. ______

C Work with your classmates. Make a list of the words from 2B.

PROBLEM SOLVING

A Listen. Look at the pictures.

Tony's Problem

Midtown Clinic 10 a.m.

English Class 9 a.m.-12 p.m.

B Work with your classmates. Help Tony.

a. Leave class early.
b. Go to class late.

Unit 3 Review and expand 43

Grammar exercises can be used as a review at the end of the unit or for additional practice.

Problem solving tasks encourage learners to use critical thinking skills and meaningful discussion to find solutions to common problems.

Step Forward offers many different components.

Step-By-Step Lesson Plans

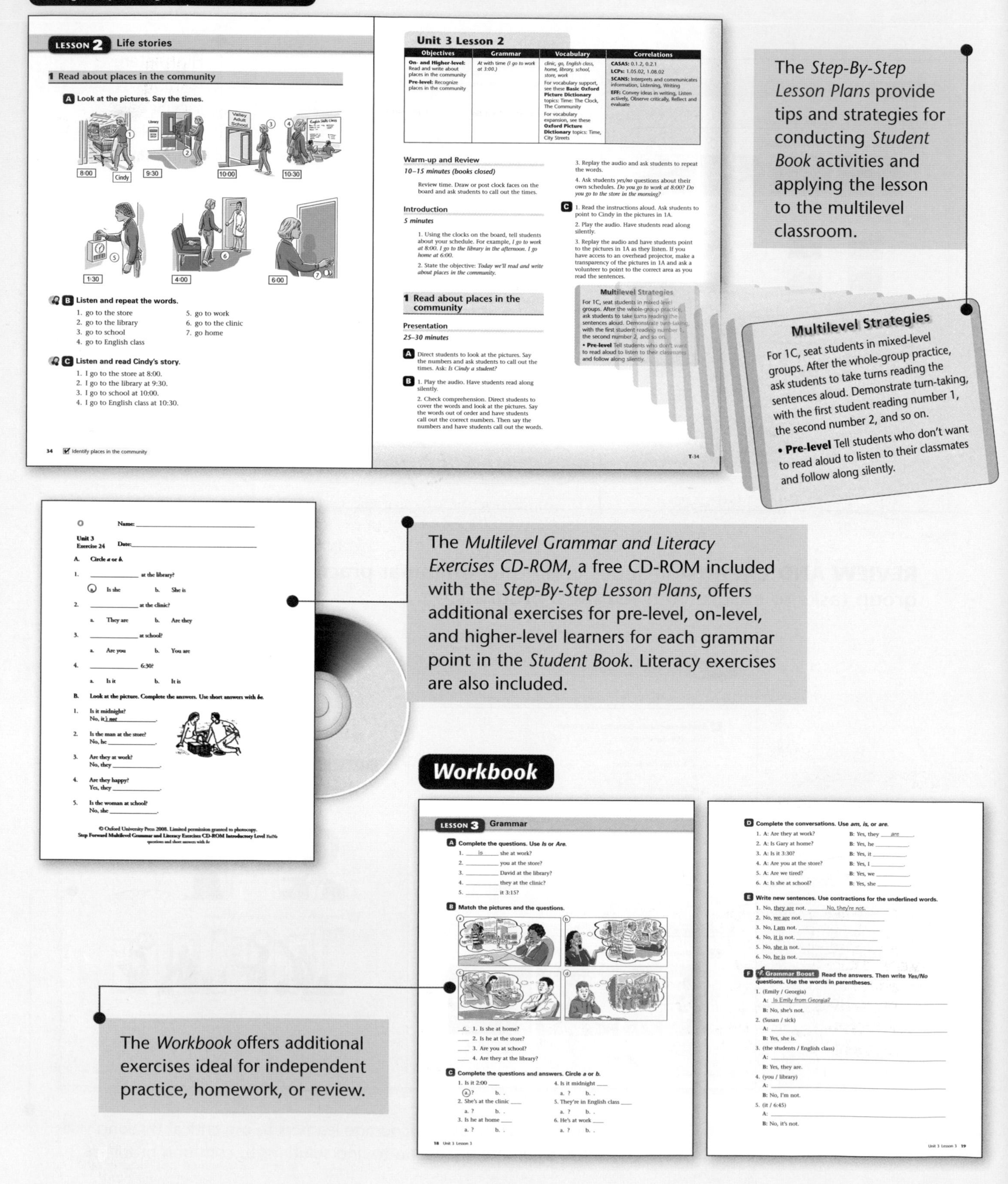

LESSON 2 Life stories

1 Read about places in the community

A Look at the pictures. Say the times.

8:00 Cindy 9:30 10:00 10:30 1:30 4:00 6:00

B Listen and repeat the words.

1. go to the store
2. go to the library
3. go to school
4. go to English class
5. go to work
6. go to the clinic
7. go home

C Listen and read Cindy's story.

1. I go to the store at 8:00.
2. I go to the library at 9:30.
3. I go to school at 10:00.
4. I go to English class at 10:30.

34 Identify places in the community

Unit 3 Lesson 2

Objectives	Grammar	Vocabulary	Correlations
On- and Higher-level: Read and write about places in the community Pre-level: Recognize places in the community	At with time (I go to work at 3:00.)	clinic, go, English class, home, library, school, store, work For vocabulary support, see these Basic Oxford Picture Dictionary topics: Time: The Clock, The Community For vocabulary expansion, see these Oxford Picture Dictionary topics: Time, City Streets	CASAS: 0.1.2, 0.2.1 LCPs: 1.05.02, 1.08.02 SCANS: Interprets and communicates information, Listening, Writing EFF: Convey ideas in writing, Listen actively, Observe critically, Reflect and evaluate

Warm-up and Review

10–15 minutes (books closed)

Review time. Draw or post clock faces on the board and ask students to call out the times.

Introduction

5 minutes

1. Using the clocks on the board, tell students about your schedule. For example, *I go to work at 8:00. I go to the library in the afternoon. I go home at 6:00.*

2. State the objective: *Today we'll read and write about places in the community.*

1 Read about places in the community

Presentation

25–30 minutes

A Direct students to look at the pictures. Say the numbers and ask students to call out the times. Ask: *Is Cindy a student?*

B 1. Play the audio. Have students read along silently.

2. Check comprehension. Direct students to cover the words and look at the pictures. Say the words out of order and have students call out the correct numbers. Then say the numbers and have students call out the words.

3. Replay the audio and ask students to repeat the words.

4. Ask students *yes/no* questions about their own schedules. *Do you go to work at 8:00? Do you go to the store in the morning?*

C 1. Read the instructions aloud. Ask students to point to Cindy in the pictures in 1A.

2. Play the audio. Have students read along silently.

3. Replay the audio and have students point to the pictures in 1A as they listen. If you have access to an overhead projector, make a transparency of the pictures in 1A and ask a volunteer to point to the correct area as you read the sentences.

T-34

The *Step-By-Step Lesson Plans* provide tips and strategies for conducting *Student Book* activities and applying the lesson to the multilevel classroom.

Multilevel Strategies

For 1C, seat students in mixed-level groups. After the whole-group practice, ask students to take turns reading the sentences aloud. Demonstrate turn-taking, with the first student reading number 1, the second number 2, and so on.

• **Pre-level** Tell students who don't want to read aloud to listen to their classmates and follow along silently.

Name: ______

Unit 3 Exercise 24 Date: ______

A. Circle *a* or *b*.

1. ______ at the library?
 a. Is she b. She is
2. ______ at the clinic?
 a. They are b. Are they
3. ______ at school?
 a. Are you b. You are
4. ______ 6:30?
 a. Is it b. It is

B. Look at the picture. Complete the answers. Use short answers with *be*.

1. Is it midnight? No, it's not.
2. Is the man at the store? No, he ______.
3. Are they at work? No, they ______.
4. Are they happy? Yes, they ______.
5. Is the woman at school? No, she ______.

© Oxford University Press 2008. Limited permission granted to photocopy.
Step Forward Multilevel Grammar and Literacy Exercises CD-ROM Introductory Level Yes/No questions and short answers with *be*

The *Multilevel Grammar and Literacy Exercises CD-ROM*, a free CD-ROM included with the *Step-By-Step Lesson Plans*, offers additional exercises for pre-level, on-level, and higher-level learners for each grammar point in the *Student Book*. Literacy exercises are also included.

Workbook

LESSON 3 Grammar

A Complete the questions. Use *Is* or *Are*.

1. Is she at work?
2. ______ you at the store?
3. ______ David at the library?
4. ______ they at the clinic?
5. ______ it 3:15?

B Match the pictures and the questions.

c 1. Is she at home?
__ 2. Is he at the store?
__ 3. Are you at school?
__ 4. Are they at the library?

C Complete the questions and answers. Circle *a* or *b*.

1. Is it 2:00 __ a. ? b. .
2. She's at the clinic __ a. ? b. .
3. Is he at home __ a. ? b. .
4. Is it midnight __ a. ? b. .
5. They're in English class __ a. ? b. .
6. He's at work __ a. ? b. .

18 Unit 3 Lesson 3

D Complete the conversations. Use *am*, *is*, or *are*.

1. A: Are they at work? B: Yes, they are.
2. A: Is Gary at home? B: Yes, he ______.
3. A: Is it 3:30? B: Yes, it ______.
4. A: Are you at the store? B: Yes, I ______.
5. A: Are we tired? B: Yes, we ______.
6. A: Is she at school? B: Yes, she ______.

E Write new sentences. Use contractions for the underlined words.

1. No, they are not. No, they're not.
2. No, we are not.
3. No, I am not.
4. No, it is not.
5. No, she is not.
6. No, he is not.

F Grammar Boost Read the answers. Then write *Yes/No* questions. Use the words in parentheses.

1. (Emily / Georgia) A: Is Emily from Georgia? B: No, she's not.
2. (Susan / sick) A: ______ B: Yes, she is.
3. (the students / English class) A: ______ B: Yes, they are.
4. (you / library) A: ______ B: No, I'm not.
5. (it / 6:45) A: ______ B: No, it's not.

Unit 3 Lesson 3 19

The *Workbook* offers additional exercises ideal for independent practice, homework, or review.

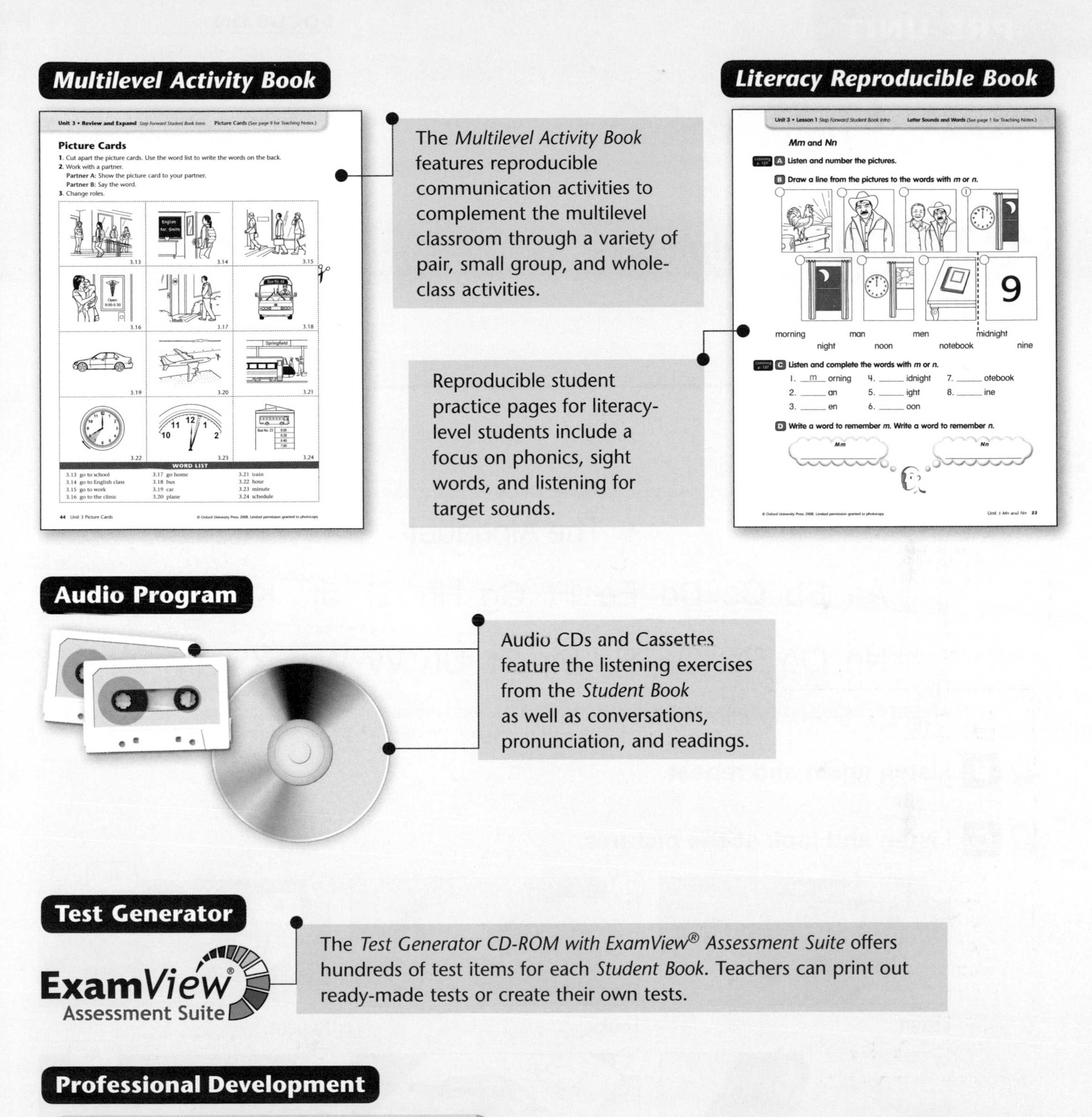

Multilevel Activity Book

Unit 3 • Review and Expand *Step Forward Student Book Intro* Picture Cards (See page 9 for Teaching Notes.)

Picture Cards

1. Cut apart the picture cards. Use the word list to write the words on the back.
2. Work with a partner.
   Partner A: Show the picture card to your partner.
   Partner B: Say the word.
3. Change roles.

WORD LIST

3.13 go to school	3.17 go home	3.21 train
3.14 go to English class	3.18 bus	3.22 hour
3.15 go to work	3.19 car	3.23 minute
3.16 go to the clinic	3.20 plane	3.24 schedule

44 Unit 3 Picture Cards © Oxford University Press 2008. Limited permission granted to photocopy.

The *Multilevel Activity Book* features reproducible communication activities to complement the multilevel classroom through a variety of pair, small group, and whole-class activities.

Literacy Reproducible Book

Unit 3 • Lesson 1 *Step Forward Student Book Intro* Letter Sounds and Words (See page 1 for Teaching Notes.)

Mm and *Nn*

A Listen and number the pictures.

B Draw a line from the pictures to the words with *m* or *n*.

morning night man noon men notebook midnight nine

C Listen and complete the words with *m* or *n*.

1. _m_ orning 2. ___ an 3. ___ en 4. ___ idnight 5. ___ ight 6. ___ oon 7. ___ otebook 8. ___ ine

D Write a word to remember *m*. Write a word to remember *n*.

© Oxford University Press 2008. Limited permission granted to photocopy. Unit 3 *Mm and Nn* 33

Reproducible student practice pages for literacy-level students include a focus on phonics, sight words, and listening for target sounds.

Audio Program

Audio CDs and Cassettes feature the listening exercises from the *Student Book* as well as conversations, pronunciation, and readings.

Test Generator

The *Test Generator CD-ROM with ExamView® Assessment Suite* offers hundreds of test items for each *Student Book*. Teachers can print out ready-made tests or create their own tests.

Professional Development

Professional Development Task 8

Imagine you want your learners to practice listening carefully during a group task. One behavior you could demonstrate would be leaning forward. Make a list of at least three other behaviors or expressions that careful listeners use.

The *Professional Development Program* offers instructors research-based teaching strategies and activities for single- and multilevel classes, plus Professional Development Tasks like this one.

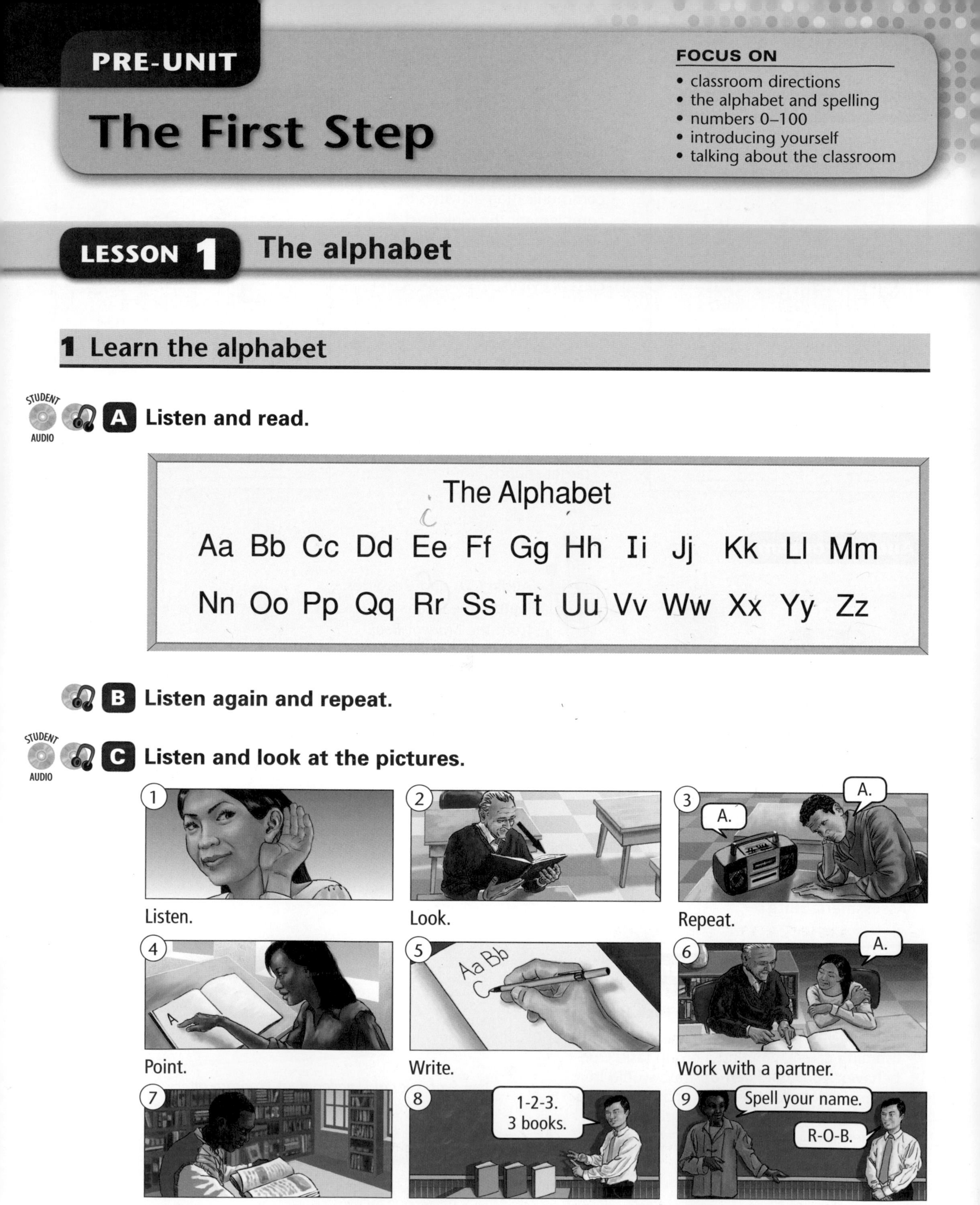

PRE-UNIT

The First Step

FOCUS ON

- classroom directions
- the alphabet and spelling
- numbers 0–100
- introducing yourself
- talking about the classroom

LESSON 1 The alphabet

1 Learn the alphabet

STUDENT AUDIO

A Listen and read.

The Alphabet

Aa Bb Cc Dd Ee Ff Gg Hh Ii Jj Kk Ll Mm

Nn Oo Pp Qq Rr Ss Tt Uu Vv Ww Xx Yy Zz

B Listen again and repeat.

STUDENT AUDIO

C Listen and look at the pictures.

1 Listen.

2 Look.

3 Repeat.

4 Point.

5 Write.

6 Work with a partner.

7 Read.

8 Count.

9 Spell.

✔ Identify letters of the alphabet; spell words

STUDENT AUDIO

D **Listen and point to the letters.**

1. a i	3. g j	5. p b	7. y w
2. i e	4. h j	6. m n	8. f s

E **Work with a partner. Read the letters in 1D.**

2 Spell words

STUDENT AUDIO

A **Look at the pictures. Listen and write the letters you hear.**

1. b _o_ _o_ k

2. p ___ n

3. ___ e ___ c ___ ___

4. ___ ___ ___ d ___ ___ t

5. t e ___ ___ h ___ ___

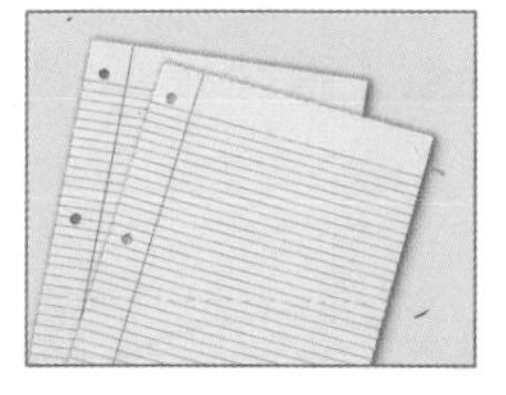

6. ___ a p ___ ___

B **Listen again and repeat.**

C **Work with a partner. Read the words in 2A.
Then spell the words.**

LESSON 2 Numbers

1 Learn the numbers 0–19

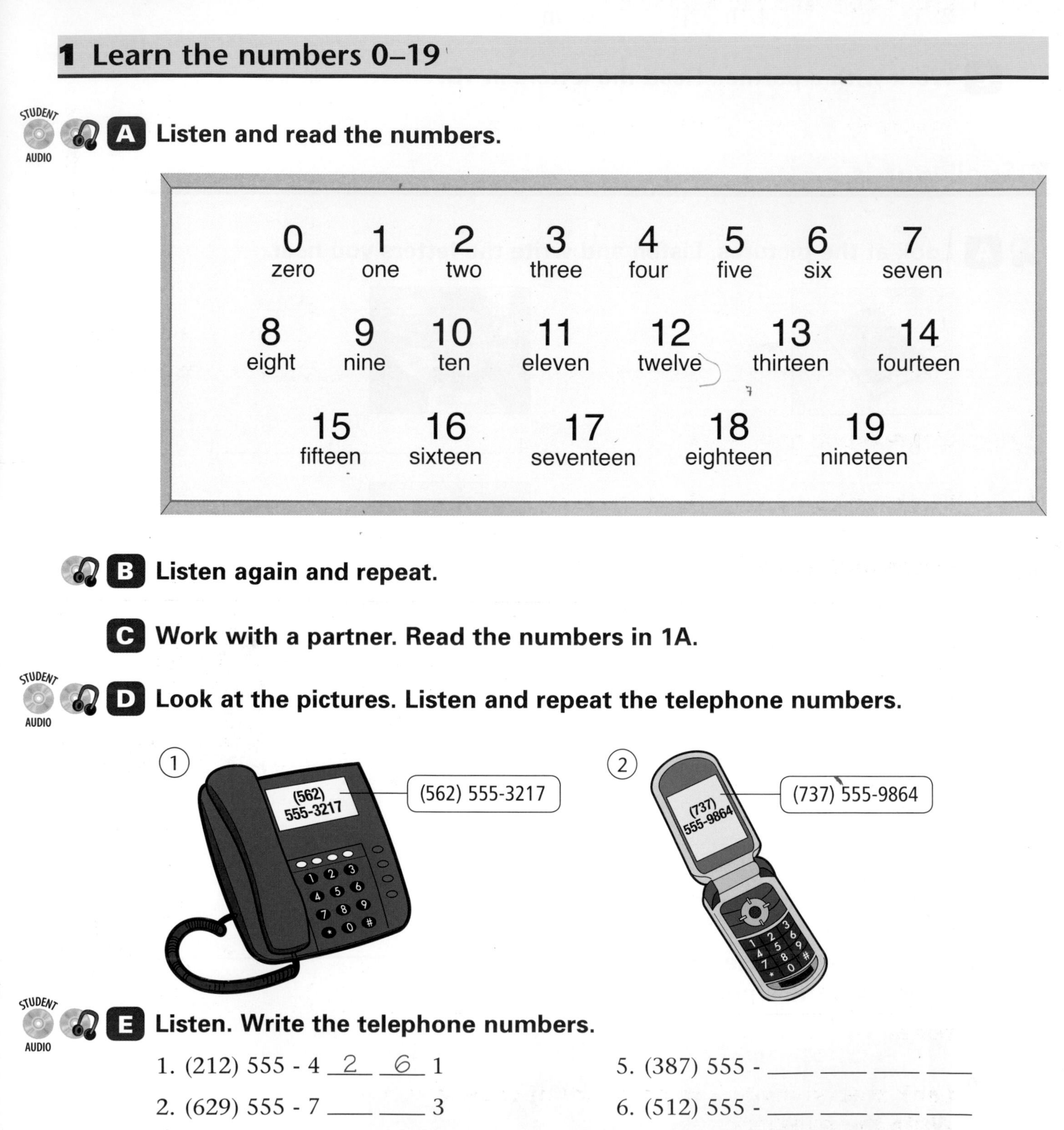

A **Listen and read the numbers.**

0	1	2	3	4	5	6	7
zero	one	two	three	four	five	six	seven

8	9	10	11	12	13	14
eight	nine	ten	eleven	twelve	thirteen	fourteen

15	16	17	18	19
fifteen	sixteen	seventeen	eighteen	nineteen

B **Listen again and repeat.**

C **Work with a partner. Read the numbers in 1A.**

D **Look at the pictures. Listen and repeat the telephone numbers.**

E **Listen. Write the telephone numbers.**

1. (212) 555 - 4 _2_ _6_ 1
2. (629) 555 - 7 ____ ____ 3
3. (748) 555 - 6 ____ ____ ____
4. (256) 555 - ____ ____ ____ 7
5. (387) 555 - ____ ____ ____ ____
6. (512) 555 - ____ ____ ____ ____
7. (936) 555 - ____ ____ ____ ____
8. (481) 555 - ____ ____ ____ ____

2 Learn the numbers 20–100

STUDENT AUDIO

A Listen and read the numbers.

20 twenty	21 twenty-one	22 twenty-two	23 twenty-three	24 twenty-four	25 twenty-five
26 twenty-six	27 twenty-seven	28 twenty-eight	29 twenty-nine	30 thirty	40 forty
50 fifty	60 sixty	70 seventy	80 eighty	90 ninety	100 one hundred

B Listen again and repeat.

C Work with a partner. Read the numbers in 2A.

STUDENT AUDIO

D Listen and repeat.

1 student

2 students

3 woman

4 women

5 man

6 men

E Look around your classroom. Count what you see. Write the numbers.

__2__ students

__2__ men

__2__ women

LESSON 3 In the classroom

1 Introduce yourself

A **Look at the pictures. Read the conversation.**

B **Listen and read.**

Lorena: Hello. I'm Lorena.
Jin: Excuse me?
Lorena: Lorena. L - O - R - E - N - A.
Jin: Hi. I'm Jin.

C **Listen again and repeat.**

D **Work with your classmates. Practice the conversation. Use your own information.**

A: Hello. I'm ____________.

B: Excuse me?

A: ____________.

B: Hi. I'm ____________.

 ☑ Use appropriate language to introduce yourself; identify classroom items

2 Talk about your classroom

A Look at the pictures. Listen and repeat the words.

1 
clock

2 

clocks

3 
desk

4 
desks

5 table

6 tables

7 
chair

8 
chairs

B Work with a partner. Talk about your classroom.

C Work with your classmates. Write about your classroom. Make a list.

1 clock
2 desks
10 tables
35 students

UNIT 1 Nice to Meet You

FOCUS ON
- classroom directions
- personal information
- subject pronouns; the verb *be*
- meeting new people
- reading a checklist

LESSON 1 Vocabulary

1 Learn classroom directions

A **Look at the pictures. Point to the student.**

STUDENT AUDIO **B** **Listen and point to the pictures.**

STUDENT AUDIO **C** **Listen and repeat the words.**

1. open
2. close
3. circle
4. say
5. check
6. sign

D **Read the new words with a partner.**

2 Talk about classroom directions

A **Look at the picture. Complete the words.**

1. s _a_ y
2. c l o ___ e
3. ___ i r c l e
4. c h ___ c k
5. s ___ g n
6. o p e ___

B **Listen and check (✔) what you hear.**

1. ___ a. Open your book. _✔_ b. Close your book.
2. ___ a. Circle the pencil. ___ b. Say *pencil.*
3. ___ a. Sign your name. ___ b. Say your name.
4. ___ a. Read number one. ___ b. Check number one.
5. ___ a. Circle your name. ___ b. Sign your name.

C **Listen and follow the directions.**

1. Circle the pen.
2. Say *pen.*
3. Close your book.
4. Open your book.
5. Sign your name. ______________________

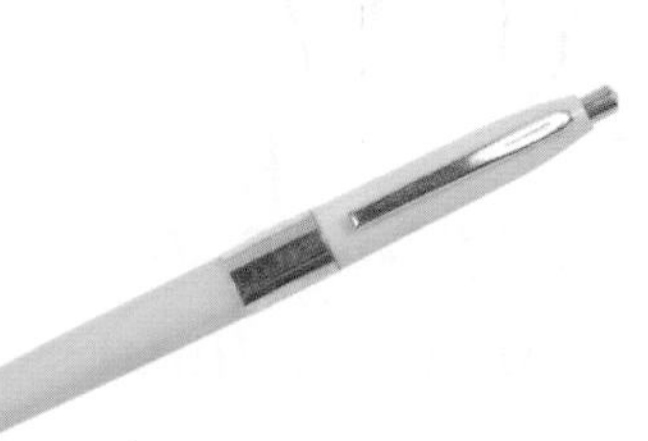

TEST YOURSELF ✔

Close your book. Write 3 classroom directions.
Check your spelling in a dictionary.

1 Read about personal information

A **Look at the ID card. Say the numbers you see.**

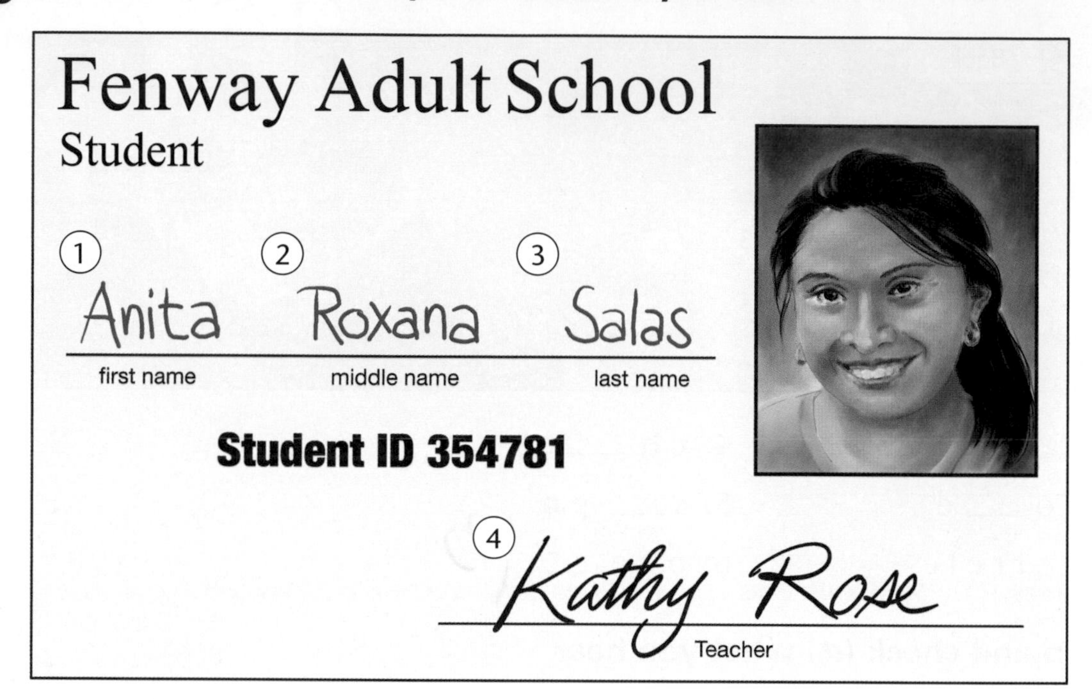
Fenway Adult School
Student
① Anita ② Roxana ③ Salas
first name middle name last name
Student ID 354781
④ Kathy Rose
Teacher

B **Listen and repeat the words.**

1. first name
2. middle name
3. last name
4. signature

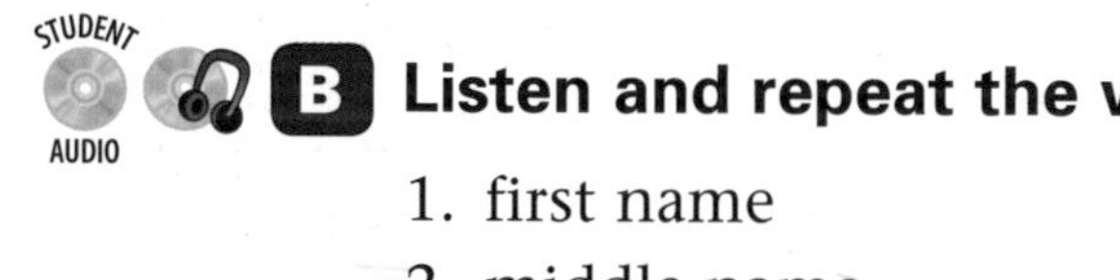

C **Listen and read Anita's story.**

1. My first name is Anita.
2. My last name is Salas.
3. I am a student.
4. My teacher is Kathy Rose.

D **Listen to Alan's story. Circle the correct word.**

1. My ____ name is Alan.	(first)	last
2. My ____ name is Woo.	first	last
3. I am a ____ .	student	signature
4. My ____ is Marsha Lee.	teacher	student

Alan

2 Write about yourself

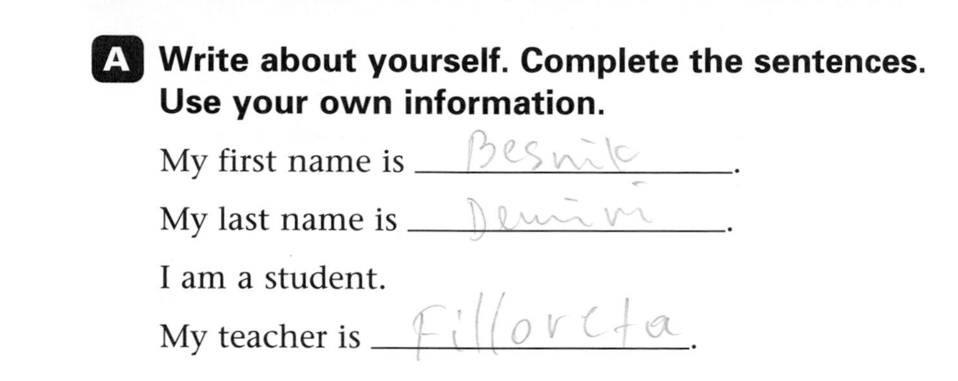

A Write about yourself. Complete the sentences. Use your own information.

My first name is Besnik.

My last name is Demiri.

I am a student.

My teacher is Filloreta.

B Read your story to a partner.

3 Listen for personal information

A Listen and point to the names.

B Listen and repeat.

Mrs. Boatman: What is your first name?
John Wong: John.

Mrs. Boatman: What is your last name?
John Wong: Wong.

C Work with a partner. Practice the conversation in 3B. Use your own information.

TEST YOURSELF ✔

Copy the sentences. Close your book. Then complete the sentences.

My first name is __________. My last name is __________.

1 Learn subject pronouns

A Look at the pictures. Read the words.

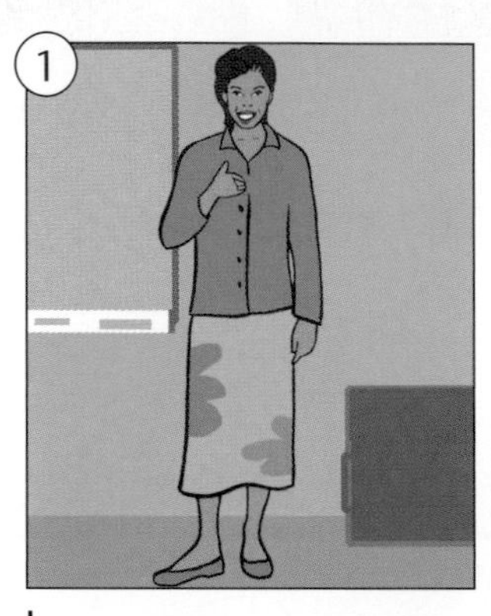

1 I

2 he

3 she

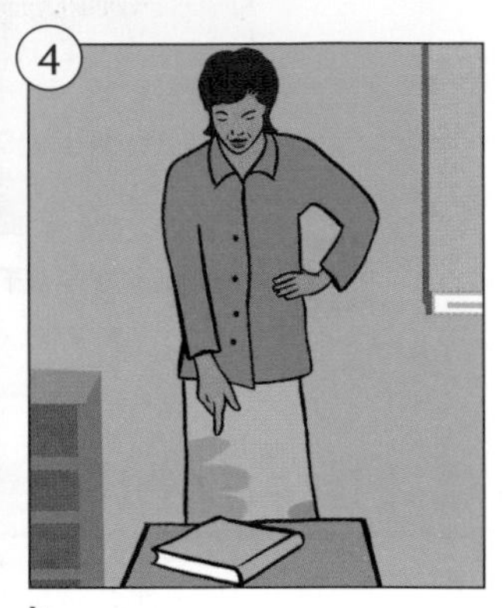

4 it

5 they

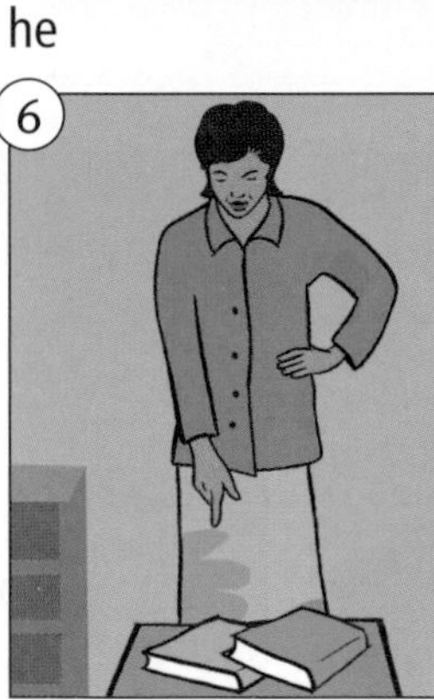

6 they

7 we

B Look at the words in 1A. Listen and repeat.

C Look at the pictures. Circle *a* or *b*.

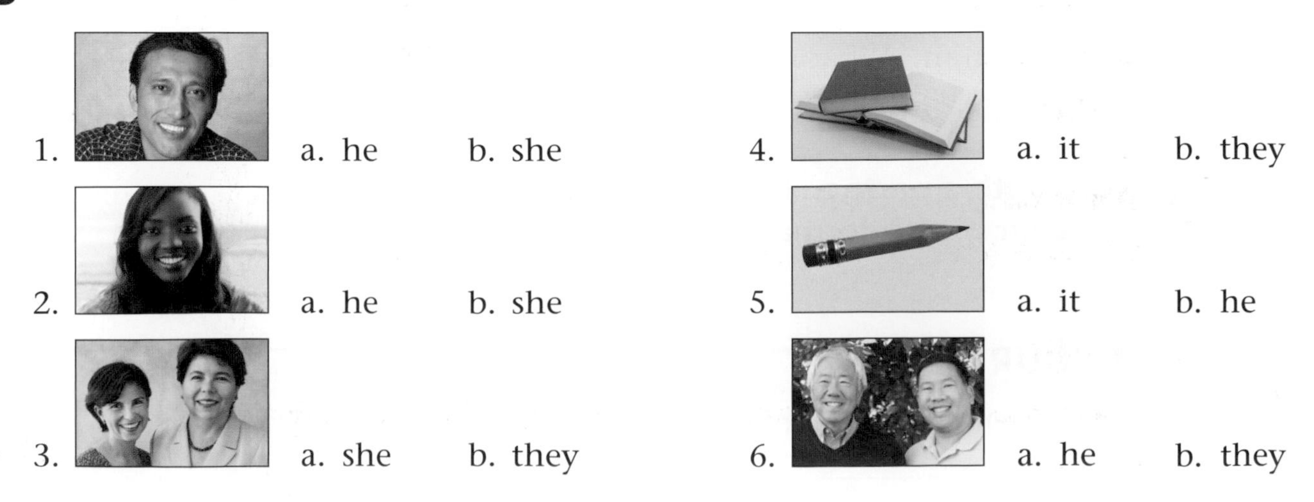

1. a. he b. she
2. a. he b. she
3. a. she b. they
4. a. it b. they
5. a. it b. he
6. a. he b. they

2 Learn the verb *be*

A Look at the pictures. Listen and repeat.

1. I am a student.

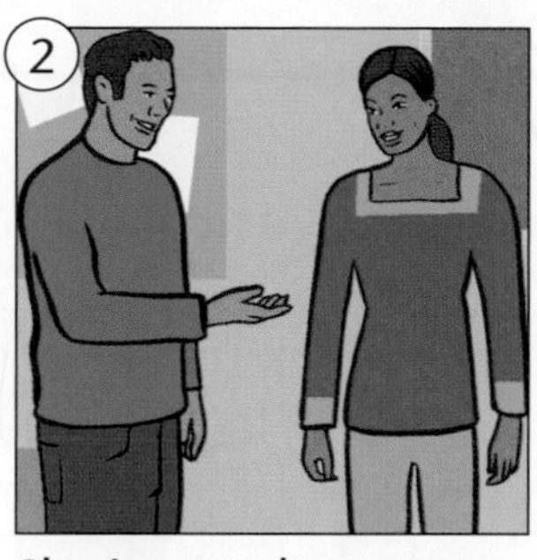

2. She is a student.

3. He is a student.

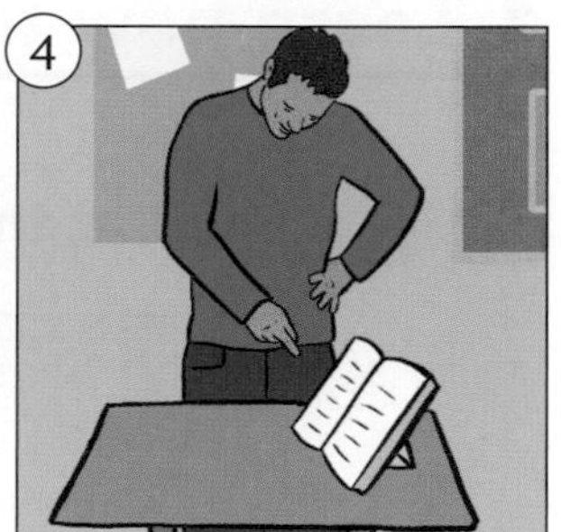

4. It is a book.

5. They are students.

6. We are students.

7. You are a student.

B Match the parts of the sentence.

__c__ 1. I	a. is a teacher.
____ 2. They	b. are students.
____ 3. It	c. am a student.
____ 4. She	d. is a pencil.

C Complete the sentences. Use *am, is,* or *are*.

1. I ___am___ a student.
2. He ________ a student.
3. They ________ teachers.
4. It ________ a pen.
5. She ________ Anna.
6. We ________ students.

D Work with a partner. Talk about your classroom.

She is a student. They are tables. It is a pencil.

TEST YOURSELF ✓

Write sentences about your classroom. Compare your sentences with a partner.

He is a student. It is a book.

LESSON 4 Everyday conversation

1 Learn how to meet new people

A **Look at the pictures. Read the conversation.**

B **Listen and read.**

Marta: Hi. I am Marta. What is your name?
Trang: My name is Trang.
Marta: Nice to meet you.
Trang: Nice to meet you, too.

C **Listen again and repeat.**

D **Work with your classmates. Practice the conversation. Use your own information.**

A: Hi. I am ____________. What is your name?

B: My name is ____________.

A: Nice to meet you.

B: Nice to meet you, too.

 ☑ Use appropriate language for interpersonal communication

2 Listen for spelling

A Listen. Circle *a* or *b*.

1. (a.) Mary — b. Mark
2. a. John — b. Joan
3. a. Mel — b. Mal
4. a. Sandy — b. Sandi
5. a. Gerry — b. Jerry
6. a. Corbin — b. Corvin

B Listen again and check your answers.

3 Practice your pronunciation

A Listen for *i* and *e* sounds.

i	*e*
1. nice	5. meet
2. write	6. read
3. five	7. repeat
4. sign	8. please

B Listen and check (✔) the sounds you hear.

	i	*e*
1.		✔
2.		
3.		
4.		

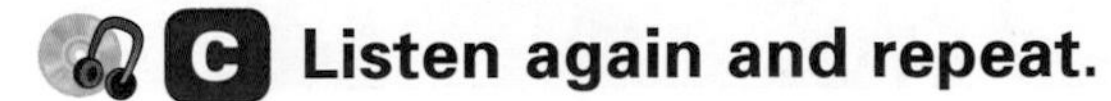

C Listen again and repeat.

TEST YOURSELF ✔

Copy the conversation. Close your book. Then add your own information and practice with a partner.

A: Hi. I am ________. What is your name?
B: My name is ________.

1 Learn *a* and *an*

STUDENT AUDIO **A** **Look at the pictures. Listen and repeat.**

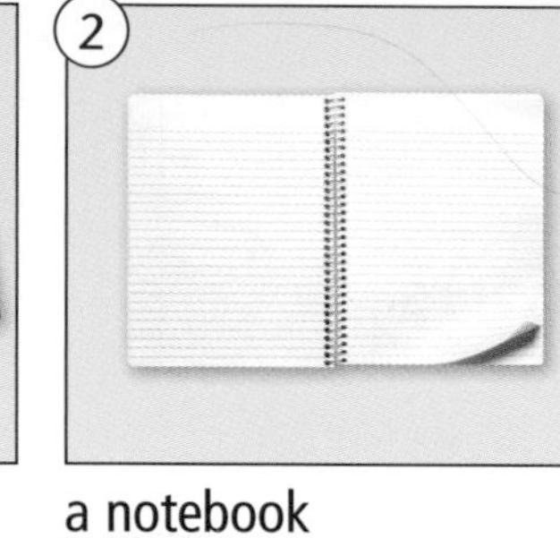
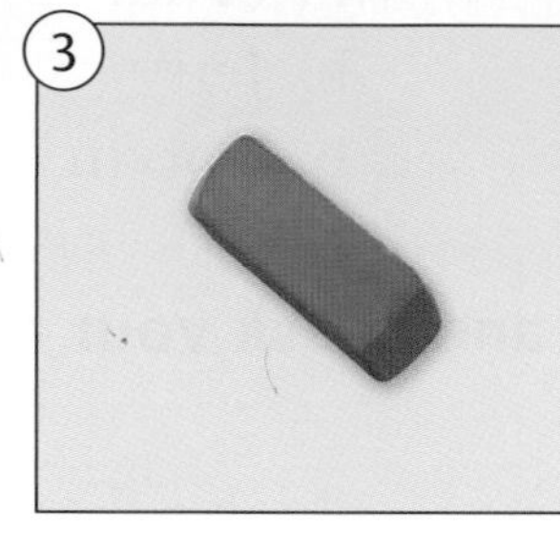

1. a binder
2. a notebook
3. an eraser
4. an English dictionary

STUDENT AUDIO **B** **Listen. Write *a* or *an*.**

1. __a__ notebook
2. ____ eraser
3. ____ binder
4. ____ English dictionary
5. ____ pen
6. ____ open book
7. ____ English class
8. ____ teacher

2 Get ready to read

A **Look at the pictures. Read the words.**

1. adult school
2. bring
3. supplies
4. pages

 ☑ Use indefinite articles; interpret a supplies checklist

B Check (✓) the supplies you bring to school.

- ☐ a pencil
- ☐ a pen
- ☐ an eraser
- ☐ a binder
- ☐ an English dictionary

3 Read a class supplies list

A Read the list.

ABC ADULT SCHOOL

Please bring these supplies to class!

- ☑ two pencils
- ☑ a pen
- ☑ an eraser
- ☐ an English dictionary
- ☑ a binder
- ☐ a notebook (100 pages)
- ☑ paper

B Look at the list. Circle *yes* or *no*.

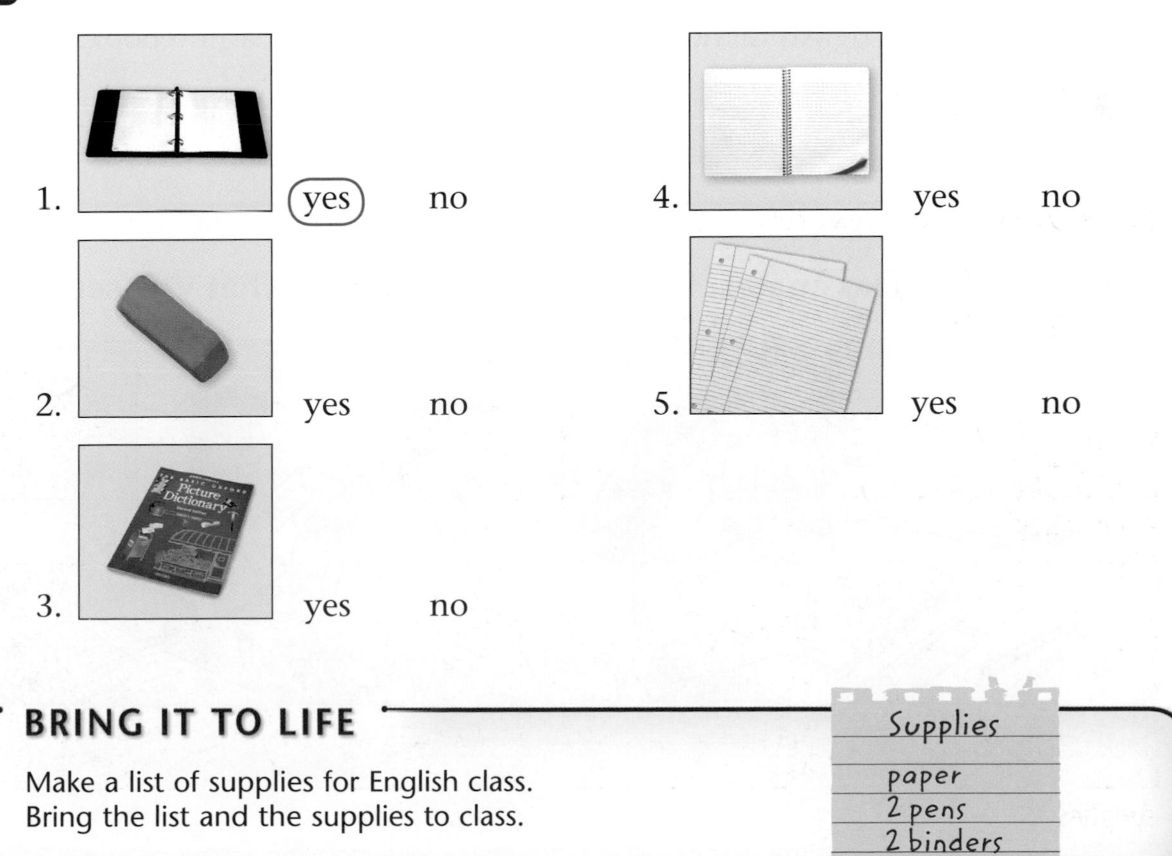

1. (yes) no
2. yes no
3. yes no
4. yes no
5. yes no

BRING IT TO LIFE

Make a list of supplies for English class.
Bring the list and the supplies to class.

UNIT 1 Review and expand

1 Grammar

A Complete the sentences. Use the words in the box.

She	They	~~I~~	It

1. ___I___ am Tony.
2. ___They___ are in my class.
3. ___IT___ is my dictionary.
4. ___SHE___ is my teacher.

B Complete the sentences. Use *am, is,* or *are*.

1. He ___is___ a teacher.
2. She ___IS___ a student.
3. They ___are___ students.
4. I ___am___ a student.
5. It ___IS___ an English dictionary.
6. Sam ___IS___ a student.
7. Ali and Chris ___are___ students.
8. Petra ___IS___ a student.
9. They ___are___ books.
10. It ___is___ a notebook.

2 Group work

A Work with 2–3 classmates. Look at the picture. Say what you see.

B **Work with your group. Look at the picture in 2A again. Write what you see. Check your spelling in a dictionary.**

1. paper
2. Teacher
3. close The book
4. Open the Boock
5. Pen
6. Pencil

C **Work with your classmates. Make a list of the words from 2B.**

PROBLEM SOLVING

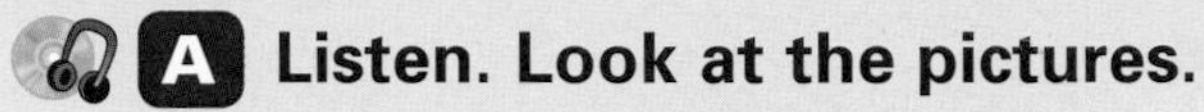

A **Listen. Look at the pictures.**

Amaya's Problem

B **Work with your classmates. Help Amaya.**

a. Ask a student.

b. Ask the teacher.

UNIT 2

How are you feeling?

FOCUS ON
- feelings
- personal information
- negative statements with *be*
- asking about feelings
- reading an envelope

LESSON 1 Vocabulary

1 Learn feeling words

A **Look at the pictures. Say what you see.**

B **Listen and point to the pictures.**

C **Listen and repeat the words.**

1. fine
2. happy
3. excited
4. sad
5. hungry
6. thirsty
7. tired
8. sick

D **Read the new words with a partner.**

 ✔ Identify appropriate language to describe feelings and emotions

2 Talk about feelings

A **Look at the picture. Complete the words.**

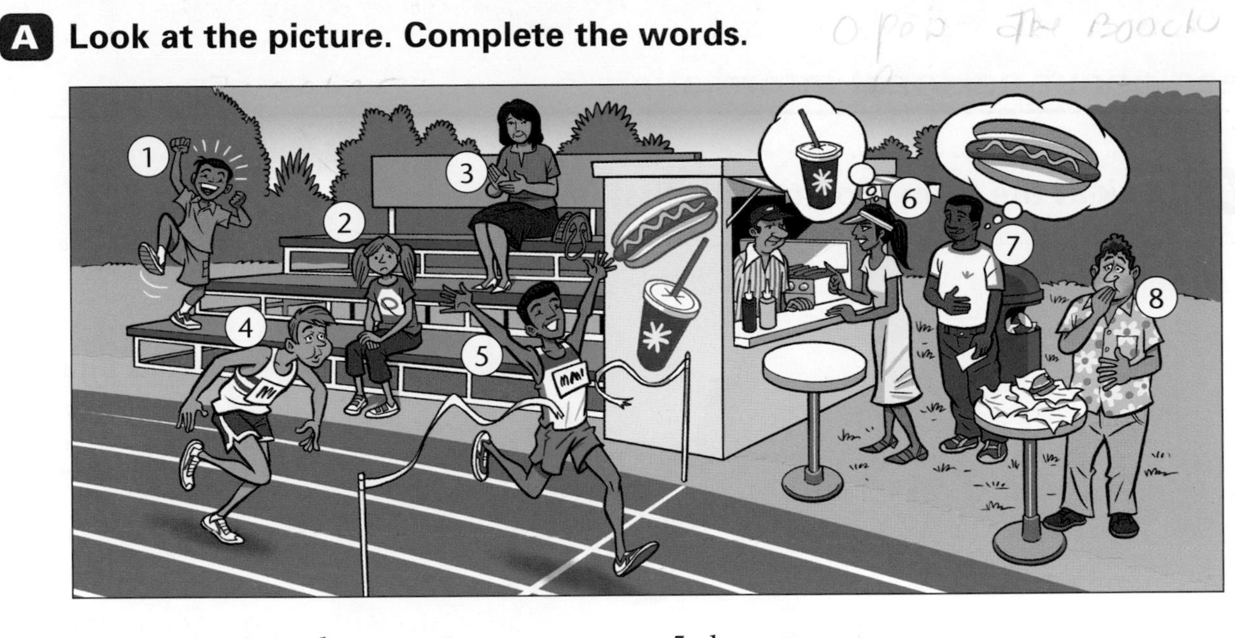

1. e x _c_ i t e d
2. s ___ d
3. ___ i n ___
4. t i r ___ d
5. h a p ___ y
6. t h i r s ___ y
7. ___ u n g r y
8. ___ i c k

B **Listen and repeat.**

I am tired.
I am tired, too.
Zita
Inez

1. **Zita:** I am tired.
   Inez: I am tired, too.
2. **Al:** I am hungry.
   Lam: I am thirsty.

C **Work with a partner. Practice the conversations. Use your own ideas.**

1. **A:** I am ___________.
   B: I am ___________, too.
2. **A:** I am ___________.
   B: I am ___________.

TEST YOURSELF ✓

Close your book. Write 3 words for feelings. Check your spelling in a dictionary.

1 Read about personal information

A **Look at the form. Point to the first name.**

B **Listen and repeat the words.**

1. city
2. state
3. birthplace
4. country

C **Listen and read Camille's story.**

1. My name is Camille.
2. I am from Haiti.
3. Now I am in Dallas, Texas.
4. I am happy in Dallas.

 ✔ Interpret a personal information form; respond to questions about personal information

D **Look at 1C. Write about Camille.**

1. name ___Camille___
2. birthplace ____________
3. city ____________, state ____________

Camille

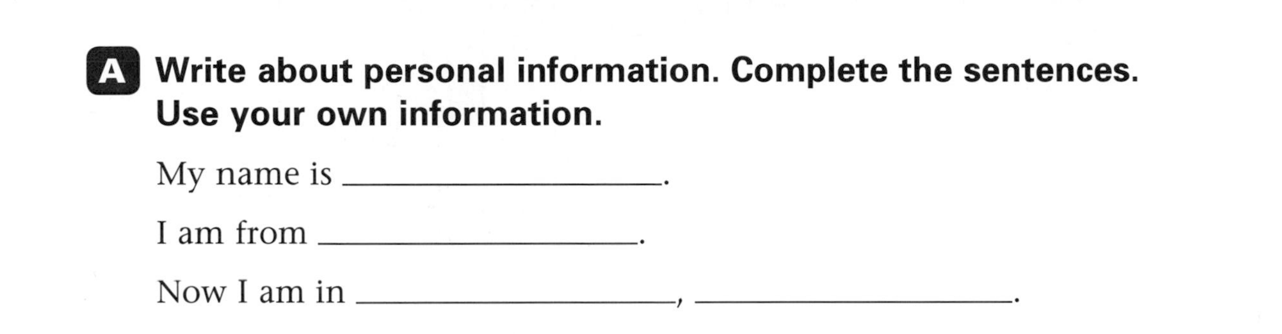

2 Write about personal information

A **Write about personal information. Complete the sentences. Use your own information.**

My name is ____________.

I am from ____________.

Now I am in ____________, ____________.

B **Read your story to a partner.**

3 Listen for countries

STUDENT AUDIO

A **Listen and point to the countries you hear.**

STUDENT AUDIO

B **Listen and repeat.**

A: Where are you from?
B: I am from Vietnam.

A: Where is Lian from?
B: She is from China.

C **Work with a partner. Practice the conversation in 3B. Use your own ideas.**

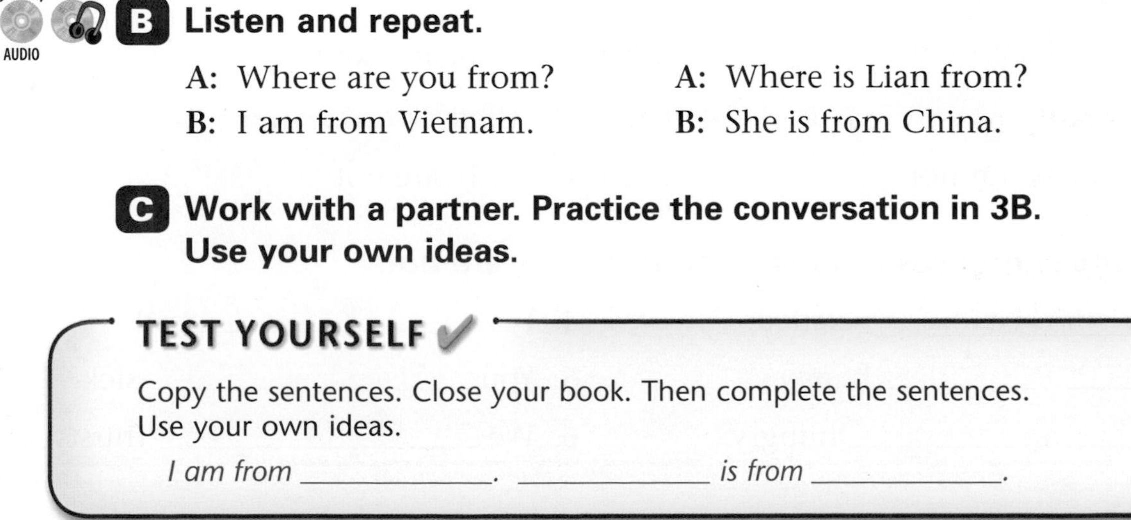

TEST YOURSELF ✓

Copy the sentences. Close your book. Then complete the sentences. Use your own ideas.

I am from ____________. ____________ *is from* ____________.

LESSON 3 Grammar

1 Learn negative statements with *be*

A Look at the pictures. Read the sentences.

1 He is not sad. He is happy.

2 She is not sick. She is tired.

 **B Study the chart. Listen and repeat.**

I	am	not	tired.
You	are		
He She It	is		
We They	are		

C Complete the sentences. Circle *a* or *b*. Then read the sentences with a partner.

1. I ____ tired.
   a. is not (b.) am not
2. She ____ tired.
   a. is not b. am not
3. We ____ tired.
   a. is not b. are not
4. They ____ tired.
   a. is not b. are not

D Complete the sentences. Use *am not, is not,* or *are not*.

1. She ____is not____ excited.
2. He ____________ happy.
3. They ____________ hungry.
4. I ____________ sad.
5. You ____________ sick.
6. We ____________ thirsty.

2 Learn contractions with *be*

 **A Look at the pictures. Listen and read the sentences.**

1 

I'm not from Texas.
I'm from Mexico.

2 

She's not tired.
She's excited.

3 

He's not happy.
He's sick.

4 

They're not in California.
They're in Colorado.

5 

It's not a city.
It's a state.

6 

You're not a student.
You're a teacher.

7 

We're not teachers.
We're students.

B Match the sentences.

c	1. I am not sad.	a. She's tired.
____	2. She is not tired.	b. They're happy.
____	3. She is tired.	c. I'm not sad.
____	4. It is not a state.	d. They're not happy.
____	5. They are happy.	e. She's not tired.
____	6. They are not happy.	f. It's not a state.

C Write new sentences. Use contractions.

1. She is not excited. She's not excited.
2. He is not a student. ________________________
3. We are not sick. ________________________

D Work with a partner. Read the sentences in 2C.

TEST YOURSELF ✓

Write sentences about feelings. Use contractions. Compare your sentences with a partner.

I'm tired. They're not happy.

LESSON 4 Everyday conversation

1 Learn to ask about feelings

A **Look at the pictures. Read the conversation.**

B **Listen and read.**

Pedro: How are you feeling?
Vanna: I'm fine. How are you feeling?
Pedro: I'm sick.
Vanna: Oh, I'm sorry.

C **Listen again and repeat.**

D **Work with a partner. Practice the conversation. Use your own ideas.**

A: How are you feeling?
B: I'm ____________.
How are you feeling?
A: I'm ____________.
B: Oh, I'm sorry.

Need help?

2 Listen for personal information

A **Listen. Circle *a* or *b*.**

1. a. How are you feeling? b. Where are you from?
2. a. Where are you from? b. What's your name?
3. a. How are you feeling? b. What's your name?

B **Listen and answer the questions. Circle *a* or *b*.**

1. (a.) I'm happy. b. My name is Pao.
2. a. I'm from China. b. My name is Leila.
3. a. I'm tired. b. I'm from China.
4. a. My name is Luis. b. I'm from Mexico.

3 Practice your pronunciation

A **Listen and count the syllables (•).**

1 syllable	2 syllables	3 syllables
fine •	hap py • •	ex cit ed • • •

B **Listen and check (✔) the correct boxes.**

	1. fine	2. thirsty	3. telephone	4. hungry	5. sad	6. signature
1 syllable	✔					
2 syllables						
3 syllables						

C **Listen again and check your answers. Then repeat the words.**

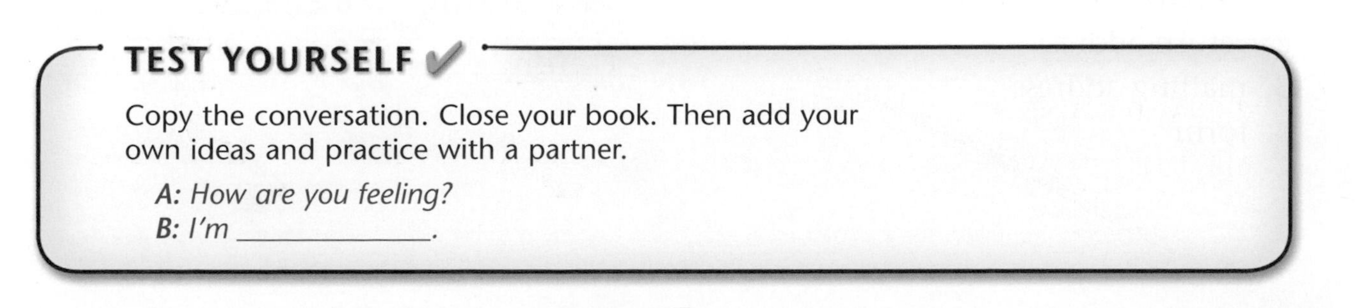

TEST YOURSELF ✔

Copy the conversation. Close your book. Then add your own ideas and practice with a partner.

A: *How are you feeling?*
B: *I'm* ____________.

1 Learn about addresses

STUDENT AUDIO

A Look at the picture. Listen and repeat.

1. address
2. zip code

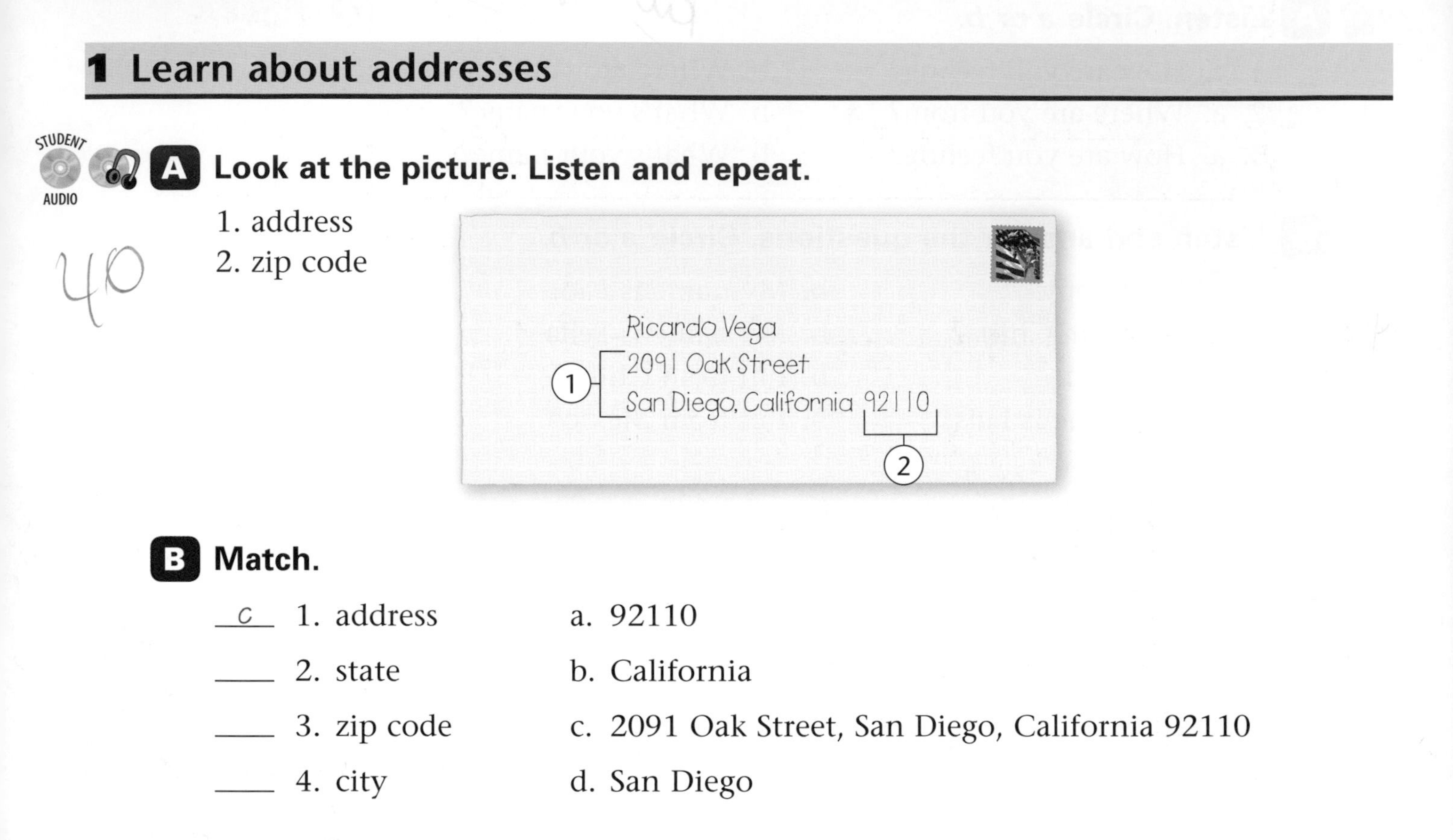

Ricardo Vega
2091 Oak Street
San Diego, California 92110
1
2

B Match.

c	1. address	a. 92110
____	2. state	b. California
____	3. zip code	c. 2091 Oak Street, San Diego, California 92110
____	4. city	d. San Diego

2 Get ready to read

A Look at the pictures. Read the words.

David Brown
16 Spring Street
Helen, GA 74112

River City Adult School
3712 Maple Street
Salem, NC 60611

River City Adult School
Student Information

David	Brown
first name	last name

16	Spring Street
number	street

Helen,	GA	74112
city	state	zip code

1. envelope
2. return address
3. mailing address
4. form

Need help?
GA = Georgia
NC = North Carolina

 Identify the information on an envelope; complete a personal information form

B **Complete the form. Use your own information.**

number	street	
city	state	zip code

3 Read a form and an envelope

A **Read the form and the envelope.**

River City Adult School
Student Information

Susan	Kirkwood	
first name	last name	
609	First Street	
number	street	
Atlanta,	GA	74354
city	state	zip code

Susan Kirkwood
609 First Street
Atlanta, GA 74354

River City Adult School
3712 Maple Street
Salem, NC 60611

B **Look at the form and envelope. Circle *a* or *b*.**

1. Susan is in ____.
   (a.) Atlanta   b. Salem
2. River City Adult School is in ____.
   a. Atlanta   b. Salem
3. The address of the school is ____.
   a. 609 First Street   b. 3712 Maple Street
4. Susan's zip code is ____.
   a. 609   b. 74354

BRING IT TO LIFE

Bring an envelope to class. Circle the mailing address. Check (✔) the return address.

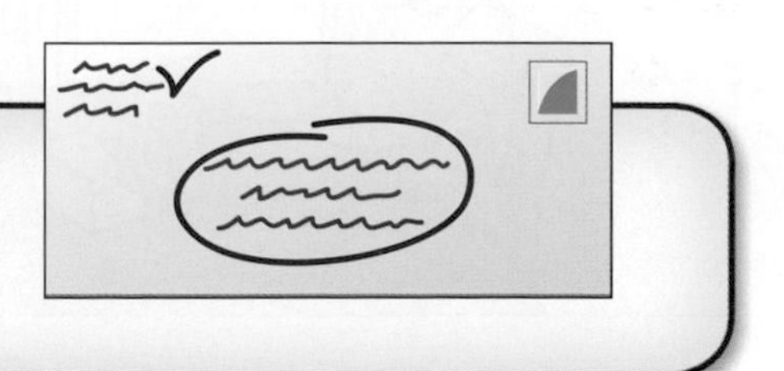

1 Grammar

A **Complete the sentences. Use contractions.**

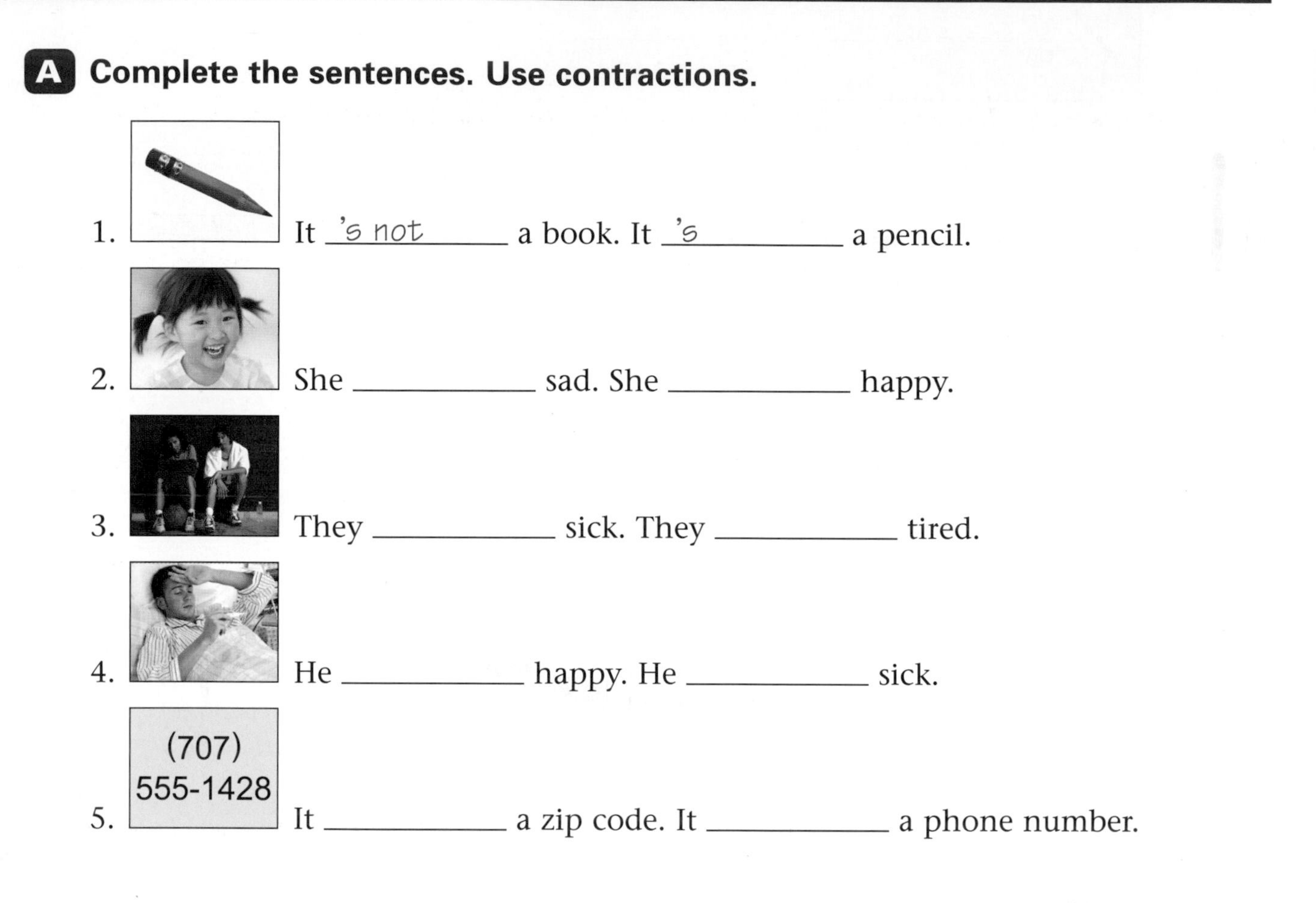

1. It _'s not_ a book. It _'s_ a pencil.
2. She ____________ sad. She ____________ happy.
3. They ____________ sick. They ____________ tired.
4. He ____________ happy. He ____________ sick.
5. (707) 555-1428 It ____________ a zip code. It ____________ a phone number.

2 Group work

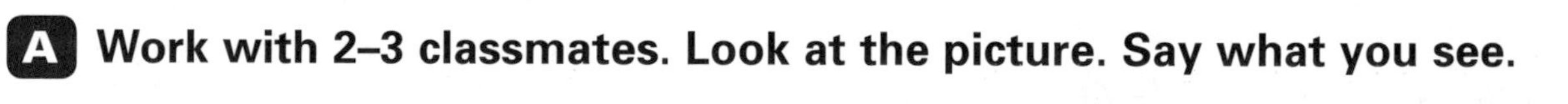

A **Work with 2–3 classmates. Look at the picture. Say what you see.**

B **Work with your group. Look at the picture in 2A again. Write what you see. Check your spelling in a dictionary.**

1. happy
2. ______
3. ______
4. ______
5. ______
6. ______

C **Work with your classmates. Make a list of the words from 2B.**

PROBLEM SOLVING

A **Listen. Look at the pictures.**

Gary's Problem

B **Work with your classmates. Help Gary.**

a. Go to the post office. Ask for help.

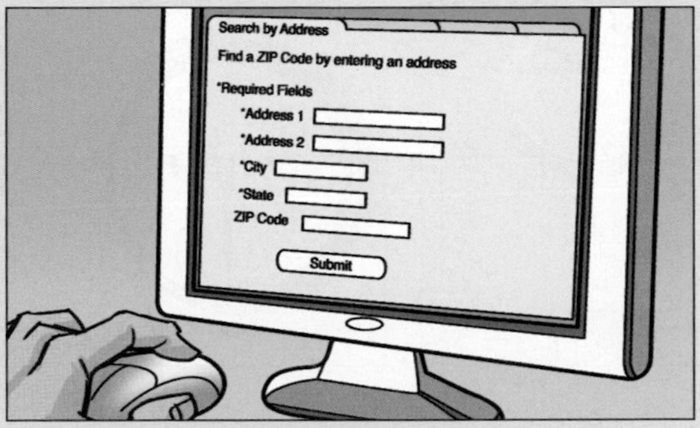

b. Look on the computer.

UNIT 3

What time is it?

FOCUS ON

- telling time
- places in the community
- *Yes/No* questions with *be*
- asking about time
- reading a bus schedule

LESSON 1 Vocabulary

1 Learn to tell time

A **Look at the pictures. Count the clocks.**

STUDENT AUDIO **B** **Listen and point to the pictures.**

1 

2 

3 

4 

5 

6 

7 

8 

9 

10 

STUDENT AUDIO **C** **Listen and repeat the words.**

1. morning
2. afternoon
3. evening
4. night
5. 2:00
6. 2:15
7. 2:30
8. 2:45
9. noon
10. midnight

D **Read the new words with a partner.**

 ☑ Interpret time with analog and digital clocks

2 Talk about time

A Look at the pictures. Complete the words.

1. m __o__ __r__ n i n g
2. n ___ o n
3. a ___ t e r n o o n
4. e ___ e n i n g
5. n i g ___ t
6. m i d n ___ g h t

43

B Listen and repeat.

A: What time is it?

B: It's 6:30.

C Work with a partner. Point to the clocks in 1B and 2A. Practice the conversation.

A: What time is it?

B: It's ______________.

TEST YOURSELF

Close your book. Write 3 times of day. Check your spelling in a dictionary.

LESSON 2 Life stories

1 Read about places in the community

A **Look at the pictures. Say the times.**

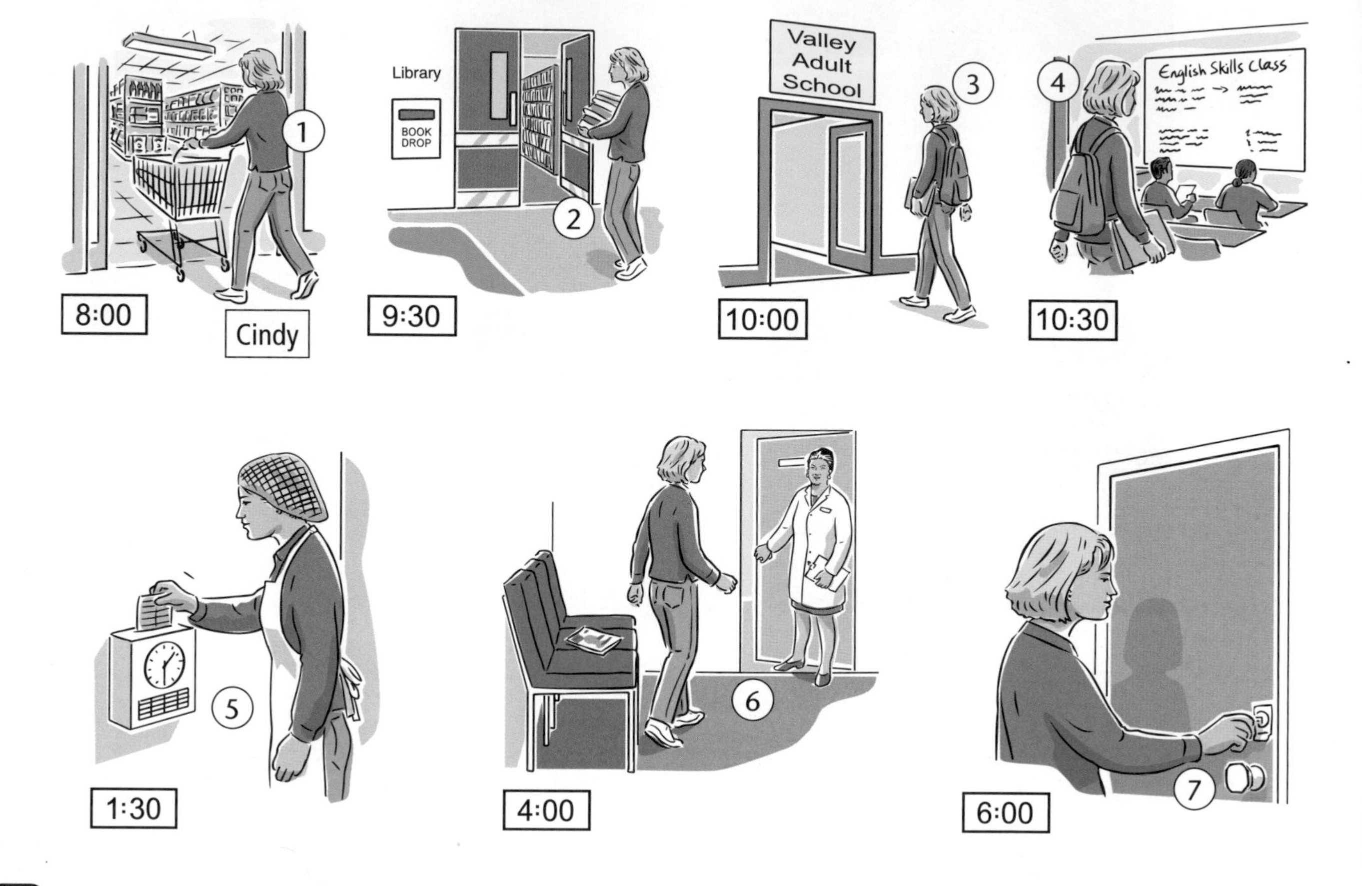

B **Listen and repeat the words.**

1. go to the store
2. go to the library
3. go to school
4. go to English class
5. go to work
6. go to the clinic
7. go home

C **Listen and read Cindy's story.**

1. I go to the store at 8:00.
2. I go to the library at 9:30.
3. I go to school at 10:00.
4. I go to English class at 10:30.

STUDENT AUDIO

D **Listen to Rick's story. Circle the correct word.**

1. I go to ____ at 9:00.	(school)	the store
2. I go to ____ at 1:00.	the clinic	the library
3. I go to English ____ at 2:30.	class	the clinic
4. I go to ____ at 6:00.	home	work

Rick

2 Write about your day

A **Write about your day. Complete the sentences. Use your own ideas.**

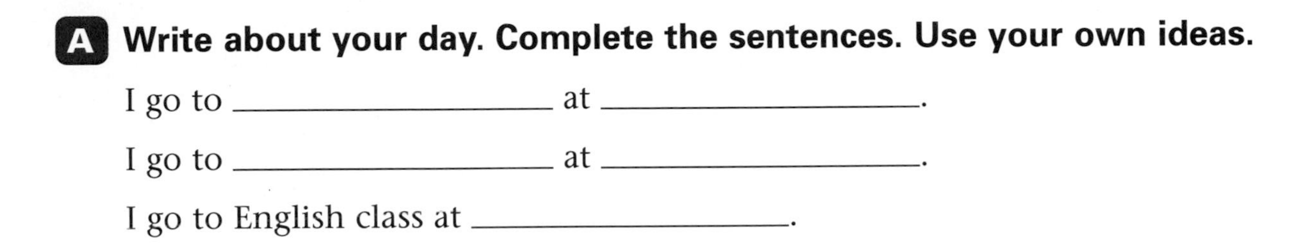

I go to ____________________ at ____________________.

I go to ____________________ at ____________________.

I go to English class at ____________________.

B **Read your story to a partner.**

3 Listen for *a.m.* and *p.m.*

A **Look at the pictures. Read the times and sentences.**

8 a.m. = 8:00 in the morning
I go to work at 8 a.m.

8 p.m. = 8:00 in the evening
I go home at 8 p.m.

STUDENT AUDIO

B **Listen. Circle *morning* or *evening*.**

1. (morning)	evening	3. morning	evening
2. morning	evening	4. morning	evening

STUDENT AUDIO

C **Listen again. Write the times you hear.**

1. 7 a.m. 2. __________ 3. __________ 4. __________

TEST YOURSELF ✓

Copy the sentences. Close your book. Then complete the sentences.
Use your own ideas.

I go to ________ at ________ in the morning. I go ________ at ________ .

LESSON 3 Grammar

1 Learn *Yes/No* questions with *be*

A Look at the pictures. Read the questions.

1 Are you at school?

2 Is it 6:00?

3 Is he at the clinic?

B Study the chart. Listen and repeat.

Is	he she	at school?
	it	6:00?
Are	you they	at home?

C Complete the questions. Use *Is* or *Are*. Then read the questions with a partner.

1. __Is__ he at school?
2. ______ she at school?
3. ______ it 6:00?
4. ______ you at home?
5. ______ they at home?

D Complete the statements and questions. Use *?* or *.*

1. She's at the clinic __.__
2. Are you at work ____
3. Is it 5:00 ____
4. He's at the library ____
5. It's closed ____
6. She's at home ____
7. Is he at the clinic ____
8. They're at the store ____

 ☑ Use *Yes/No* questions and short answers with *be* to talk about time and location

2 Learn short answers with *be*

A **Listen. Repeat the questions and answers.**

1

A: Are you at the store?
B: <u>Yes, I am.</u>
B: Are you at work?
A: <u>No, I'm not.</u>

2

A: Is she at work?
B: <u>Yes, she is.</u>
A: Is she at the clinic?
B: <u>No, she's not.</u>

3

A: Is he at school?
B: <u>Yes, he is.</u>
A: Is he at the library?
B: <u>No, he's not.</u>

4

A: Is it 10 a.m.?
B: <u>Yes, it is.</u>
A: Is it 10 p.m.?
B: <u>No, it's not.</u>

5

A: Are they at the library?
B: <u>Yes, they are.</u>
A: Are they at home?
B: <u>No, they're not.</u>

6

A: Are we happy?
B: <u>Yes, we are.</u>
A: Are we hungry?
B: <u>No, we're not.</u>

B **Read the questions. Complete the answers. Use short answers with *be*.**

1. A: Is it 4 p.m.?
   B: No, it 's not.
2. A: Is she at the store?
   B: Yes, she is.
3. A: Are you at school?
   B: Yes, I am.
4. A: Are they at the store?
   B: No, they aren't.

C **Work with a partner. Ask the questions. Answer with *Yes, I am.* or *No, I'm not.***

1. Are you at school?
2. Are you at the library?
3. Are you a student?
4. Are you a teacher?
5. Are you at home?
6. Are you in English class?
7. Are you from Mexico?
8. Are you from China?

TEST YOURSELF ✓

Write *Yes/No* questions and short answers with *be*.
Compare your sentences with a partner.

Are you at the library? No, I'm not.

LESSON 4 Everyday conversation

1 Learn to ask about time

A **Look at the pictures. Read the conversation.**

B **Listen and read.**

Alfredo: Excuse me. What time is it?
Pilar: It's 8:00.
Alfredo: Is the store open?
Pilar: No, it's not.

C **Listen again and repeat.**

D **Work with a partner. Practice the conversation. Use your own ideas.**

A: Excuse me. What time is it?

B: It's __________.

A: Is the __________ open?

B: No, it's not.

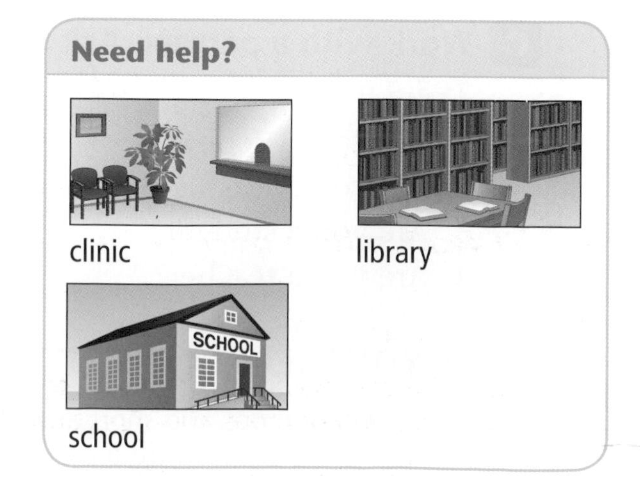

 ✔ Use appropriate language to ask for information about places in the community

2 Listen for times

A **Listen and point to the pictures.**

B **Listen again. What times do you hear? Circle *a* or *b*.**

1. (a.) 10 a.m. b. 10 p.m.
2. a. 8:00 in the morning b. 8:00 in the evening
3. a. 9 a.m. b. 9 p.m.
4. a. 10:00 in the morning b. 10:00 in the evening

3 Practice your pronunciation

A **Listen to the questions.**

1. Is the store open?↗
2. Are you at the office?↗

B **Listen and repeat the questions.**

1. Is it 4:00?↗
2. Is Daniel at the store?↗
3. Is the class in the morning?↗
4. Are you at home?↗
5. Are they happy?↗
6. Is he at the clinic?↗
7. Are they at work?↗
8. Are you hungry?↗

C **Work with a partner. Read the questions in 3B.**

TEST YOURSELF ✓

Copy the conversation. Close your book. Then add your own ideas and practice with a partner.

A: *Is the* ____________ *open?*
B: ____________.

LESSON 5 Real-life reading

1 Learn about kinds of transportation

A Look at the pictures. Listen and repeat.

1 bus 2 car 3 plane 4 train

B Listen. Circle *a* or *b*.

1. (a.) b.
2. a. b.
3. a. b.
4. a. b.

2 Get ready to read

A Look at the pictures. Read the words.

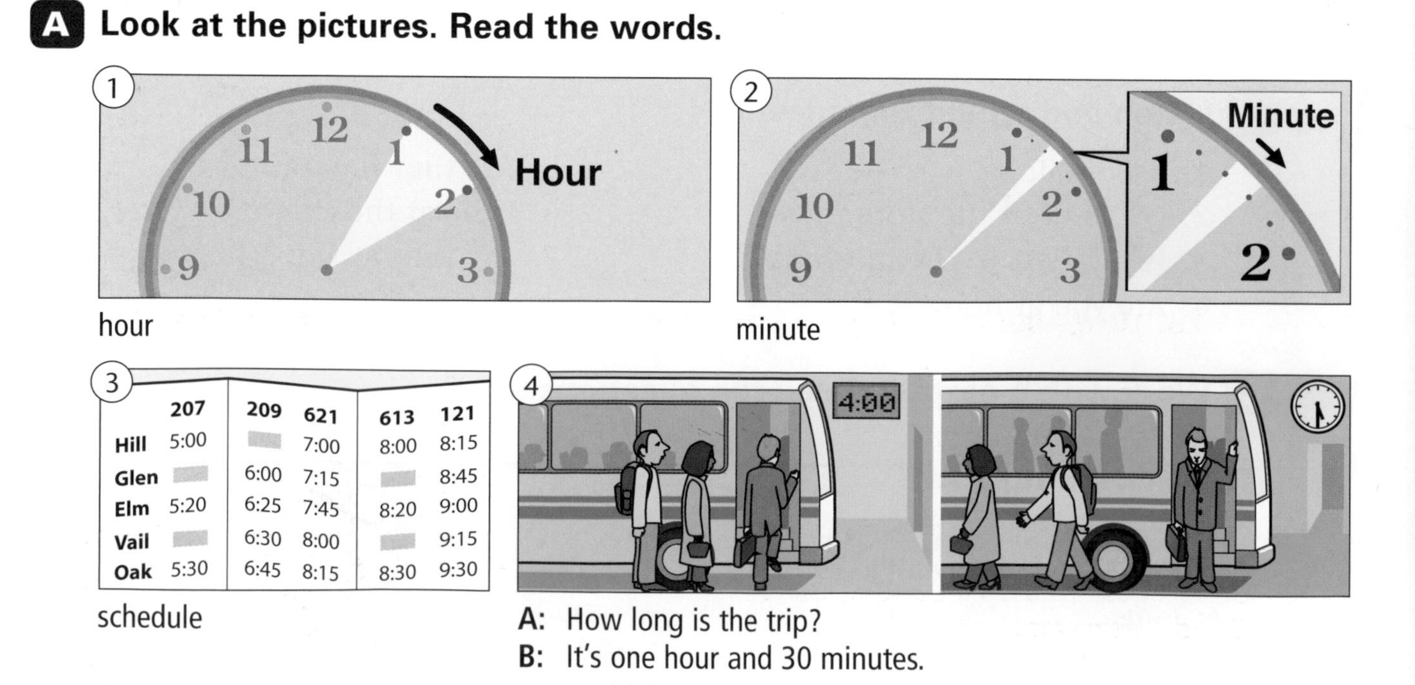

1 hour

2 minute

3

	207	209	621	613	121
Hill	5:00		7:00	8:00	8:15
Glen		6:00	7:15		8:45
Elm	5:20	6:25	7:45	8:20	9:00
Vail		6:30	8:00		9:15
Oak	5:30	6:45	8:15	8:30	9:30

schedule

4

A: How long is the trip?
B: It's one hour and 30 minutes.

B Work with your classmates. How long is your English class?

3 Read a bus schedule

A Read the bus schedule.

Bus Number	Newport	Springfield	Salem	Sundale
23	7:00 a.m.	——	10:00 a.m.	10:30 a.m.
61	7:30 a.m.	9:00 a.m.	10:50 a.m.	11:20 a.m.
94	9:30 a.m.	11:00 a.m.	——	1:10 p.m.
57	4:00 p.m.	——	7:00 p.m.	7:30 p.m.

B Look at the schedule. Circle *yes* or *no*.

1. Bus 94 is at Springfield. Is it 10:00 a.m.? yes (no)
2. Bus 61 is at Newport. Is it 7:30 a.m.? yes no
3. Bus 23 is at Sundale. Is it 10:30 a.m.? yes no
4. Bus 57 is at Salem. Is it 7:30 p.m.? yes no

C Look at the schedule. Answer the questions for Carlos. Circle *a* or *b*.

1. How long is the trip to Sundale on Bus 23?
   a. 2 hours and 30 minutes
   b. 3 hours and 30 minutes
2. How long is the trip to Sundale on Bus 61?
   a. 3 hours and 30 minutes
   b. 3 hours and 50 minutes
3. How long is the trip to Sundale on Bus 94?
   a. 2 hours and 40 minutes
   b. 3 hours and 40 minutes

Carlos is in Newport.

BRING IT TO LIFE

Bring a bus or train schedule to class.
Circle 1 new word.

UNIT 3 Review and expand

1 Grammar

A Read the questions. Complete the answers.

1. **A:** Is Deenah at the store?
   B: No, ___she's not___.
2. **A:** Is Monica at the clinic?
   B: Yes, ______________________.
3. **A:** Is Bob at home?
   B: Yes, ______________________.
4. **A:** Are the students at the library?
   B: Yes, ______________________.
5. **A:** Is it 11:00?
   B: No, ______________________.
6. **A:** Is he at work?
   B: No, ______________________.
7. **A:** Is she at home?
   B: No, ______________________.

2 Group work

 **Work with 2–3 classmates. Look at the pictures. Say what you see.**

B **Work with your group. Look at the pictures in 2A again. Write what you see. Check your spelling in a dictionary.**

1. clinic
2. ______________________
3. ______________________
4. ______________________
5. ______________________
6. ______________________

C **Work with your classmates. Make a list of the words from 2B.**

PROBLEM SOLVING

A **Listen. Look at the pictures.**

Tony's Problem

B **Work with your classmates. Help Tony.**

a. Leave class early.

b. Go to class late.

UNIT 4

What day is it?

FOCUS ON
- days
- months
- *on* and *at*; information questions
- saying goodbye
- ordinal numbers

LESSON 1 Vocabulary

1 Learn the days of the week

A **Look at the calendar. What time is English class?**

B **Listen and point to the days.**

55

Sunday ①	Monday ②	Tuesday ③	Wednesday ④	Thursday ⑤	Friday ⑥	Saturday ⑦
	1	9:00 – 12:00 English class 2	3:00 clinic 3	4	5	6
⑧						

⑨

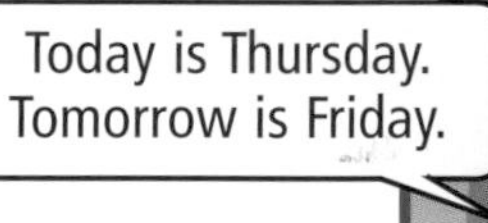

C **Listen and repeat the words.**

56

1. Sunday	4. Wednesday	7. Saturday	10. today
2. Monday	5. Thursday	8. day	11. tomorrow
3. Tuesday	6. Friday	9. week	12. weekend

D **Read the new words with a partner.**

 ☑ Identify the days of the week

2 Talk about the days of the week

A **Look at the picture. Complete the words.**

1. w e e __k__ e n d
2. M ___ n d a y
3. T u e s ___ a y
4. ___ e d n e s d a y
5. T h ___ r s d a y
6. F r i d a ___
7. S a t u ___ d a y
8. S u n d ___ y
9. w e ___ k

STUDENT AUDIO 57

B **Listen and repeat.**

A: What day is it?
B: It's Thursday.

C **Work with a partner. Point to the days in 2A. Practice the conversation.**

A: What day is it?
B: It's __________.

TEST YOURSELF ✓

Close your book. Write 3 days of the week. Check your spelling in a dictionary.

LESSON 2 Life stories

1 Read about the months

A **Look at the picture. Point to the number 24.**

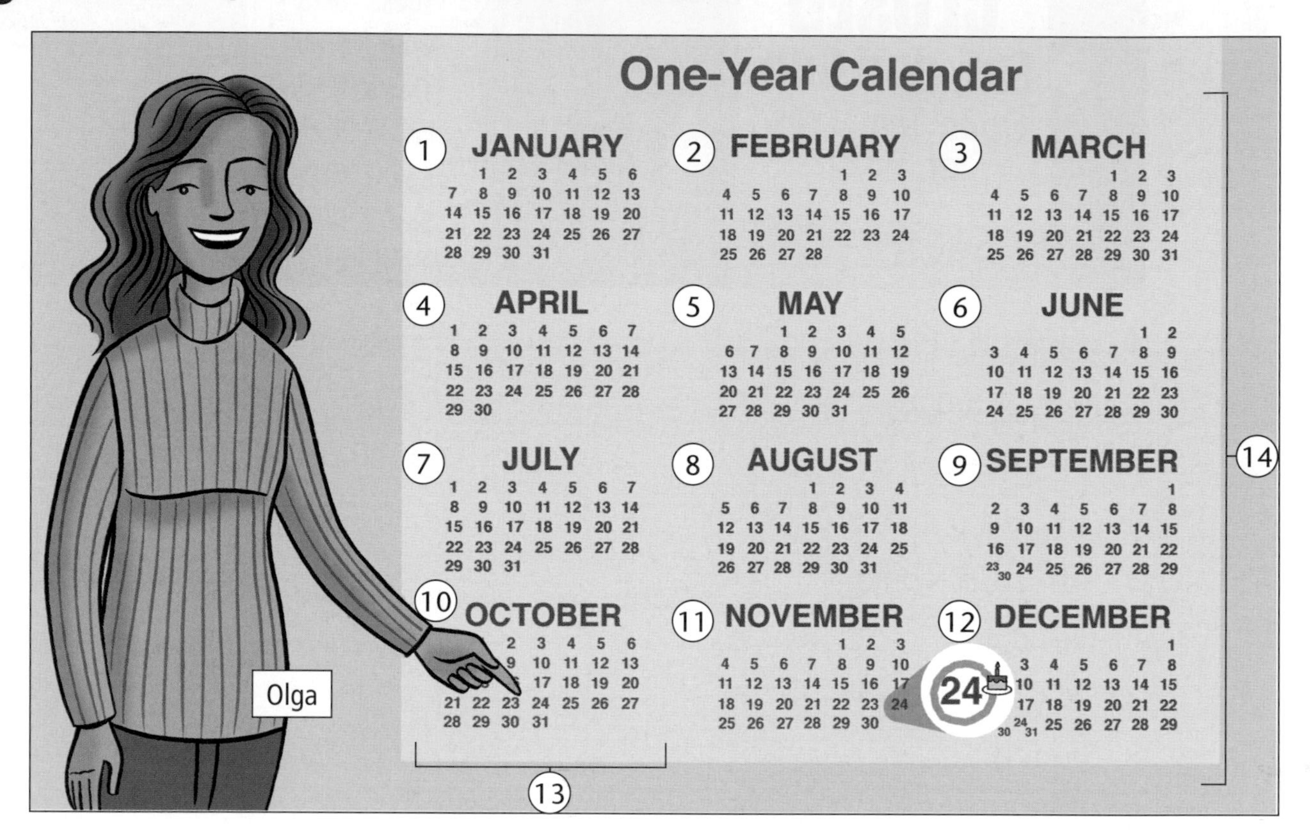

B **Listen and repeat the words.**

1. January
2. February
3. March
4. April
5. May
6. June
7. July
8. August
9. September
10. October
11. November
12. December
13. month
14. year

STUDENT AUDIO

C **Listen and read Olga's story.**

1. It's October.
2. Next month is November.
3. My birthday is in November.

STUDENT AUDIO

D **Listen to Bill's story. Circle the correct word.**

1. It's ____. April August
2. Next month is ____. March May
3. My birthday is in ____. June July

Bill

2 Write about the months

Write about the months. Complete the sentences. Use your own information.

It's ____________________.

Next month is ____________________.

My birthday is in ____________________.

B **Read your story to a partner.**

3 Listen for years

A **Listen and repeat the years.**

1. 1948
2. 1952
3. 1963
4. 1975
5. 1986
6. 2000
7. 2008
8. 2011

STUDENT AUDIO

B **Listen. Circle *a* or *b*.**

1. a. 1964 b. 1946
2. a. 2007 b. 2008
3. a. 1985 b. 1958
4. a. 1972 b. 1992
5. a. March b. May
6. a. February 1956 b. February 1965

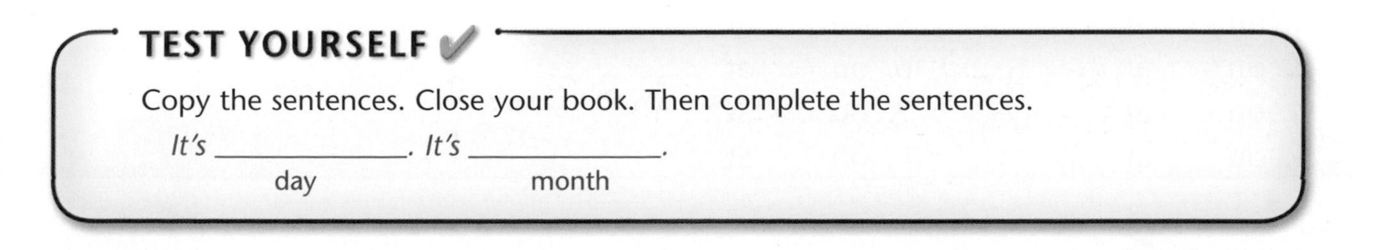
TEST YOURSELF

Copy the sentences. Close your book. Then complete the sentences.

It's ______________ (day). *It's* ______________ (month).

LESSON 3 Grammar

1 Learn *on* with days and *at* with times

A Look at the picture. Read the sentences.

IT'S A
BIRTHDAY
PARTY
When: Tuesday
What time: 7:00

The party is on Tuesday. The party is at 7:00.

B Study the chart. Listen and repeat.

The birthday party is The class party is	on	Tuesday Thursday	at	7:00. 5:00.

C Complete the sentences. Circle *on* or *at*. Then read the sentences with a partner.

1. The birthday party is ____ Tuesday.

   on   at

2. The birthday party is ____ 7:00.

   on   at

3. The class party is ____ 5:00.

   on   at

4. The class party is ____ Thursday.

   on   at

D Listen. Circle *on* or *at*.

1. on   at
2. on   at
3. on   at
4. on   at
5. on   at
6. on   at
7. on   at
8. on   at

2 Learn information questions

A **Listen. What time is the party?**

Abena: When is the birthday party?
Gloria: It's on Tuesday.
Abena: Where is the party?
Gloria: It's at my house.
Abena: What time is the party?
Gloria: It's at 6:00.
Abena: Are you excited?
Gloria: Yes, I am!

B **Listen again. Complete the questions.**

1. **Abena:** ___________ is the birthday party?
   Gloria: It's on Tuesday.
2. **Abena:** ___________ is the party?
   Gloria: It's at my house.
3. **Abena:** ___________ time is the party?
   Gloria: It's at 6:00.

C **Read the invitation. Answer the questions. Circle *a* or *b*.**

1. When is the party?
   (a.) It's on Thursday. b. It's at Pizza Town.
2. What time is the party?
   a. It's on Thursday. b. It's at 6:00.
3. Where is the party?
   a. Yes, it is. b. It's at Pizza Town.
4. Is the party on Thursday?
   a. Yes, it is. b. It's at Pizza Town.

D **Work with a partner. Read the questions and answers in 2C.**

TEST YOURSELF

Write sentences for a party invitation. Compare your sentences with a partner.
The party is on Friday. It's at 4:30.

LESSON 4 Everyday conversation

1 Learn to say goodbye

A **Look at the pictures. Read the conversations.**

B **Listen and read.**

Arun: Goodbye. Have a nice weekend.
Oscar: Thanks. You, too. See you Monday.

Mrs. Robledo: Bye. Have a nice evening.
Tuan: Thanks. You, too. See you tomorrow.

C **Listen again and repeat.**

D **Work with your classmates. Practice the conversation. Use your own ideas.**

A: Goodbye. Have a nice ___________.

B: Thanks. You, too. See you ___________.

2 Listen for dates with years

A Read the dates.

June 4, 2009 = 6/4/2009
April 6, 2009 = 4/6/2009
July 12, 1960 = 7/12/1960
December 7, 1960 = 12/7/1960

B Listen. Circle *a* or *b*.

1. a. 6/4/1999 (b.) 4/6/1999
2. a. 7/12/1960 b. 12/7/1960
3. a. 11/9/1982 b. 9/11/1982
4. a. 8/10/2009 b. 10/8/2009
5. a. 2/1/2007 b. 1/2/2007
6. a. 3/5/1951 b. 5/3/1951
7. a. 11/5/1974 b. 5/11/1974
8. a. 1/8/2008 b. 8/1/2008

C Work with a partner. Look at the dates in 2B. Say the months.

3 Practice your pronunciation

A Listen to the pronunciation of *t* and *th*.

See you **t**omorrow. **Th**anks. See you **Th**ursday.

B Listen and repeat the words.

t	*th*
1. tomorrow	4. Thursday
2. Tuesday	5. thirsty
3. tired	6. thanks

C Listen. Check (✔) the sounds you hear.

	1.	2.	3.	4.	5.	6.
t	✔					
th						

TEST YOURSELF ✔

Copy the conversation. Close your book. Then add your own ideas and practice with a partner.

A: Goodbye. ______________.
B: ______________.

LESSON 5 Real-life reading

1 Learn about ordinal numbers

A Look at the calendar. Listen and point to the dates.

March						
Sun.	**Mon.**	**Tues.**	**Wed.**	**Thurs.**	**Fri.**	**Sat.**
1 first	2 second	3 third	4 fourth	5 fifth	6 sixth	7 seventh
8 eighth	9 ninth	10 tenth	11 eleventh	12 twelfth	13 thirteenth	14 fourteenth
15 fifteenth	16 sixteenth	17 seventeenth	18 eighteenth	19 nineteenth	20 twentieth	21 twenty-first
22 twenty-second	23 twenty-third	24 twenty-fourth	25 twenty-fifth	26 twenty-sixth	27 twenty-seventh	28 twenty-eighth
29 twenty-ninth	30 thirtieth	31 thirty-first				

B Listen again and repeat.

C Match the numbers with the ordinals.

_c_ 1. one	a. second
___ 2. two	b. fourth
___ 3. three	c. first
___ 4. four	d. fifth
___ 5. five	e. third

2 Get ready to read

A Look at the pictures. Read the words.

1 winter break

2 registration

3 the last day of school

B **Work with your classmates. Complete the sentences.**

1. The last day of school is ________________.
2. Winter break is from ________________ to ________________.

3 Read a school calendar

A **Read the school calendar.**

Valley Adult School Calendar

Important Dates

September 5-9 .... registration

September 12 .... the first day of school

November 24-25 .... Thanksgiving holiday

December 20-January 3 .... winter break

June 20 .... the last day of school

B **Look at the calendar. Circle *a* or *b*.**

1. ____ is September 5–9.
   a. Winter break (b.) Registration
2. ____ is December 20–January 3.
   a. The first day of school b. Winter break
3. The ____ day of school is June 20.
   a. first b. last
4. The ____ day of school is September 12.
   a. first b. last

BRING IT TO LIFE

Find the calendar for your school. Bring it to class. Circle 2 new words.

May Calendar

Computer lab 5/3

Language lab 5/8

Mother's Day 5/13

Memorial Day 5/28

UNIT 4 Review and expand

1 Grammar

A Complete the questions. Circle *a* or *b*.

1. **A:** ____ is your birthday?
   B: It's on April 25.
   a. Where
   (b.) When

2. **A:** ____ time is the party?
   B: It's at 6:00.
   a. What
   b. When

3. **A:** ____ is the party?
   B: It's at my house.
   a. Where
   b. What

4. **A:** ____ the party on Thursday?
   B: Yes, it is.
   a. Is
   b. When

5. **A:** ____ is the first day of school?
   B: September 10.
   a. Where
   b. When

6. **A:** ____ you happy?
   B: Yes, I am.
   a. Are
   b. Where

B Complete the sentences. Use *on* or *at*.

1. Registration is ____on____ Thursday.
2. I go to work ________ 6:00.
3. I go to the library ________ Mondays.
4. The party is ________ December 2 ________ 7:00.

2 Group work

A Work with 2–3 classmates. Look at the picture. Say what you see.

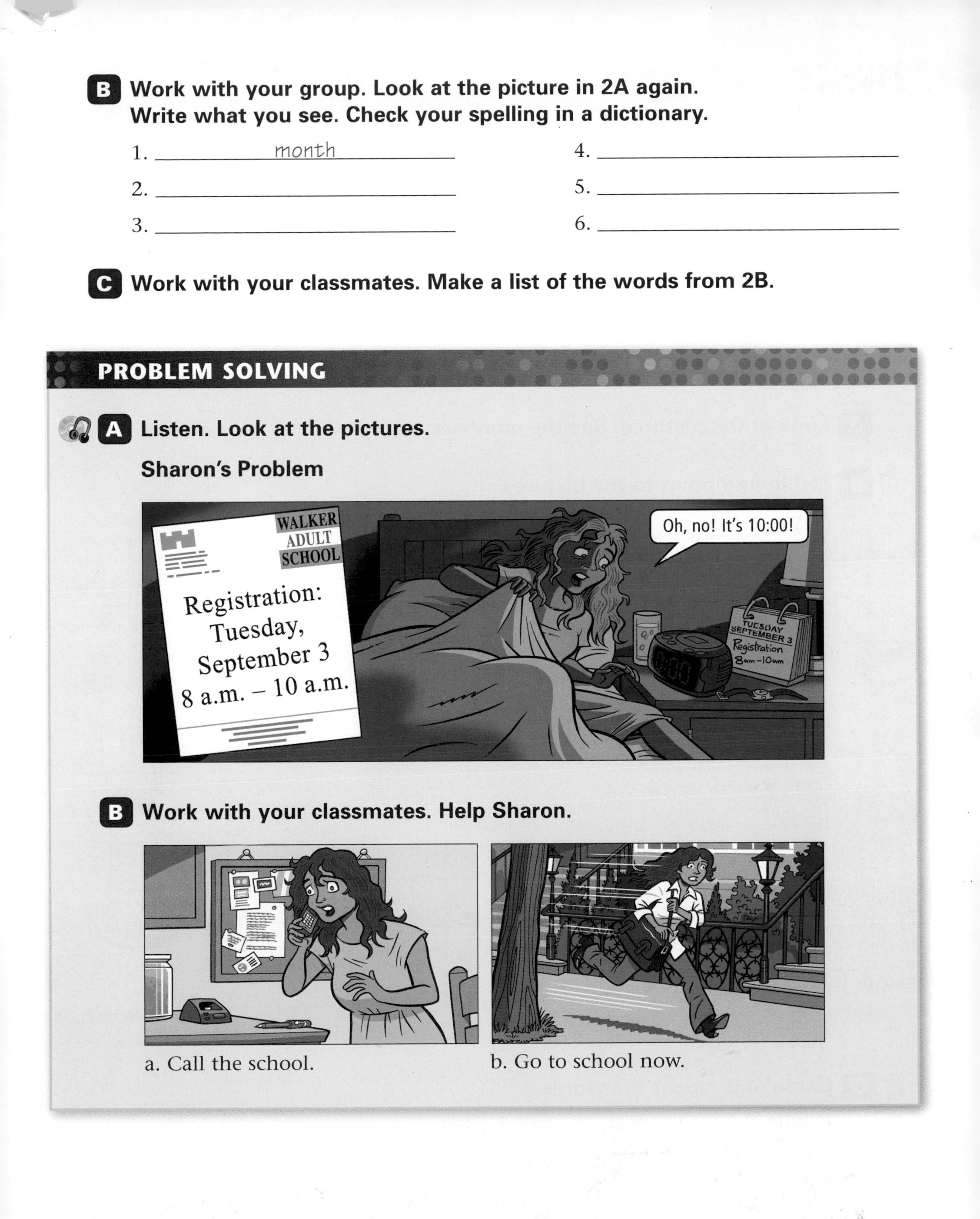

B **Work with your group. Look at the picture in 2A again. Write what you see. Check your spelling in a dictionary.**

1. ______month______
2. ____________
3. ____________
4. ____________
5. ____________
6. ____________

C **Work with your classmates. Make a list of the words from 2B.**

PROBLEM SOLVING

A **Listen. Look at the pictures.**

Sharon's Problem

B **Work with your classmates. Help Sharon.**

a. Call the school.

b. Go to school now.

UNIT 5

How much is it?

FOCUS ON
- money
- shopping
- *This, That, These,* and *Those*
- asking about prices
- reading a check

LESSON 1 Vocabulary

1 Learn words for money

A **Look at the pictures. Say the numbers.**

B **Listen and point to the pictures.**

41¢

1¢ = $0.01

5¢ = $0.05

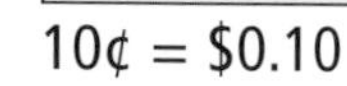

10¢ = $0.10

25¢ = $0.25

C **Listen and repeat the words.**

1. bills	4. cents	7. dime
2. dollar	5. penny	8. quarter
3. coins	6. nickel	

D **Read the new words with a partner.**

 ✔ Identify coins and currency

2 Talk about money

A Look at the picture. Complete the words.

1. p ___ ___ n y
2. d i ___ e
3. b ___ ___ l s
4. ___ o l l ___ r
5. ___ ___ i n s
6. n i c ___ ___ l
7. ___ u a ___ t e r
8. c ___ ___ t s

STUDENT AUDIO

B Listen and repeat.

1. **A:** How much is it?
   B: It's 25¢.
2. **A:** How much is it?
   B: It's $6.

C Listen. Circle *a* or *b*.

1. a. 65¢ b. 75¢
2. a. $2 b. $12
3. a. 35¢ b. 45¢
4. a. $6 b. $16
5. a. $5 b. $7
6. a. 80¢ b. 90¢

D Work with a partner. Point to the money in 2A. Practice the conversation.

A: How much is it?

B: It's ___________.

TEST YOURSELF ✓

Close your book. Write 3 words for money. Check your spelling in a dictionary.

Life stories

1 Read about shopping

A **Look at the picture. Say the numbers.**

B **Listen and repeat the words.**

1. price
2. pants
3. shirt
4. sweater
5. socks
6. shoes
7. clothes
8. cheap
9. expensive

STUDENT AUDIO **C** **Listen and read Daniela's story.**

1. Clothes Mart is a good store.
2. The clothes are good.
3. The prices are cheap.

 ✔ Identify common articles of clothing; interpret price tags

STUDENT AUDIO

D **Listen to Ken's story. Circle the correct word.**

1. Shoe World is a good ____. (store) sock
2. The ____ are good. sweaters shoes
3. The ____ are cheap. shoes socks

Ken

2 Write about shopping

A **Write about shopping. Complete the sentences. Use your own ideas.**

________________ is a good store.

The ________________ are good.

The ________________ are cheap.

B **Read your story to a partner.**

3 Listen for prices

A **Listen and repeat.**

1. $1.50
2. $2.30
3. $5.45
4. $12.25
5. $15.50
6. $7.60

B **Listen and write the prices.**

1. $ 3 . 2 5
2. $____.____ ____
3. $____.____ ____
4. $____.____ ____
5. $____.____ ____
6. $____.____ ____

TEST YOURSELF ✓

Copy the sentences. Close your book. Then complete the sentences.

The ____________ is cheap. It's $____________.

LESSON 3 Grammar

1 Learn *This* and *That*

A Look at the pictures. Listen and repeat the sentences.

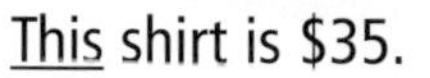
This shirt is $35.

That shirt is $42.

This sweater is $22.

That sweater is $54.

B Look at 1A. Write *This* or *That*.

1. ___________ shirt is $35.
2. ___________ shirt is $42.
3. ___________ sweater is $22.
4. ___________ sweater is $54.

C Look at the pictures. Circle *a* or *b*. Then read the sentences with a partner.

1. ____ sweater is $12.

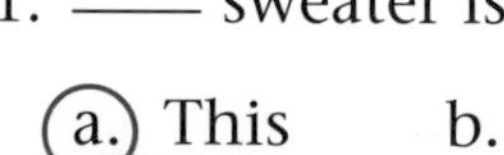
(a.) This   b. That

2. ____ sweater is $9.99.

a. This   b. That

3. ____ dictionary is $5.99.

a. This   b. That

4. ____ dictionary is $42.

a. This   b. That

✔ Use demonstrative pronouns to talk about prices

2 Learn *These* and *Those*

A **Look at the pictures. Listen and repeat the sentences.**

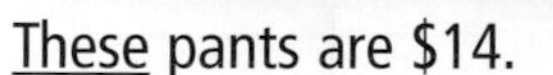

<u>These</u> pants are $14.

<u>Those</u> pants are $45.

B **Match the pictures with the sentences.**

__b__ 1. These pants are $45.

____ 2. Those pants are $45.

____ 3. These shoes are $34.50.

____ 4. Those shoes are $34.50.

____ 5. These pens are $3.99.

____ 6. Those pens are $3.99.

C **Complete the sentences. Circle *a* or *b*.**

1. ____ pencil is 25¢.
   (a.) This b. These
2. ____ shoes are $30.
   a. That b. Those
3. ____ clock is expensive.
   a. That b. Those
4. ____ notebooks are cheap.
   a. This b. These

D **Work with a partner. Read the sentences in 2B and 2C.**

TEST YOURSELF ✔

Write sentences using *This*, *That*, *These*, or *Those*. Compare your sentences with a partner.

This shirt is expensive. Those pencils are 30¢.

LESSON 4 Everyday conversation

1 Learn to talk about prices

A Look at the pictures. Read the conversation.

B Listen and read.

George: How much is the shirt?
Kumi: It's $35.
George: How much are the shoes?
Kumi: They're $33.
George: That's cheap!

C Listen again and repeat.

D Work with a partner. Practice the conversation. Use your own ideas.

A: How much is the ____________?
B: It's ____________.
A: How much are the ____________?
B: They're ____________.
A: That's ____________!

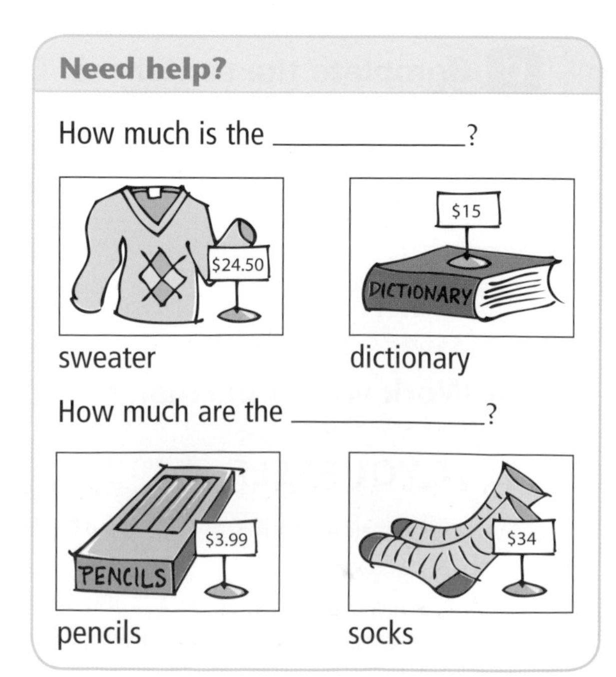

Need help?
How much is the ____________?
$24.50
sweater
$15
DICTIONARY
dictionary
How much are the ____________?
$3.99
PENCILS
pencils
$34
socks

2 Listen for change amounts

A **Look at the money. What coins do you see?**

B **Listen. Circle *a* or *b*.**

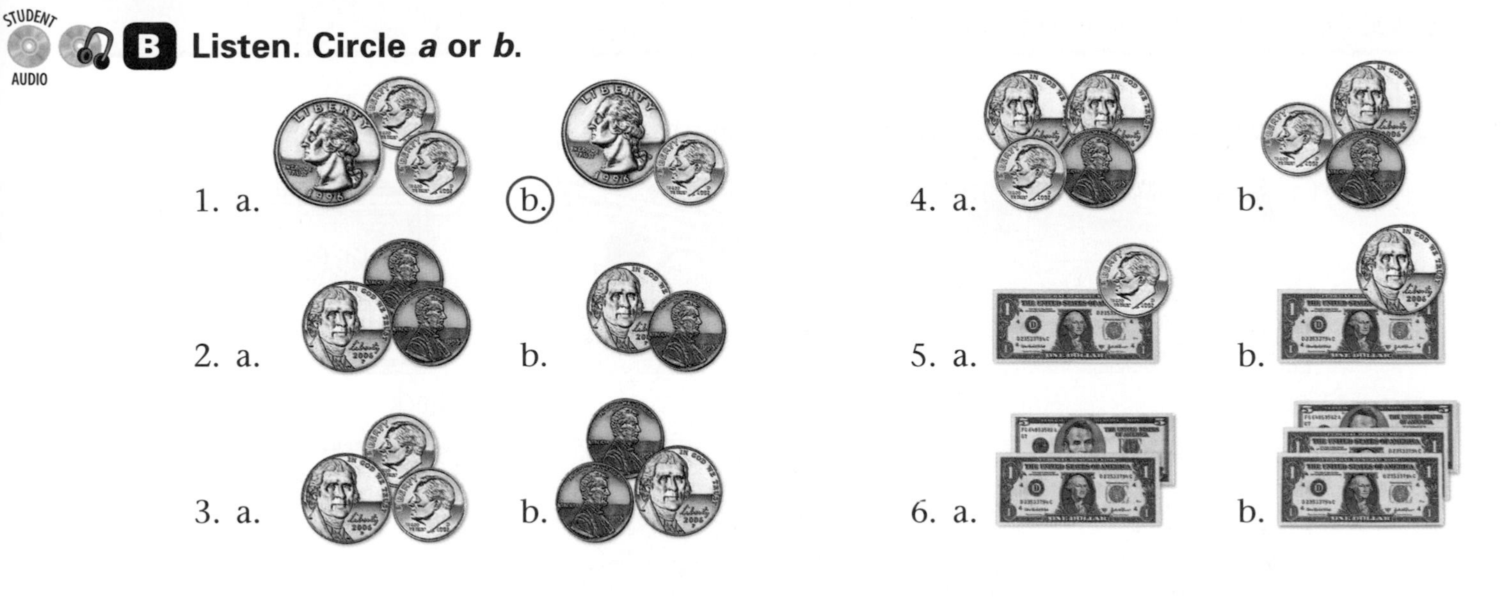

3 Real-life math

A **Look at the picture. Say the prices.**

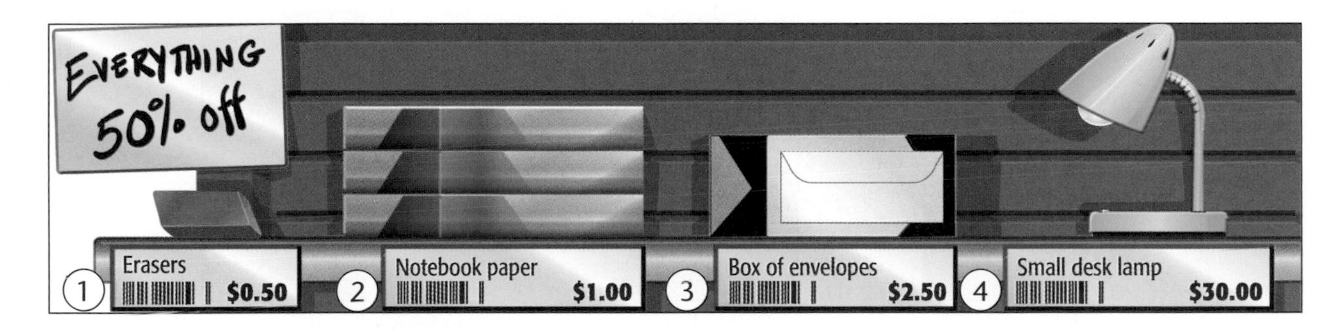

B **Do the math. Write the sale price.**

1. $0.50 × 0.5 = $ 0.25	An eraser is $ 0.25.
2. $1.00 × 0.5 = $______	The paper is $______.
3. $2.50 × 0.5 = $______	The envelopes are $______.
4. $30.00 × 0.5 = $______	A lamp is $______.

TEST YOURSELF ✔

Copy the conversation. Close your book. Then add your own ideas and practice with a partner.

A: *How much is ______?*
B: *It's ______.*

1 Learn about ways to pay

STUDENT AUDIO **A** **Look at the pictures. Listen and repeat.**

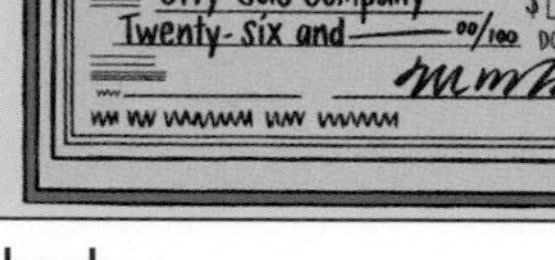

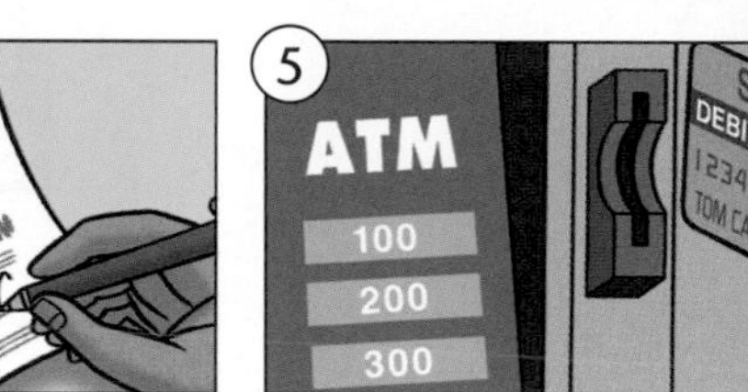

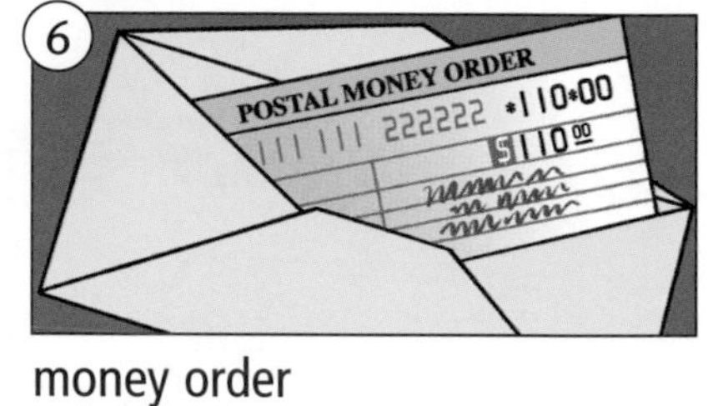

1. pay
2. cash
3. check
4. credit card
5. debit card
6. money order

STUDENT AUDIO **B** **Listen. Circle *a* or *b*.**

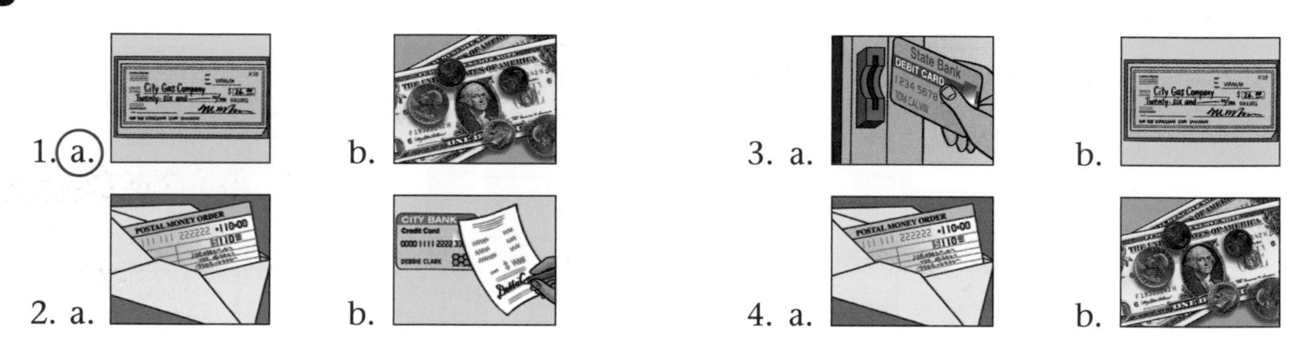

1. (a.) b.
2. a. b.
3. a. b.
4. a. b.

2 Get ready to read

A **Look at the pictures. Read the words.**

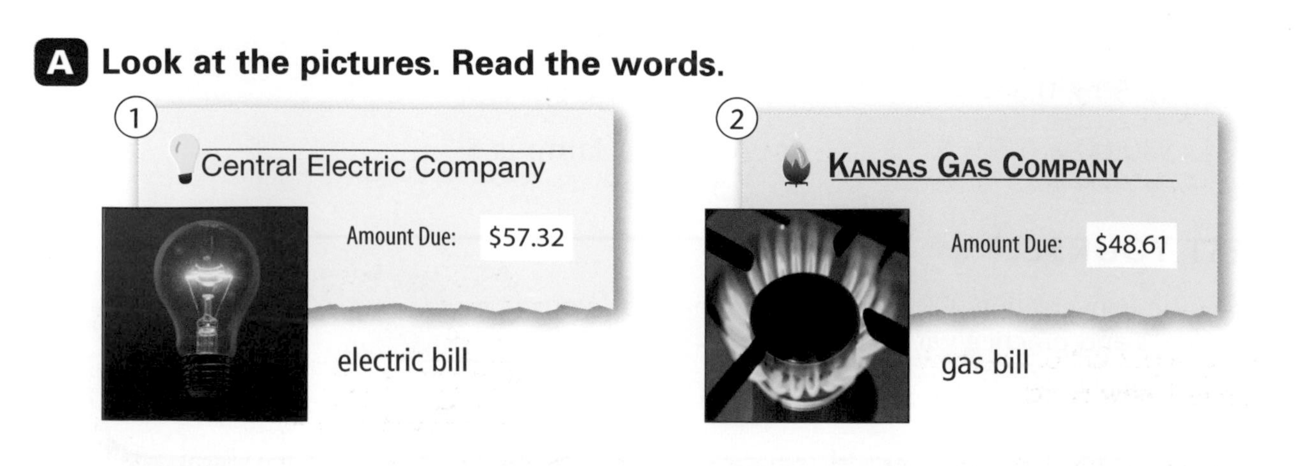

1. electric bill
2. gas bill

B **Complete the sentences with *expensive* or *cheap*.**

1. My gas bill is ________________.
2. My electric bill is ________________.

3 Read a check

A **Read the bill and the check.**

Central Electric Company

Amount Due: $56.23

Joel and Ana Marino
4219 Brook Street
Topeka, Kansas 61401

2529

Date 7/12/2009

PAY TO THE ORDER OF Central Electric Company $ 56.23

fifty-six and 23/100 DOLLARS

FOR electric bill Joel Marino

87255654653 06128745379

B **Look at the gas bill. Complete the check.**

KANSAS GAS COMPANY

Amount Due: $32.89

State Bank

2530

Date ____________

PAY TO THE ORDER OF ______________________________ $ [ ]

______________________________ DOLLARS

FOR ________________ ________________

12345470053 06457820579

BRING IT TO LIFE

Bring a gas bill or an electric bill to class.
Circle 1 new word.

1 Grammar

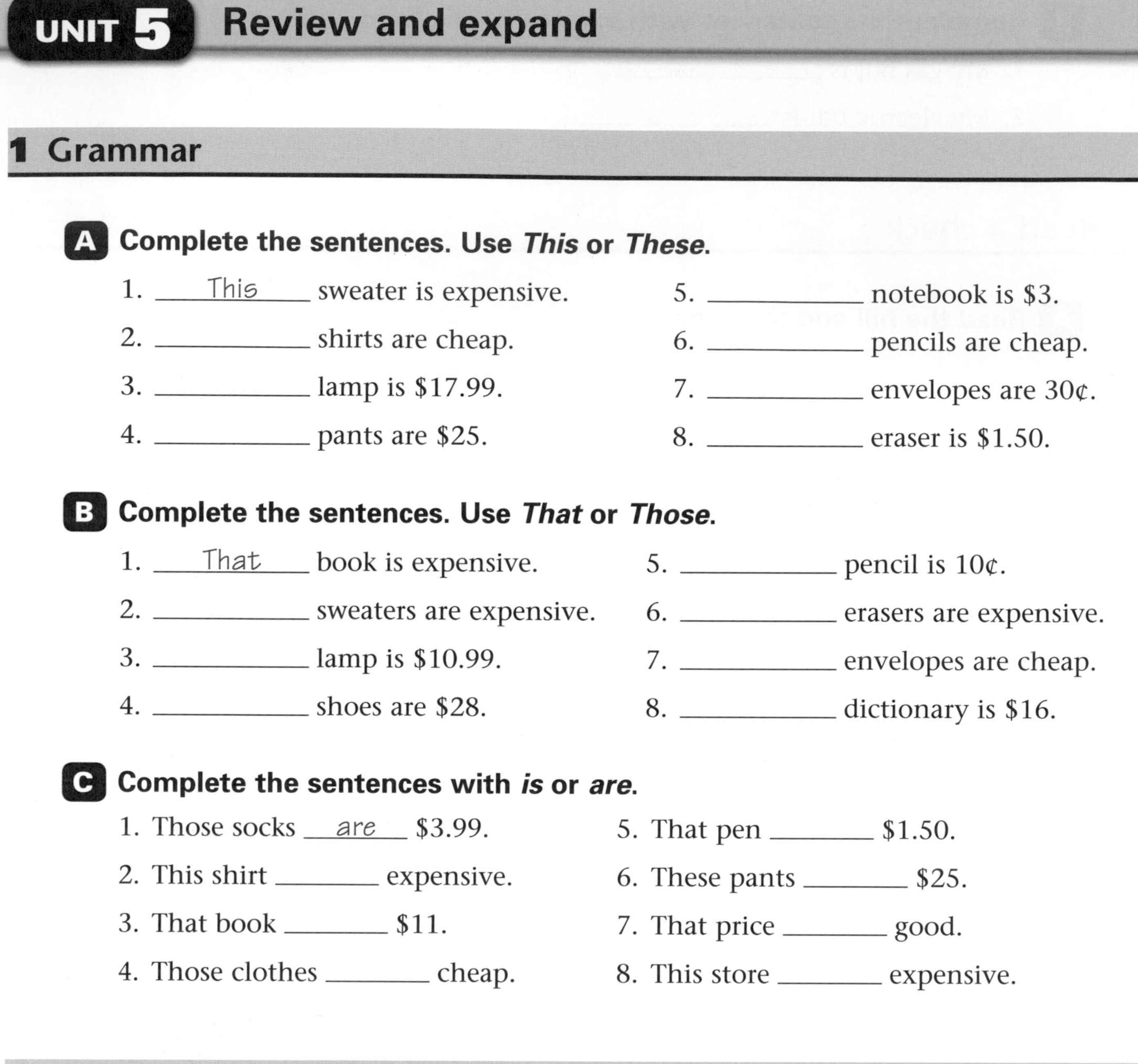

A Complete the sentences. Use *This* or *These*.

1. This sweater is expensive.
2. ________ shirts are cheap.
3. ________ lamp is $17.99.
4. ________ pants are $25.
5. ________ notebook is $3.
6. ________ pencils are cheap.
7. ________ envelopes are 30¢.
8. ________ eraser is $1.50.

B Complete the sentences. Use *That* or *Those*.

1. That book is expensive.
2. ________ sweaters are expensive.
3. ________ lamp is $10.99.
4. ________ shoes are $28.
5. ________ pencil is 10¢.
6. ________ erasers are expensive.
7. ________ envelopes are cheap.
8. ________ dictionary is $16.

C Complete the sentences with *is* or *are*.

1. Those socks are $3.99.
2. This shirt ________ expensive.
3. That book ________ $11.
4. Those clothes ________ cheap.
5. That pen ________ $1.50.
6. These pants ________ $25.
7. That price ________ good.
8. This store ________ expensive.

2 Group work

A Work with 2–3 classmates. Look at the picture. Say what you see.

B **Work with your group. Look at the picture in 2A again. Write what you see. Check your spelling in a dictionary.**

1. shirt
2. ______________
3. ______________
4. ______________
5. ______________
6. ______________

C **Work with your classmates. Make a list of the words from 2B.**

PROBLEM SOLVING

A **Listen. Look at the pictures.**

Ivan's Problem

$20.15

$20.05

B **Work with your classmates. Help Ivan.**

$20.15

$15.00

a. Ask for a dime.

b. Go home.

c. Buy cheaper shoes.

UNIT 6

That's My Son

FOCUS ON
- family members
- marital status
- the simple present
- talking about family and friends
- the U.S. school system

LESSON 1 Vocabulary

1 Learn about friends and family members

A **Look at the pictures. Count the men and women.**

B **Listen and point to the pictures.**

C **Listen and repeat the words.**

1. parents	4. baby	7. friend
2. mother	5. girl	8. husband
3. father	6. boy	9. wife

D **Read the new words with a partner.**

 ☑ Identify friends and family members

2 Talk about families

A Look at the picture. Complete the words.

1. w _i_ f _e_
2. h ___ s ___ a n d
3. ___ a ___ h e r
4. p ___ r e n t ___
5. m ___ t h e ___
6. b a ___ y
7. b ___ y
8. ___ i r l
9. f r i ___ ___ d

B Listen and repeat.

1. **A:** Is this the father?
   B: No, that's the mother.
2. **A:** Is this the boy?
   B: Yes, that's the boy.

C Work with a partner. Point to the people in 2A. Practice the conversations.

A: Is this the ___________?

B: No, that's the ___________.

A: Is this the ___________?

B: Yes, that's the ___________.

TEST YOURSELF ✓

Close your book. Write 4 family words. Check your spelling in a dictionary.

LESSON 2 Life stories

1 Read about families

A **Look at the pictures. Point to the girls.**

B **Listen and repeat the words.**

1. children
2. child
3. daughter
4. son
5. brother
6. sister

C **Listen and read Sandra's story.**

1. These are my children.
2. This is my son.
3. He's seven years old.
4. This is my daughter.
5. She's ten years old.

D **Listen to Freddy's story. Circle the correct word.**

Freddy

1. These are my ____. (children) child
2. This is my ____. daughter brother
3. ____ twenty years old. He's She's
4. This is my ____. son sister
5. ____ fifteen years old. He's She's

2 Write about your family or friends

A **Write about your family or friends. Complete the sentences. Show or draw a picture.**

This is my ____________________.

He's ____________________ years old.

This is my ____________________.

She's ____________________ years old.

B **Read your story to a partner.**

3 Listen for marital status

A **Listen and repeat the sentences.**

We're married.

I'm single.

We're divorced.

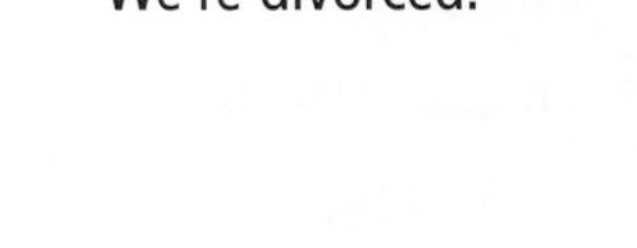

B **Listen. Circle *a* or *b*.**

1. a. married (b.) divorced
2. a. married b. single
3. a. single b. divorced
4. a. married b. divorced

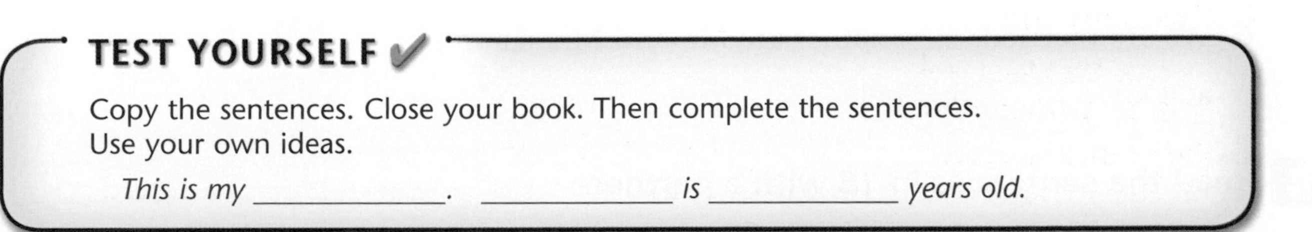

TEST YOURSELF ✓

Copy the sentences. Close your book. Then complete the sentences. Use your own ideas.

This is my ______________. ______________ *is* ______________ *years old.*

LESSON 3 Grammar

1 Learn possessive adjectives

A Look at the pictures. Listen and read the sentences.

1. I am a student.
My name is Marie.

2. You are my friend.
Your name is Silvia.

3. He is my brother.
His name is Claude.

4. She is my sister.
Her name is Brigitte.

5. They are my friends.
Their names are Annie and Donna.

6. We are married.
Our names are Mr. and Mrs. Laurent.

B Complete the sentences. Circle *a* or *b*.

1. I'm a student. ____ name is Marie.
   a. Your (b.) My
2. You are my friend. ____ name is Silvia.
   a. Your b. My
3. He is my brother. ____ name is Claude.
   a. My b. His
4. She is my sister. ____ name is Brigitte.
   a. His b. Her
5. They are my friends. ____ names are Annie and Donna.
   a. Her b. Their
6. We are married. ____ names are Mr. and Mrs. Laurent.
   a. Our b. Their

C Read the sentences in 1B with a partner.

2 Learn the simple present

A Look at the pictures. Read the sentences.

1. He lives in California.

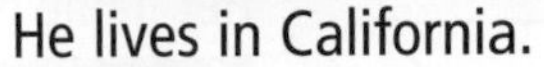

2. She lives in New York.

3. He lives in Texas.

4. They live in Florida.

B Study the chart. Listen and repeat.

I You	live	in New York.
He She	lives	
We They	live	

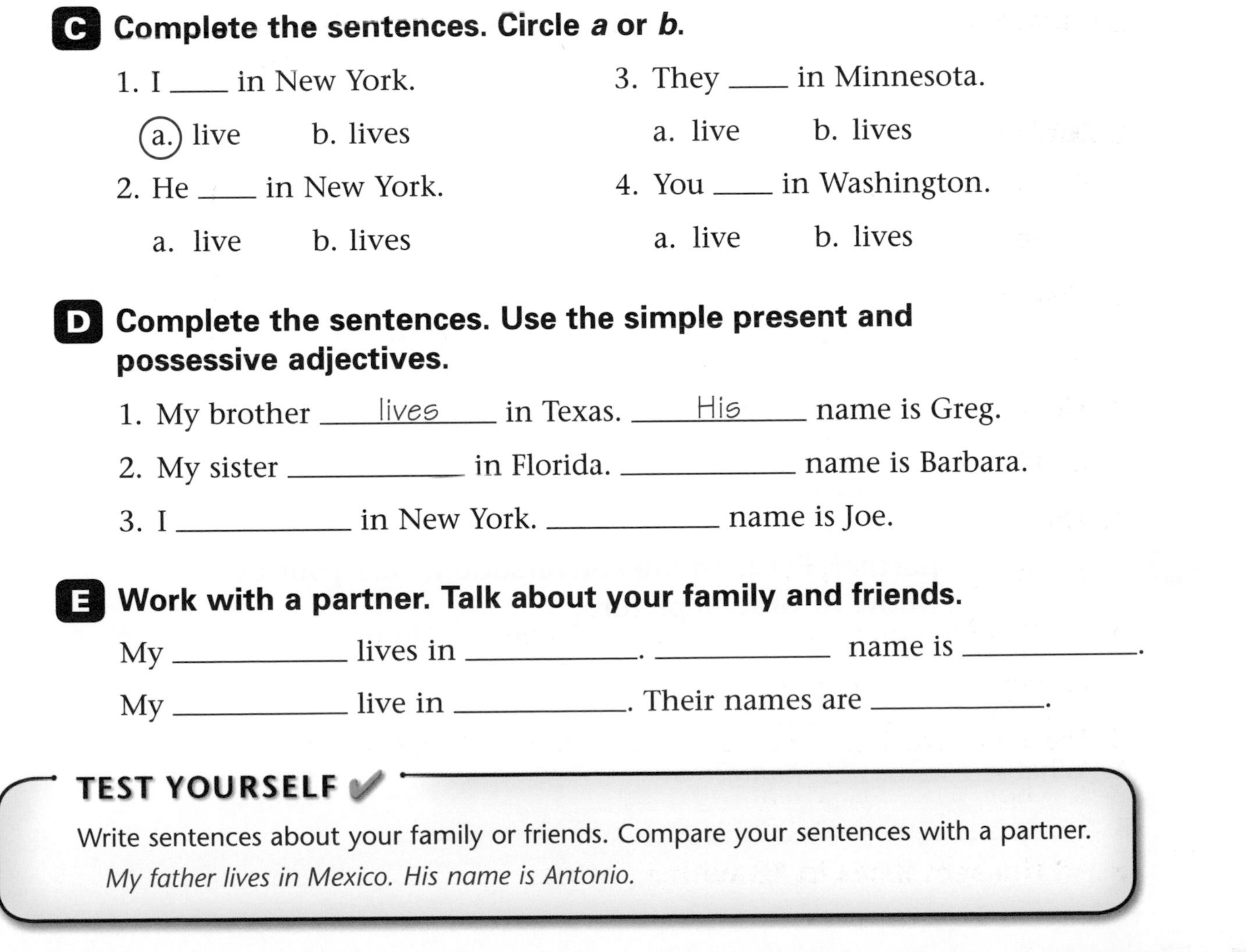

C Complete the sentences. Circle *a* or *b*.

1. I ____ in New York.
   (a.) live b. lives
2. He ____ in New York.
   a. live b. lives
3. They ____ in Minnesota.
   a. live b. lives
4. You ____ in Washington.
   a. live b. lives

D Complete the sentences. Use the simple present and possessive adjectives.

1. My brother __lives__ in Texas. __His__ name is Greg.
2. My sister ________ in Florida. ________ name is Barbara.
3. I ________ in New York. ________ name is Joe.

E Work with a partner. Talk about your family and friends.

My ________ lives in ________. ________ name is ________.

My ________ live in ________. Their names are ________.

TEST YOURSELF ✔

Write sentences about your family or friends. Compare your sentences with a partner.

My father lives in Mexico. His name is Antonio.

LESSON 4 Everyday conversation

1 Learn to talk about families and friends

A **Look at the pictures. Read the conversation.**

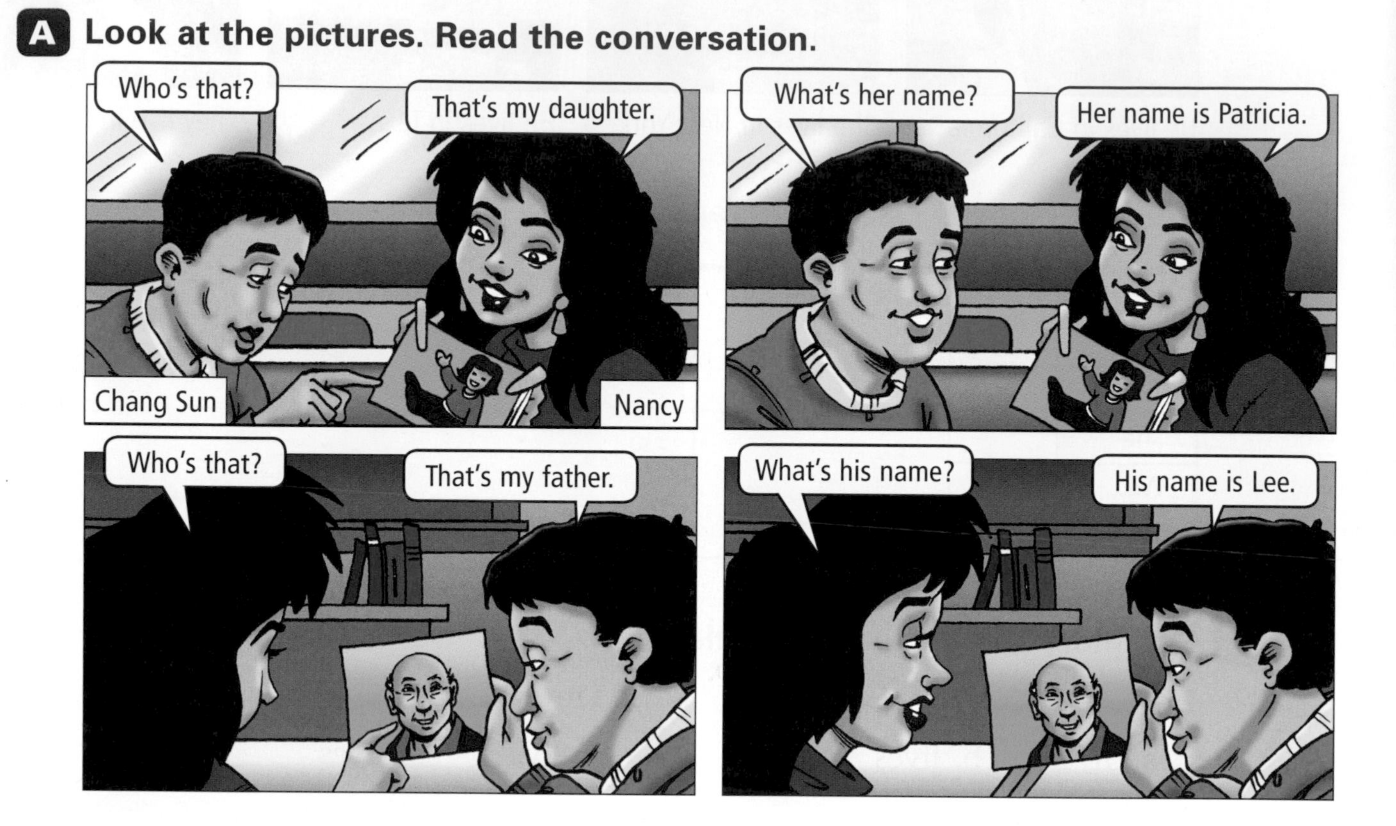

B **Listen and read.**

Chang Sun: Who's that?
Nancy: That's my daughter.
Chang Sun: What's her name?
Nancy: Her name is Patricia.

Nancy: Who's that?
Chang Sun: That's my father.
Nancy: What's his name?
Chang Sun: His name is Lee.

C **Listen again and repeat.**

D **Work with a partner. Practice the conversation. Use your own information. Show or draw a picture.**

A: Who's that?

B: That's my __________.

A: What's __________ name?

B: __________ name is __________.

2 Listen for titles

A **Look at the pictures. Listen to the sentences.**

1

I'm Mr. Jain.
I'm single.

2

I'm Mr. Cohen.
I'm married.

3

I'm Mrs. Cohen.
I'm married.

4

I'm Miss Diaz.
I'm single.

5

I'm Ms. Lim.
I'm single.

6

I'm Ms. Flores.
I'm married.

B **Listen. Circle *a* or *b*.**

1. (a.) I'm Mr. Jones. b. I'm Mrs. Jones.
2. a. I'm Mr. Wong. b. I'm Miss Wong.
3. a. I'm Mrs. Park. b. I'm Ms. Park.
4. a. I'm Mrs. Chavez. b. I'm Mr. Chavez.

3 Real-life math

A **Look at the ruler.**

1 inch

1 2 3 4 5 6 7 8 9 10 11 12

12 inches = 1 foot

B **Do the math and complete the sentence.**

Her son is 10 years old. He is 50 inches tall.

Her son is ____ feet and ____ inches tall.

Need help?
1 foot
2 feet

TEST YOURSELF ✓

Copy the conversation. Close your book. Then add your own ideas and practice with a partner.

A: Who's that?
B: ______________.

LESSON 5 Real-life reading

1 Learn about schools in the U.S.

A **Look at the chart.**

	Age	Grades		School
	5–6 years old	Kindergarten		Elementary school
	6–11 years old	First grade Second grade	Third grade Fourth grade	Elementary school
		Fifth grade		Elementary or middle school
	11–14 years old	Sixth grade		Elementary or middle school
		Seventh grade	Eighth grade	Middle or junior high school
	14–18 years old	Ninth grade Tenth grade	Eleventh grade Twelfth grade	High school

B **Complete the sentences. Circle *a* or *b*.**

1. His daughter is eight years old. She's in ____ grade.
   a. eighth   (b.) third
2. Her son is five years old. He's in ____.
   a. fifth grade   b. kindergarten
3. Their son is in third grade. He's in ____.
   a. elementary school   b. high school
4. My daughter is in eleventh grade. She's ____ years old.
   a. eleven   b. seventeen

2 Get ready to read

A **Look at the pictures. Read the words.**

come   every day   on time   do homework

 ✔ Identify school requirements; interpret a note from a teacher

B **Check (✔) the sentences about you.**

☐ I come to class every day.

☐ I come to class on time.

☐ I do my homework.

3 Read a note

A **Read the note from the teacher.**

ME Marshall Elementary School

Dear Mr. and Mrs. Santos,

Lila comes to class every day.
She comes to class on time.
She does her homework.
She is a good student.

Selma Romero

Ms. Selma Romero
Fourth-grade teacher

B **Look at the note. Circle *a* or *b*.**

1. Lila is in ____.
   a. third grade (b.) fourth grade
2. Ms. Romero is the ____.
   a. mother b. teacher
3. Mrs. Santos is the ____.
   a. mother b. father
4. Lila is in ____.
   a. middle school b. elementary school

BRING IT TO LIFE

Find the names of the elementary school, middle school (or junior high), and high school in your community. Tell the class.

First Elementary
King Middle School
Kent High School

UNIT 6 Review and expand

1 Grammar

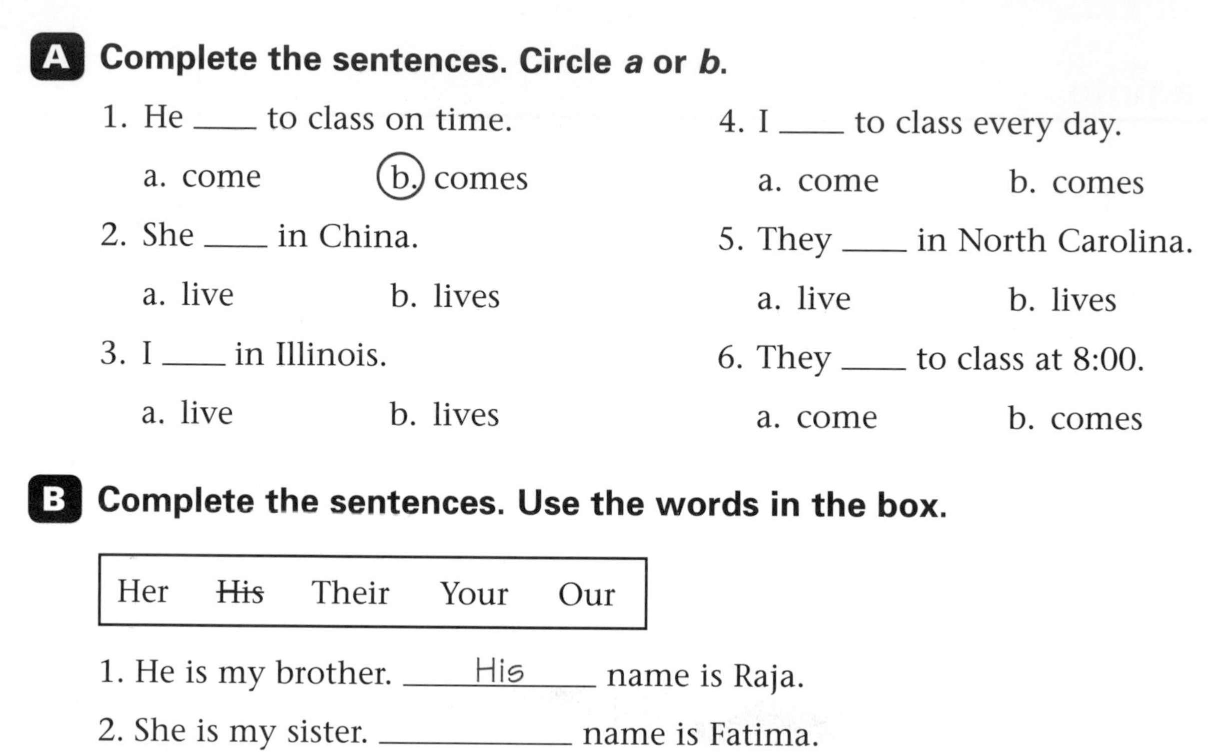

A Complete the sentences. Circle *a* or *b*.

1. He ____ to class on time.
   a. come (b.) comes
2. She ____ in China.
   a. live b. lives
3. I ____ in Illinois.
   a. live b. lives
4. I ____ to class every day.
   a. come b. comes
5. They ____ in North Carolina.
   a. live b. lives
6. They ____ to class at 8:00.
   a. come b. comes

B Complete the sentences. Use the words in the box.

Her	~~His~~	Their	Your	Our

1. He is my brother. ___His___ name is Raja.
2. She is my sister. __________ name is Fatima.
3. You are my friend. __________ name is Alonso.
4. They are good students. __________ names are Oscar and Tina.
5. We are married. __________ names are Paul and Alicia.

2 Group work

A Work with 2–3 classmates. Look at the picture. Say what you see.

B **Work with your group. Look at the picture in 2A again. Write what you see. Check your spelling in a dictionary.**

1. family
2. ______
3. ______
4. ______
5. ______
6. ______

C **Work with your classmates. Make a list of the words from 2B.**

PROBLEM SOLVING

A **Listen. Look at the pictures.**

Rosa's Problem

4th Grade

TEST PAPER

B **Work with your classmates. Help Rosa.**

MON TUES WEDS THURS FRI SAT SUN

a. Say, "No more baseball."

b. Say, "Only play baseball on Saturday."

c. Talk to the teacher.

UNIT 7 Do we need apples?

FOCUS ON
- food
- food preferences
- the simple present
- asking for help in a store
- reading a shopping list

LESSON 1 Vocabulary

1 Learn about fruit and vegetables

A **Look at the pictures. Say the prices.**

STUDENT AUDIO **B** **Listen and point to the pictures.**

STUDENT AUDIO **C** **Listen and repeat the words.**

1. fruit	4. grapes	7. broccoli
2. bananas	5. oranges	8. cabbage
3. apples	6. vegetables	9. corn

D **Read the new words with a partner.**

 ☑ Identify fruit and vegetables

 Talk about fruit and vegetables

A Look at the picture. Complete the words.

1. b a n __a__ __n__ __a__ s
2. ___ r ___ p e s
3. o ___ a n g e ___
4. ___ p ___ l e s
5. ___ r u ___ t
6. ___ o ___ n
7. b r o c c ___ ___ i
8. c a b ___ ___ ___ e
9. ___ ___ g e ___ a b l e s

B Listen and repeat.

1. Where are the apples?
2. Where are the bananas?
3. Where are the grapes?
4. Where are the vegetables?
5. Where is the broccoli?
6. Where is the cabbage?
7. Where is the corn?
8. Where is the fruit?

C Work with a partner. Read the questions in 2B. Point to the fruit and vegetables in 2A.

TEST YOURSELF ✓

Close your book. Write 2 words for fruit. Then write 2 words for vegetables. Check your spelling in a dictionary.

LESSON 2 Life stories

1 Read about food

A Look at the pictures. What food do you see?

B Listen and repeat the words.

1. cheese
2. eggs
3. milk
4. bread
5. chicken
6. pork
7. beef
8. lamb
9. meat
10. rice

C Listen and read Barbara's story.

1. I like cheese.
2. I don't like pork.
3. My husband likes beef.
4. My daughter likes chicken.
5. We all like rice.

D Listen to Don's story. Circle the correct word.

1. I like ____. (meat) milk
2. I don't like ____. chicken cheese
3. My wife likes ____. lamb rice
4. My son likes ____. rice eggs
5. We all like ____. bread beef

Don

2 Write about food you like

A Write about food. Complete the sentences. Use your own ideas.

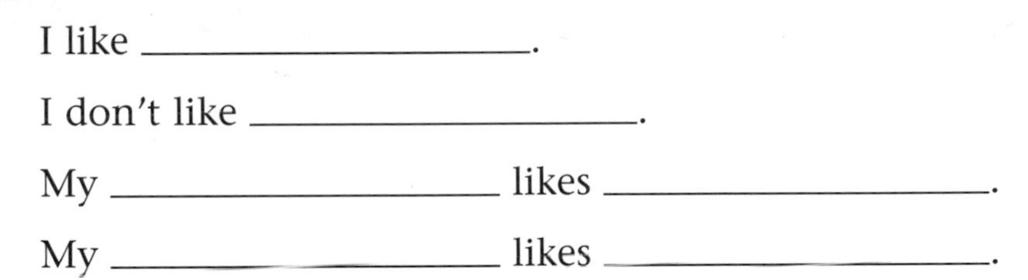

I like ______________.

I don't like ______________.

My ______________ likes ______________.

My ______________ likes ______________.

B Read your story to a partner.

3 Listen for food groups

A Listen and check (✔) the boxes.

	fruit	vegetable	meat
pork			✔
grapes			
cabbage			

B Listen. Circle *a* or *b*.

1. a. pork (b.) broccoli
2. a. oranges b. lamb
3. a. grapes b. corn
4. a. cabbage b. chicken
5. a. beef b. bananas
6. a. apples b. corn

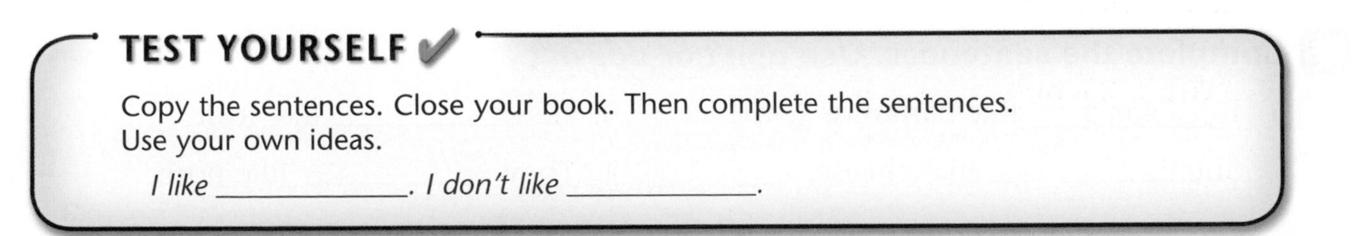

TEST YOURSELF ✔

Copy the sentences. Close your book. Then complete the sentences.
Use your own ideas.

I like ______________. I don't like ______________.

LESSON 3 Grammar

1 Learn negative statements with the simple present

A Look at the pictures. Read the sentences.

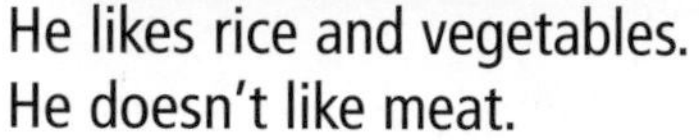

1. He likes rice and vegetables.
He doesn't like meat.

2. She likes bananas.
She doesn't like cabbage.

3. They like chicken.
They don't like rice.

B Study the chart. Listen and repeat.

I You	don't like	
He She	doesn't like	cabbage.
We They	don't like	

C Complete the sentences. Circle *a* or *b*. Then read the sentences with a partner.

1. I ____ cabbage.
   a. doesn't like (b.) don't like
2. She ____ cabbage.
   a. doesn't like b. don't like
3. They ____ bananas.
   a. doesn't like b. don't like
4. He ____ pork.
   a. doesn't like b. don't like
5. I ____ lamb.
   a. doesn't like b. don't like
6. We ____ broccoli.
   a. doesn't like b. don't like

D Complete the sentences. Use *don't* or *doesn't*.

1. I __don't__ like bananas.
2. She ________ like cheese.
3. He ________ like fruit.
4. They ________ like pork.

2 Learn *Yes/No* questions with the simple present

A Listen and look at the pictures. Read the conversations.

1

A: Do you need rice?
B: Yes, I do.
A: Do you need bread?
B: No, I don't.

2

A: Does he need milk?
B: Yes, he does.
A: Does he need eggs?
B: No, he doesn't.

3

A: Do they need oranges?
B: Yes, they do.
A: Do they need apples?
B: No, they don't.

4

A: Do we need broccoli?
B: Yes, we do.
A: Do we need cabbage?
B: No, we don't.

B Match the questions with the answers.

_c_ 1. Do you need rice? | a. No, they don't.
___ 2. Does she need chicken? | b. Yes, he does.
___ 3. Do they need apples? | c. Yes, I do.
___ 4. Does he need broccoli? | d. No, she doesn't.

C Complete the questions. Use *Do* or *Does*.

1. __Does__ she need rice?
2. ______ they need grapes?
3. ______ you like cabbage?
4. ______ she like pork?
5. ______ they like chicken?
6. ______ we need eggs?

D Work with a partner. Ask and answer the questions in 2C. Use your own ideas.

TEST YOURSELF ✓

Write questions with *like*. Write the answers. Compare your questions and answers with a partner.

Do you like bananas? Yes, I do.

LESSON 4 Everyday conversation

1 Learn to ask for help in a store

A **Look at the pictures. Read the conversation.**

Can I help you?
Yes, I need apples.
Clerk
Rosita
Here you go.
Thanks.
You're welcome.

B **Listen and read.**

Clerk: Can I help you?
Rosita: Yes, I need apples.
Clerk: Here you go.
Rosita: Thanks.
Clerk: You're welcome.

C **Listen again and repeat.**

D **Work with a partner. Practice the conversation. Use your own ideas.**

A: Can I help you?
B: Yes, I need ___________.
A: Here you go.
B: Thanks.
A: You're welcome.

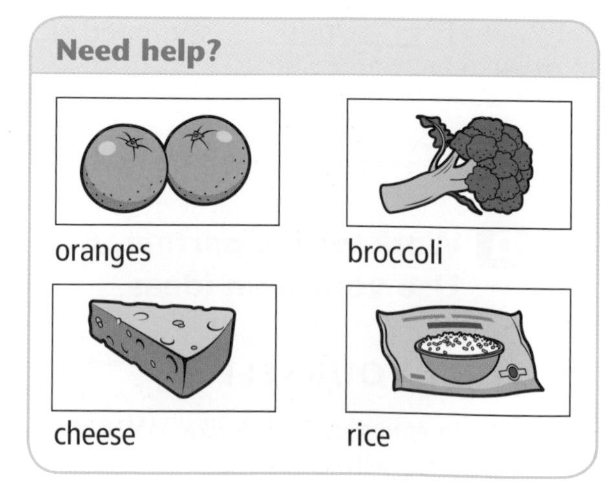

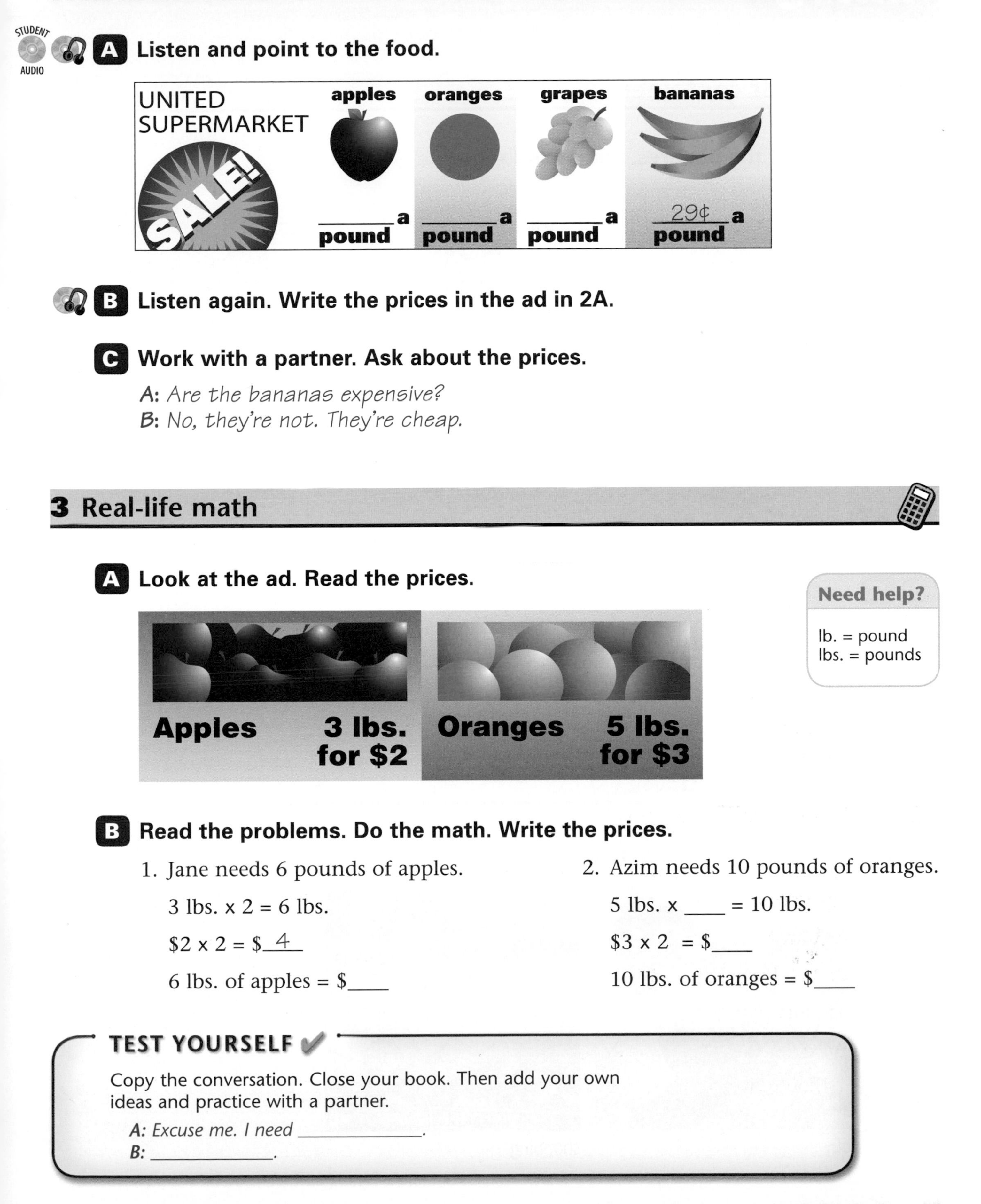

2 Listen for prices

STUDENT AUDIO

A **Listen and point to the food.**

B **Listen again. Write the prices in the ad in 2A.**

C **Work with a partner. Ask about the prices.**

A: *Are the bananas expensive?*
B: *No, they're not. They're cheap.*

3 Real-life math

A **Look at the ad. Read the prices.**

Need help?

lb. = pound
lbs. = pounds

B **Read the problems. Do the math. Write the prices.**

1. Jane needs 6 pounds of apples.

   3 lbs. x 2 = 6 lbs.

   $2 x 2 = $ 4

   6 lbs. of apples = $____

2. Azim needs 10 pounds of oranges.

   5 lbs. x ____ = 10 lbs.

   $3 x 2 = $____

   10 lbs. of oranges = $____

TEST YOURSELF ✓

Copy the conversation. Close your book. Then add your own ideas and practice with a partner.

A: Excuse me. I need ____________.
B: ____________.

1 Learn about containers

A Look at the pictures. Listen and repeat.

1. a can of coffee
2. a can of soup

3. a bottle of water

4. a bottle of juice

5. a box of cereal

6. a box of tea

B Listen. Circle *a* or *b*.

1. (a.) can	b. box	4. a. can	b. bottle
2. a. bottle	b. box	5. a. box	b. bottle
3. a. can	b. bottle	6. a. box	b. can

2 Get ready to read

A Look at the pictures. Read the words.

1. buy
2. shopping

B **Check (✓) the sentence about you.**

☐ I like shopping.

☐ I don't like shopping.

3 Read a shopping list

 **Read the shopping list.**

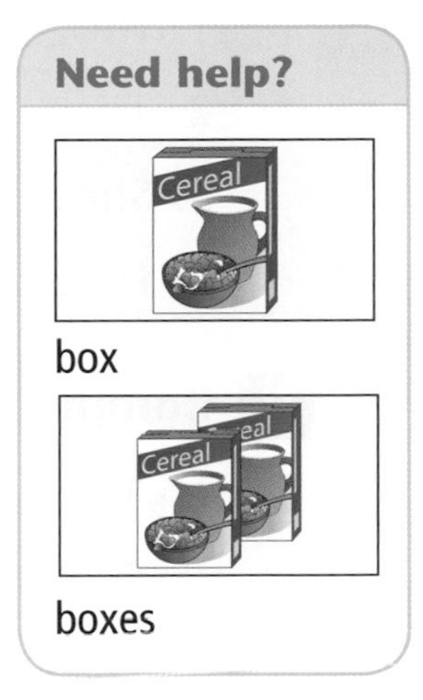

B **Look at the shopping list. Circle *a* or *b*.**

1. Do they need soup?
   a. No, they don't. (b.) Yes, they do.
2. Do they need cabbage?
   a. No, they don't. b. Yes, they do.
3. Do they need orange juice?
   a. No, they don't. b. Yes, they do.
4. Do they need fruit?
   a. No, they don't. b. Yes, they do.
5. Do they need milk?
   a. No, they don't. b. Yes, they do.

BRING IT TO LIFE

Bring a shopping list to class. Talk about the food you need.

Shopping List
coffee (1 can)
water (6 bottles)
juice (2 bottles)
tea
cereal (3 boxes)
apples
corn

UNIT 7 Review and expand

1 Grammar

A **Complete the sentences. Use *don't like* or *doesn't like*.**

1. He ___doesn't like___ lamb.
2. They ________________ cheese.
3. She ________________ oranges.
4. I ________________ corn.

B **Complete the questions and answers. Use *do, don't, does,* or *doesn't*.**

1. **A:** ___Does___ he need broccoli?
   B: Yes, he does.
2. **A:** ________ she need pork?
   B: No, she doesn't.
3. **A:** ________ they need juice?
   B: Yes, they do.
4. **A:** ________ they need coffee?
   B: No, they don't.
5. **A:** Does he like vegetables?
   B: Yes, he ________.
6. **A:** Do you like lamb?
   B: No, I ________.
7. **A:** Does she like eggs?
   B: No, she ________.
8. **A:** Do they need cheese?
   B: Yes, they ________.

 Group work

A **Work with 2–3 classmates. Look at the picture. Say what you see.**

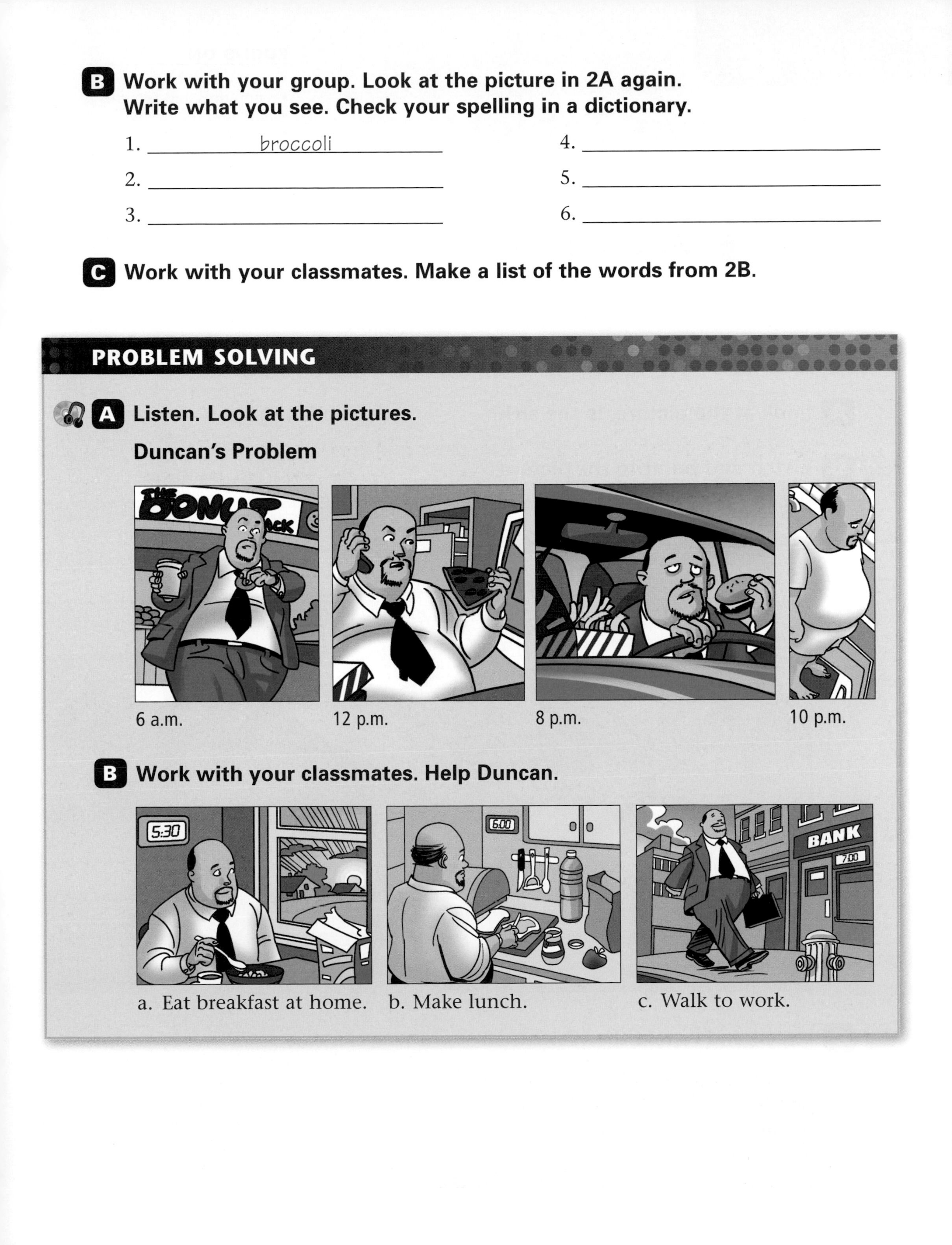

B **Work with your group. Look at the picture in 2A again. Write what you see. Check your spelling in a dictionary.**

1. broccoli
2. ______
3. ______
4. ______
5. ______
6. ______

C **Work with your classmates. Make a list of the words from 2B.**

PROBLEM SOLVING

A **Listen. Look at the pictures.**

Duncan's Problem

6 a.m. 12 p.m. 8 p.m. 10 p.m.

B **Work with your classmates. Help Duncan.**

a. Eat breakfast at home.

b. Make lunch.

c. Walk to work.

UNIT 8 Take Two Tablets

FOCUS ON
- parts of the body
- symptoms and ailments
- *have* and *has*
- making a doctor's appointment
- reading medicine labels

LESSON 1 Vocabulary

1 Learn parts of the body

A Look at the picture. Is she sick?

B Listen and point to the picture.

STUDENT AUDIO **C** Listen and repeat the words.

1. head	4. nose	7. hand
2. eye	5. arm	8. leg
3. ear	6. stomach	9. foot

D Read the new words with a partner.

2 Talk about parts of the body

A Look at the picture. Complete the words.

1. h e _a_ _d_
2. e a ___
3. e y ___
4. ___ ___ s c
5. h ___ n ___
6. a r ___
7. s ___ ___ m a c h
8. ___ o o ___
9. ___ e g

B Look at the pictures. Listen and follow the directions.

1
Point to your head.
2
Point to your leg.

C Work with a partner. Give directions. Listen and follow your partner's directions.

Point to your ___________.

TEST YOURSELF ✓

Close your book. Write 4 parts of the body. Check your spelling in a dictionary.

1 Read about health problems

A **Look at the picture. What parts of the body do you see?**

B **Listen and repeat the words.**

1. a cold
2. a cough
3. an earache
4. a sore throat
5. a headache
6. a stomachache
7. a fever
8. the flu

STUDENT AUDIO

C **Listen and read Paula's story.**

1. My family is sick.
2. My daughter has a cold.
3. My son has an earache.
4. My husband has a sore throat.
5. I have a headache.

D **Listen to Carl's story. Circle the correct word.**

1. My family is ____.	sad	(sick)
2. My brother has ____.	a fever	the flu
3. My sister has ____.	a sore throat	a stomachache
4. My mother has ____.	a cold	a cough
5. I have ____.	a cold	a cough

Carl

2 Write about health problems

A **Write about health problems. Complete the sentences. Use your own ideas.**

My ____________ has ____________.

My ____________ has ____________.

My ____________ has ____________.

I have ____________.

B **Read your story to a partner.**

3 Listen and complete a medical form

A **Listen and point to the health problems you hear.**

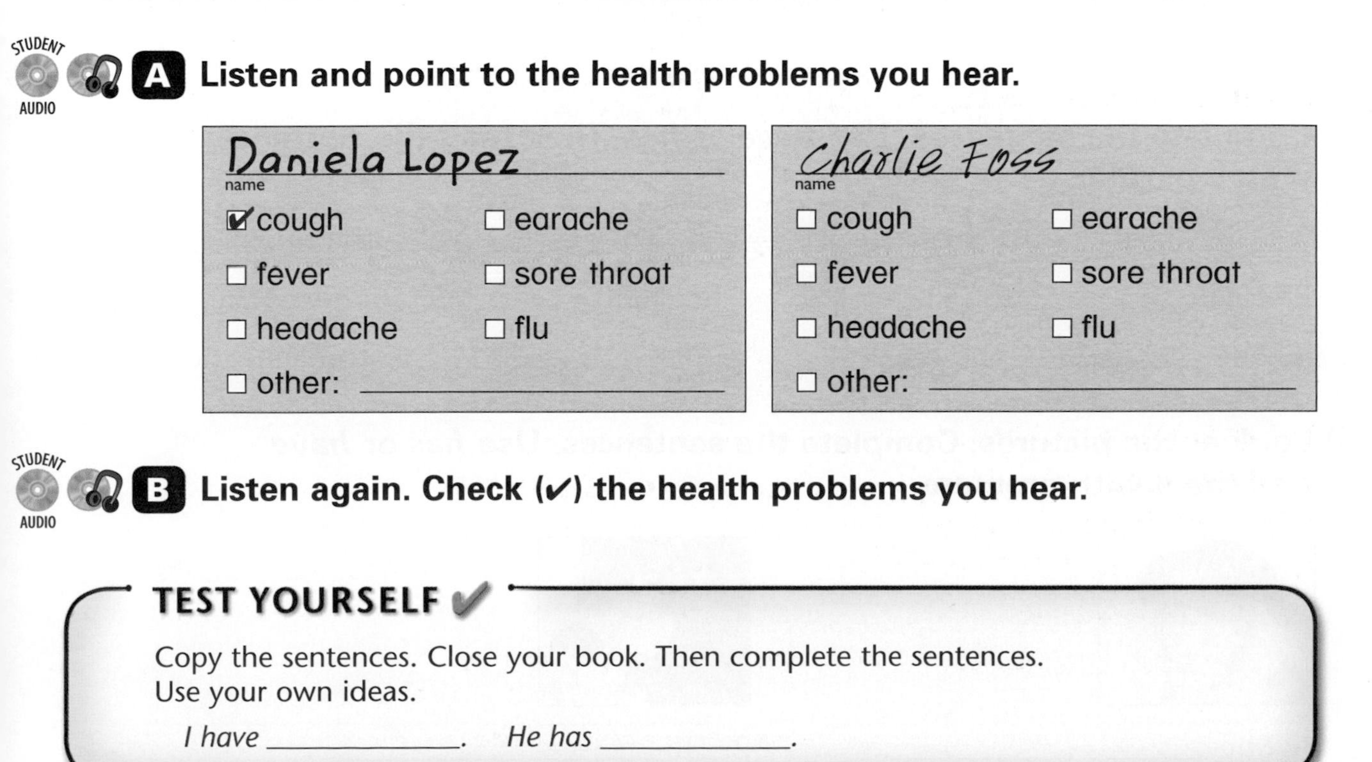

Daniela Lopez
name

☑ cough	☐ earache
☐ fever	☐ sore throat
☐ headache	☐ flu
☐ other: ________	

Charlie Foss
name

☐ cough	☐ earache
☐ fever	☐ sore throat
☐ headache	☐ flu
☐ other: ________	

B **Listen again. Check (✓) the health problems you hear.**

TEST YOURSELF ✓

Copy the sentences. Close your book. Then complete the sentences. Use your own ideas.

I have ____________. *He has* ____________.

LESSON 3 Grammar

1 Learn *have* and *has*

A **Look at the pictures. Read the sentences.**

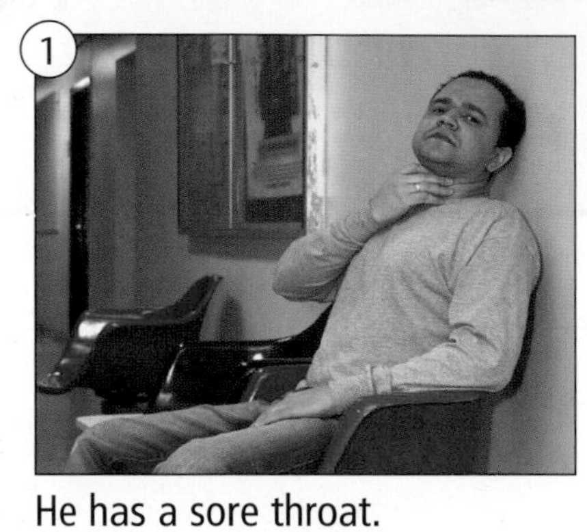

1 He has a sore throat.

2 She has a fever.

3 She has an earache.

B **Study the chart. Listen and repeat.**

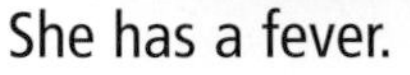

I You	have	the flu.
He She	has	
We They	have	

C **Complete the sentences. Use *have* or *has*. Then read the sentences with a partner.**

1. I ___have___ the flu.
2. He ____________ the flu.
3. She ____________ the flu.
4. They ____________ the flu.
5. Matt ____________ a headache.
6. Jill ____________ a stomachache.

D **Look at the pictures. Complete the sentences. Use *has* or *have* and the health problem.**

1. She ____________________.

2. He ____________________.

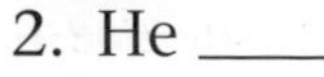

Use *have* and *has* to describe symptoms and ailments

2 Learn *Yes/No* questions with *have*

A **Look at the pictures. Listen to the questions and answers.**

Dr. Tam: Do you have a sore throat?
Eva: Yes, I do.
Dr. Tam: Do you have a stomachache?
Eva: No, I don't.

Dr. Garcia: Does he have a fever?
Flor: Yes, he does.
Dr. Garcia: Does he have an earache?
Flor: No, he doesn't.

Dr. Barr: Do they have coughs?
Vinh: Yes, they do.
Dr. Barr: Do they have fevers?
Vinh: No, they don't.

Girls: Do we have fevers?
Dr. Cantu: No, you don't.
Girls: Do we have the flu?
Dr. Cantu: No, you don't.

B **Complete the questions and answers.**

1. **A:** _Does he have_ a sore throat?
   B: Yes, he does.
2. **A:** __________ a stomachache?
   B: No, I don't.
3. **A:** Does he have the flu?
   B: Yes, __________.
4. **A:** Does he have an earache?
   B: No, __________.

C **Complete the questions and sentences. Use *have* or *has*.**

1. Does he _have_ a cough?
2. Do you __________ the flu?
3. She __________ a cold.
4. I __________ a headache.
5. He __________ a stomachache.
6. Does she __________ a sore throat?

D **Work with a partner. Read the conversations in 2B.**

TEST YOURSELF ✔

Write questions and answers about health problems. Compare your questions and answers with a partner.

Does Olivia have a headache? No, she doesn't.

1 Learn how to make a doctor's appointment

A **Look at the pictures. Read the conversation.**

B **Listen and read.**

Receptionist: Hello, Downtown Clinic.
Kara: This is Kara Woods. I need to see the doctor.
Receptionist: What's the matter?
Kara: I have a stomachache.
Receptionist: Is 2:00 OK?
Kara: Yes, thank you.

C **Listen again and repeat.**

D **Work with a partner. Practice the conversation. Use your own ideas.**

A: Hello, Downtown Clinic.

B: Hello. I need to see the doctor.

A: What's the matter?

B: I have a ____________.

A: Is ____________ OK?

B: Yes, thank you.

Need help?

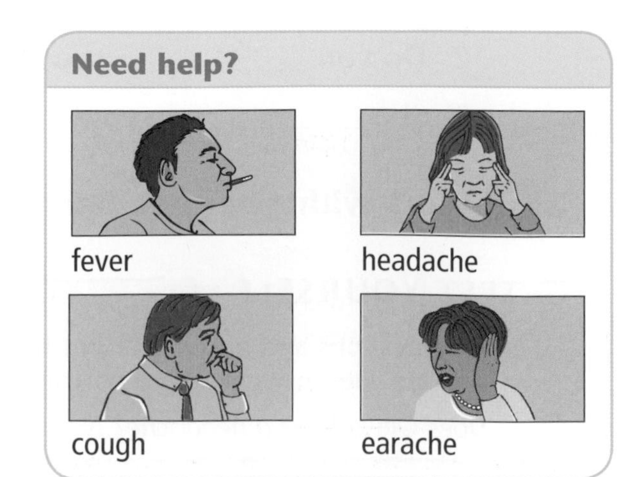

2 Listen for medical appointment information

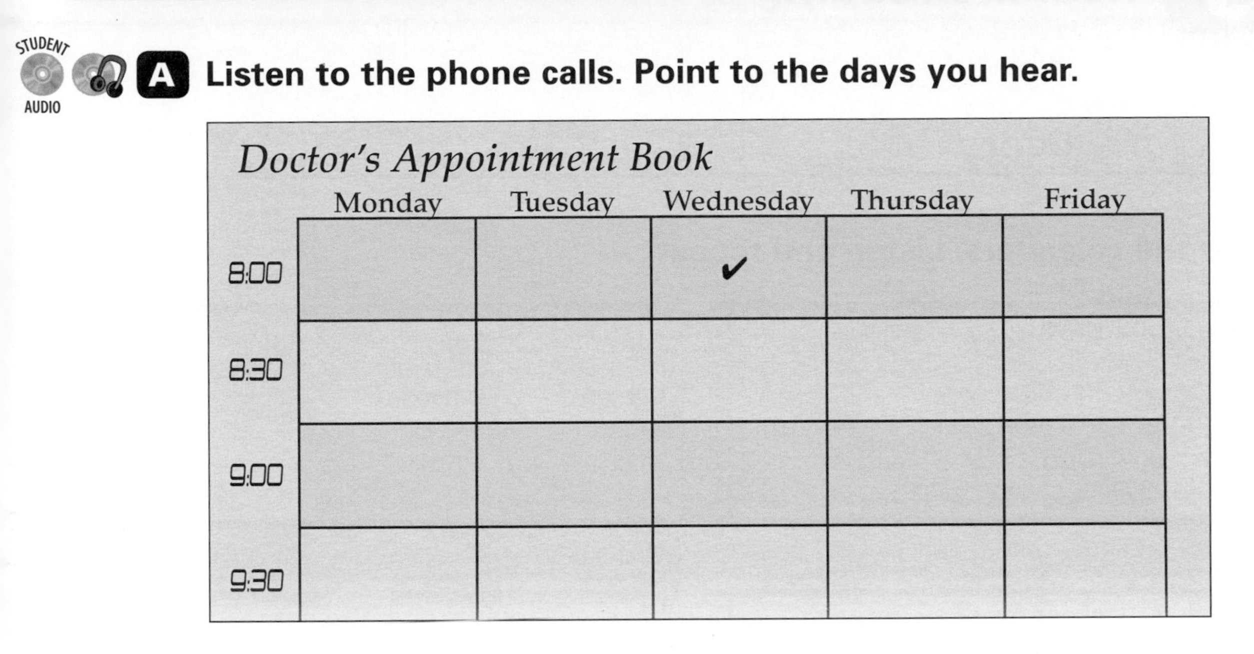

A Listen to the phone calls. Point to the days you hear.

Doctor's Appointment Book

	Monday	Tuesday	Wednesday	Thursday	Friday
8:00			✔		
8:30					
9:00					
9:30					

B Listen again. Check (✔) the day and time in the calendar.

3 Practice your pronunciation

A Listen for the different sounds of *a*.

matter	ache
have	say
has	name
sad	plane
hand	

B Listen and write these words in the chart.

~~hand~~	grapes	happy	day

C Listen again and check your answers.

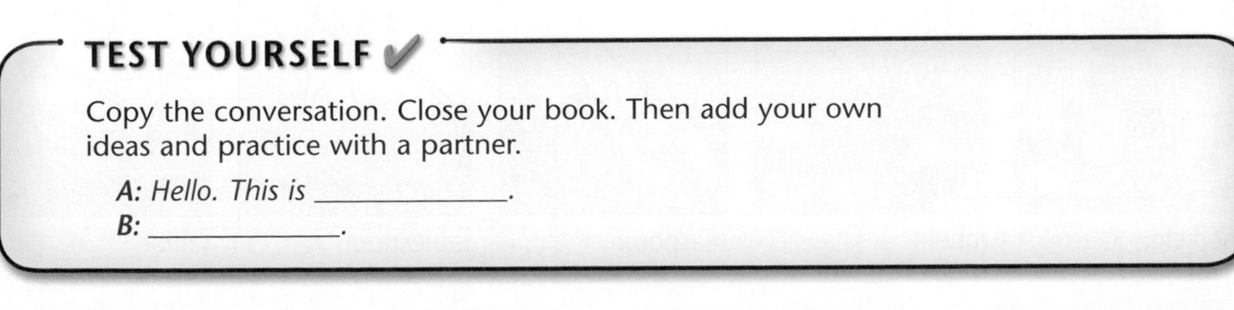

TEST YOURSELF ✔

Copy the conversation. Close your book. Then add your own ideas and practice with a partner.

A: *Hello. This is* ____________.
B: ____________.

1 Learn about frequency

STUDENT AUDIO

A Look at the calendars. Listen and repeat.

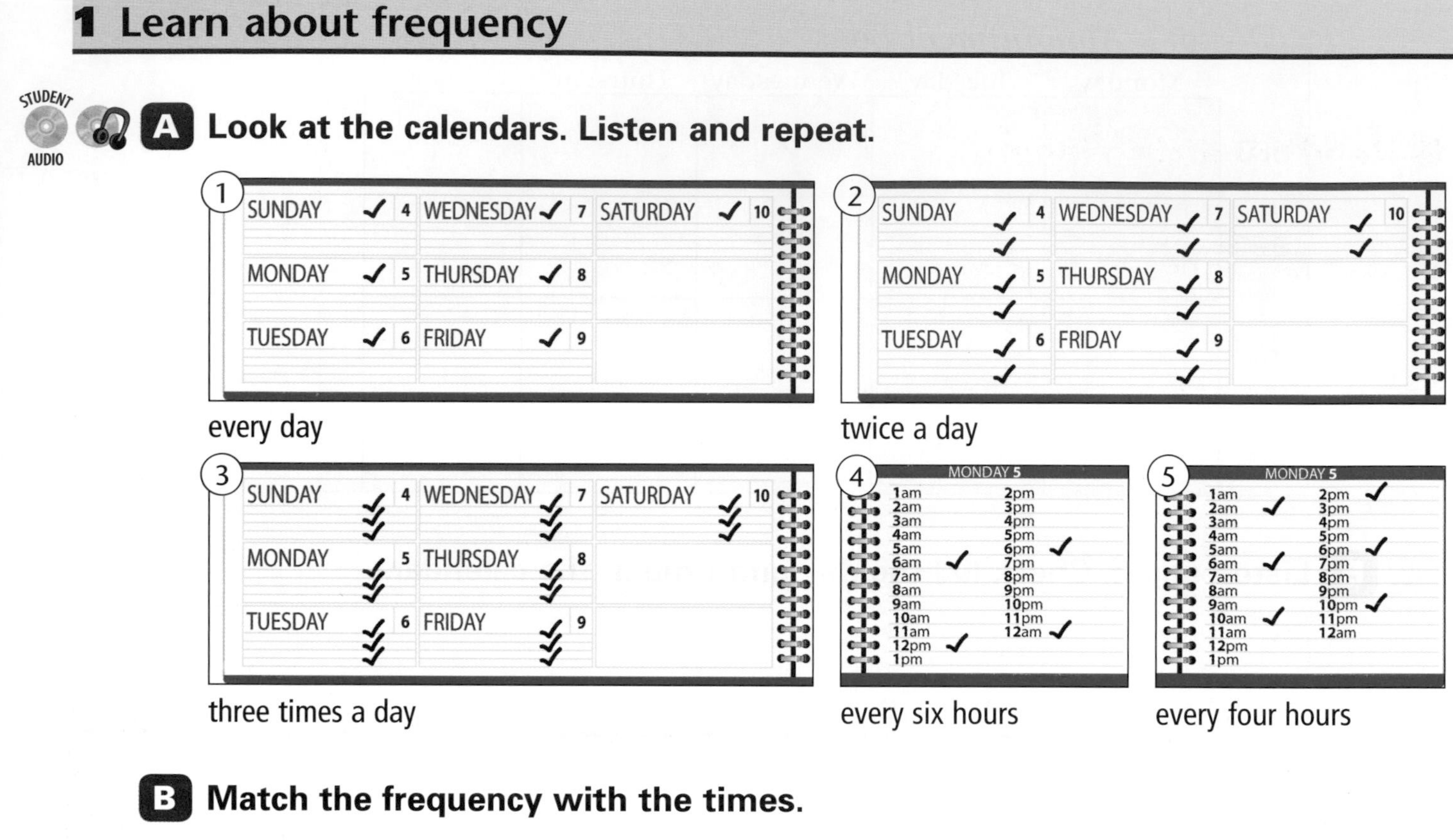

every day

twice a day

three times a day

every six hours

every four hours

B Match the frequency with the times.

_c_ 1. every four hours

____ 2. every day

____ 3. every six hours

____ 4. twice a day

____ 5. three times a day

a. 8 a.m., 8 p.m.

b. 8 a.m., 2 p.m., 8 p.m., 2 a.m.

c. 8 a.m., 12 p.m., 4 p.m., 8 p.m., 12 a.m., 4 a.m.

d. 8 a.m., 4 p.m., 12 a.m.

e. Sun., Mon., Tues., Wed., Thurs., Fri., Sat.

2 Get ready to read

A Look at the pictures. Read the words.

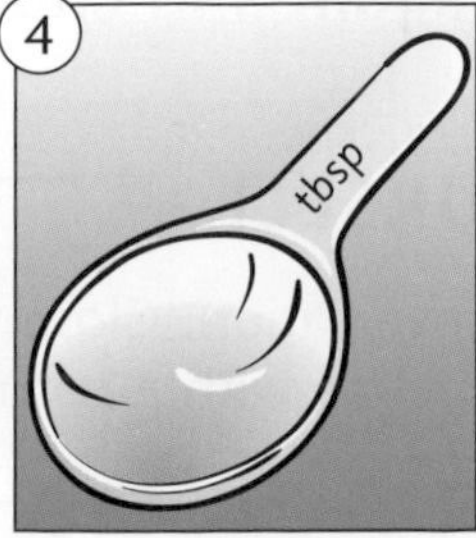

1 medicine

2 label

3 teaspoon

4 tablespoon

5 tablet

B What medicine do you have at home? Check (✓) the boxes.

☐ I have medicine for headaches.

☐ I have medicine for earaches.

☐ I have medicine for coughs.

3 Read medicine labels

A Read the medicine labels.

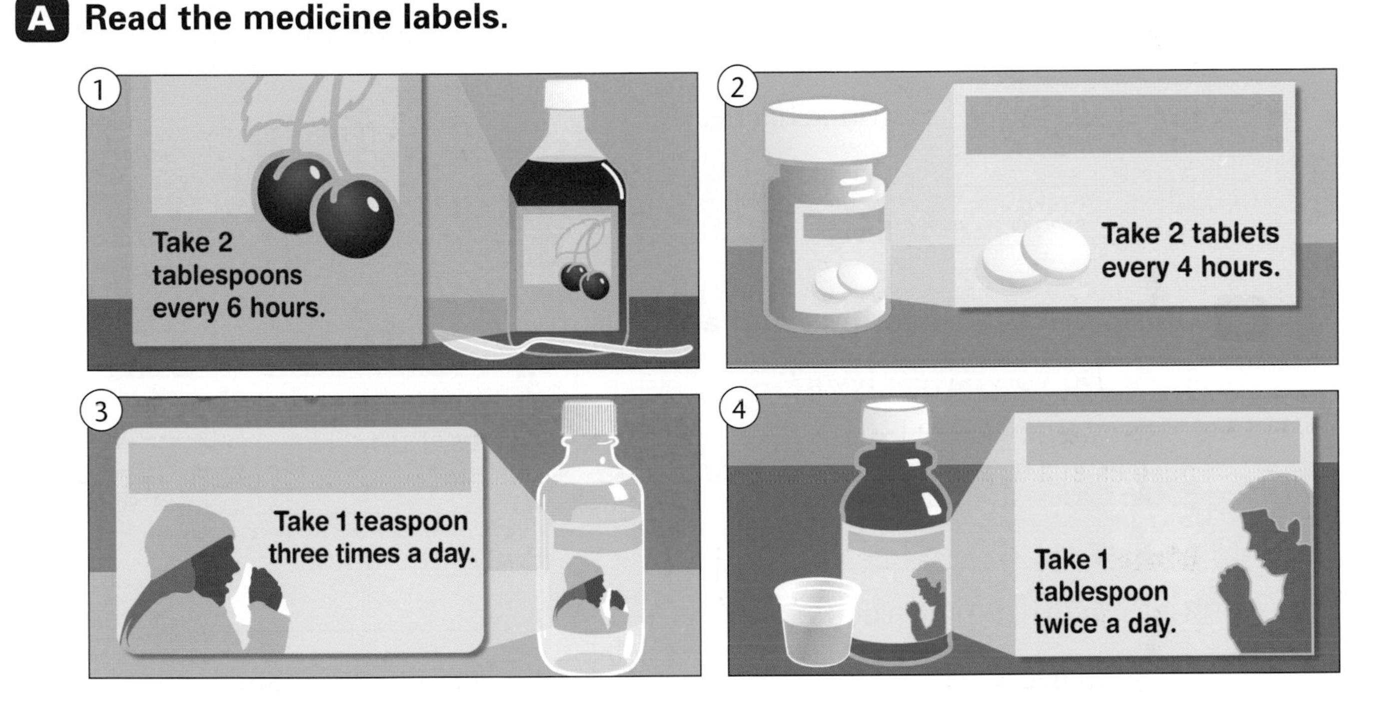

1
Take 2 tablespoons every 6 hours.
2
Take 2 tablets every 4 hours.
3
Take 1 teaspoon three times a day.
4
Take 1 tablespoon twice a day.

B Look at the medicine labels. Circle *a* or *b*.

1. Medicine 1: ____.
   a. take six tablespoons　　(b.) take two tablespoons
2. Medicine 2: ____.
   a. take every two hours　　b. take every four hours
3. Medicine 3: ____.
   a. take three times a day　　b. take every three hours
4. Medicine 4: ____.
   a. take one teaspoon　　b. take one tablespoon

BRING IT TO LIFE

Bring in medicine from the store or from a doctor.
Circle one new word.

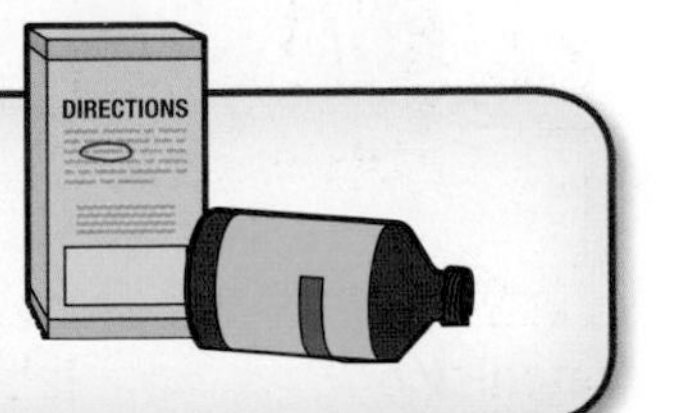

DIRECTIONS

UNIT 8 Review and expand

1 Grammar

A Complete the sentences. Use *have* or *has*.

1. He ___has___ a headache.
2. She ________ a sore throat.
3. They ________ the flu.
4. I ________ a stomachache.
5. He ________ a cold.
6. We ________ fevers.

B Complete the questions and answers.

1. **A:** Do you have a fever?
   B: Yes, ___I do___.
2. **A:** Does she have a cold?
   B: Yes, ________.
3. **A:** Do they have the flu?
   B: Yes, ________.
4. **A:** ________ a cough?
   B: Yes, I do.
5. **A:** ________ a sore throat?
   B: Yes, he does.
6. **A:** ________ a headache?
   B: Yes, she does.

2 Group work

A Work with 2–3 classmates. Look at the picture. Say what you see.

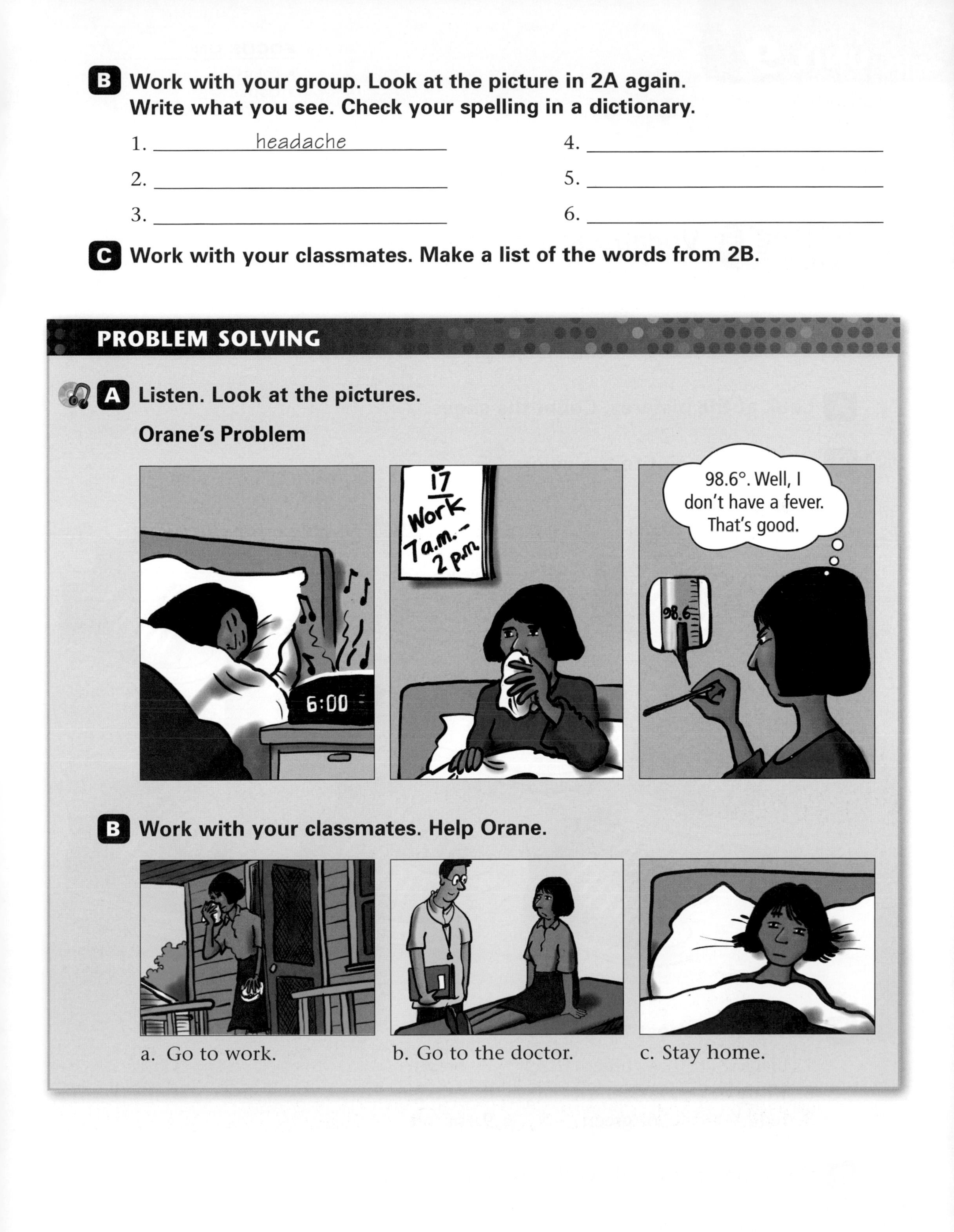

B **Work with your group. Look at the picture in 2A again. Write what you see. Check your spelling in a dictionary.**

1. headache
2. ______________________
3. ______________________
4. ______________________
5. ______________________
6. ______________________

C **Work with your classmates. Make a list of the words from 2B.**

PROBLEM SOLVING

A **Listen. Look at the pictures.**

Orane's Problem

B **Work with your classmates. Help Orane.**

a. Go to work.

b. Go to the doctor.

c. Stay home.

What size?

FOCUS ON

- colors
- clothes
- the present continuous
- shopping for clothes
- weather

Vocabulary

1 Learn colors

A **Look at the pictures. Count the shoes.**

STUDENT AUDIO **B** **Listen and point to the colors.**

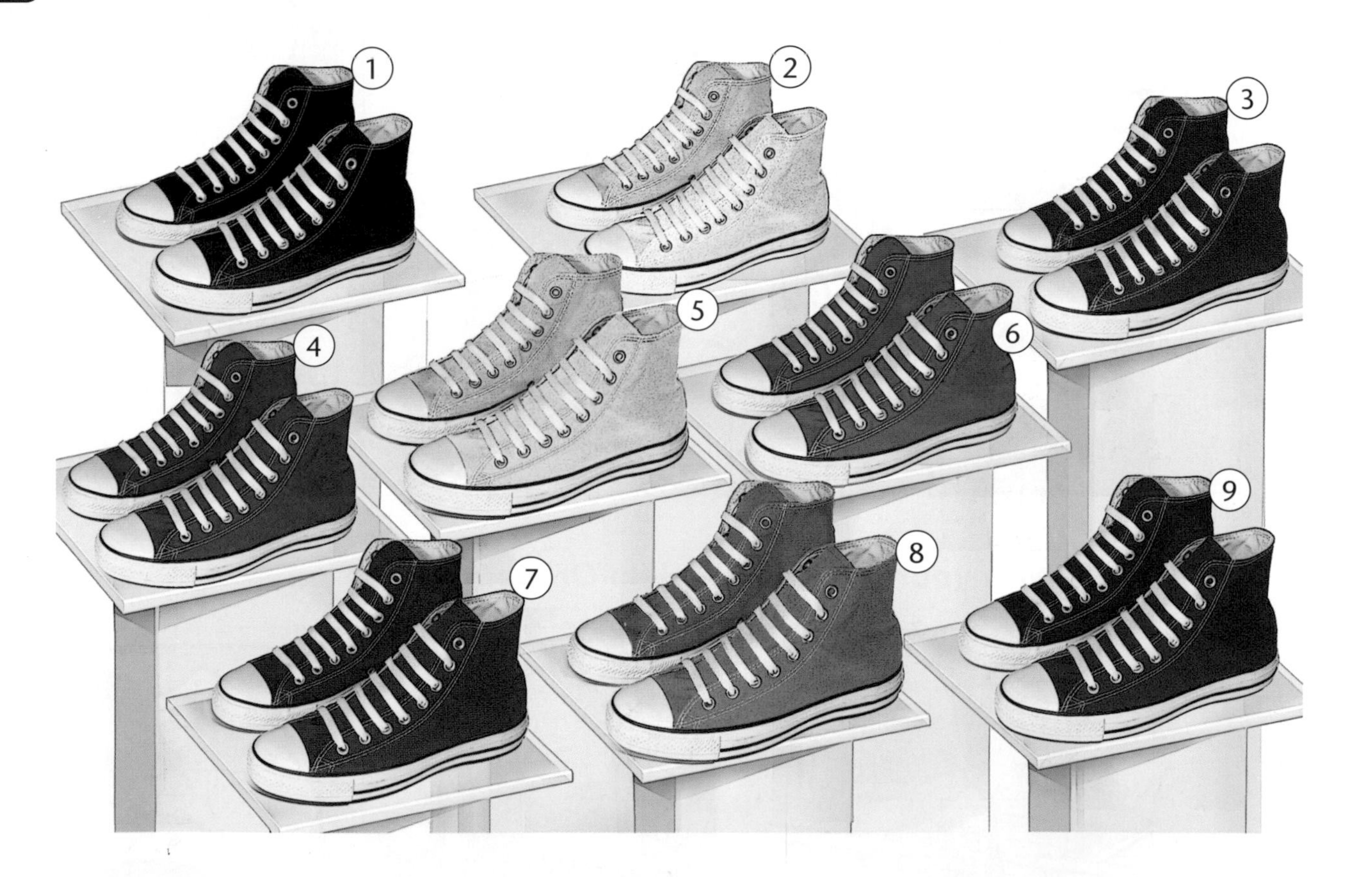

C **Listen and repeat the words.**

1. black	4. blue	7. brown
2. white	5. yellow	8. orange
3. red	6. green	9. purple

D **Read the new words with a partner.**

2 Talk about colors

A **Look at the picture. Complete the words.**

1. r _e_ d
2. g r ___ e ___
3. ___ h i ___ e
4. b ___ ___ c k
5. ___ r ___ w ___
6. ___ r ___ n g ___
7. y ___ l ___ o w
8. ___ l ___ e
9. ___ u ___ p l e

STUDENT AUDIO

B **Listen and repeat.**

A: What color is this sweater?
B: It's red.
A: What color is this shirt?
B: It's purple.

C **Work with a partner. Point to the clothes in 2A. Practice the conversation.**

A: What color is this ___________?

B: It's ___________.

TEST YOURSELF ✓

Close your book. Write 5 colors. Check your spelling in a dictionary.

1 Read about clothes

A **Look at the pictures. Say the months.**

July

October

February

STUDENT AUDIO **B** **Listen and repeat the words.**

1. cap
2. T-shirt
3. shorts
4. jacket
5. dress
6. coat
7. belt
8. boots

STUDENT AUDIO **C** **Listen and read Justine's story.**

1. It's July.
2. I'm wearing white shorts.
3. I'm wearing a red T-shirt.
4. I'm wearing a blue cap.

STUDENT AUDIO

D **Listen to Ben's story. Circle the correct word.**

1. It's ____. (January) June
2. I'm wearing a blue ____. cap coat
3. I'm wearing brown ____. boots belt
4. I'm wearing a brown ____. belt boot

Ben

2 Write about your clothes

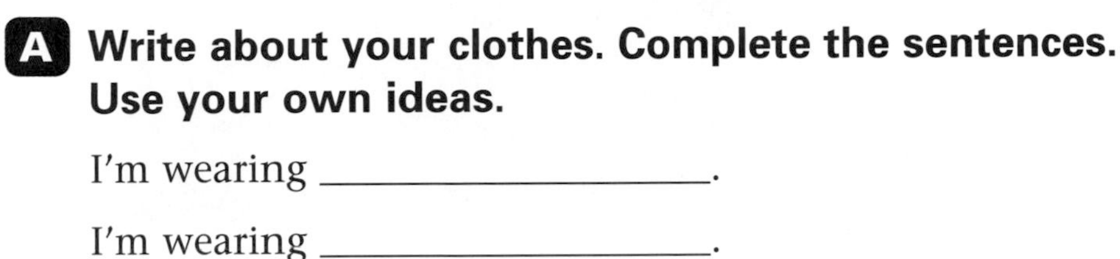

A **Write about your clothes. Complete the sentences. Use your own ideas.**

I'm wearing ______________________.

I'm wearing ______________________.

I'm wearing ______________________.

B **Read your story to a partner.**

3 Listen for clothes and colors

STUDENT AUDIO

A **Listen. Circle *a* or *b*.**

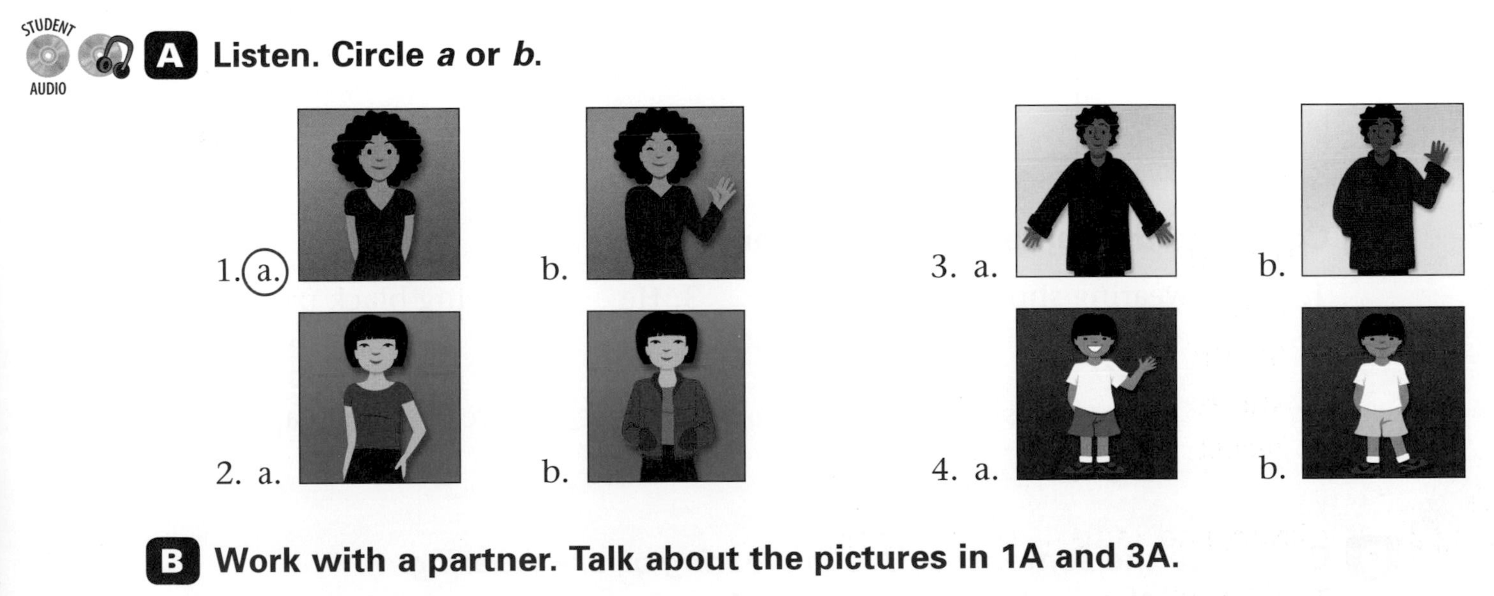

1. (a.) b.
2. a. b.
3. a. b.
4. a. b.

B **Work with a partner. Talk about the pictures in 1A and 3A.**

It's a red dress. It's a red sweater.

TEST YOURSELF ✔

Copy the sentences. Close your book. Then complete the sentences. Use your own ideas.

It's March. I'm wearing ______________. *It's June. I'm wearing* ______________.

1 Learn statements with the present continuous

A **Look at the pictures. Read the sentences.**

1 I am wearing black pants.

2 She is wearing a blue dress.

3 It is wearing shoes.

B **Study the chart. Listen and repeat.**

I	am	wearing	shoes.
You	are		
He She It	is		
We They	are		

C **Complete the sentences. Circle *a* or *b*.**

1. I ____ wearing shoes.
   a. is (b.) am
2. You ____ wearing shoes.
   a. are b. is
3. He ____ wearing black pants.
   a. are b. is
4. They ____ wearing red caps.
   a. are b. is

D **Complete the sentences. Use *is wearing* or *are wearing*. Then read the sentences with a partner.**

1. She __is wearing__ a green sweater.
2. They ________________ white coats.
3. He ________________ blue pants.
4. You ________________ a purple dress.

2 Learn *Yes/No* questions with the present continuous

A Look at the pictures. Listen and read the questions and answers.

1

A: Are you wearing a dress?
B: Yes, I am.

2

A: Is Ed reading a book?
B: Yes, he is.

3

A: Is Min reading a book?
B: No, she's not.

4

A: Is the cat sleeping?
B: Yes, it is.

5

A: Are we going to the library?
B: No, we're not.

6

A: Are they wearing red shoes?
B: No, they're not.

B Complete the questions. Use the present continuous.

1. A: ___Are___ you wearing a skirt?
   B: Yes, I am.
2. A: __________ Irene wearing an orange T-shirt?
   B: Yes, she is.
3. A: Is Cho __________ brown shoes?
   B: Yes, he is.
4. A: Is Ana __________ a jacket?
   B: Yes, she is.

C Work with a partner. Read the conversations in 2A and 2B.

TEST YOURSELF ✔

Write questions and answers about your classmates. Compare your sentences with a partner.

Is Galina wearing a dress? No, she's not.
Is Azim wearing blue pants? Yes, he is.

1 Learn about shopping for clothes

A **Look at the pictures. Read the conversation.**

B **Listen and read.**

Hector: Excuse me. I'm looking for a T-shirt.
Clerk: What size?
Hector: Small.
Clerk: Here's a small.
Hector: Thanks.

C **Listen again and repeat.**

D **Work with a partner. Practice the conversation. Use your own ideas.**

A: I'm looking for a __________.

B: What size?

A: __________.

B: Here's a __________.

A: Thanks.

Need help?

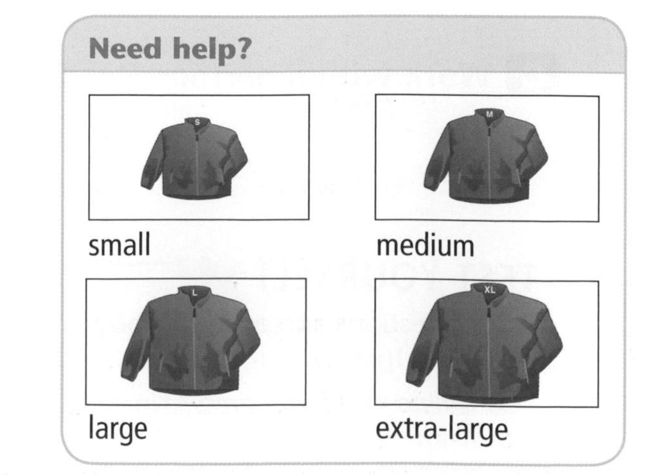

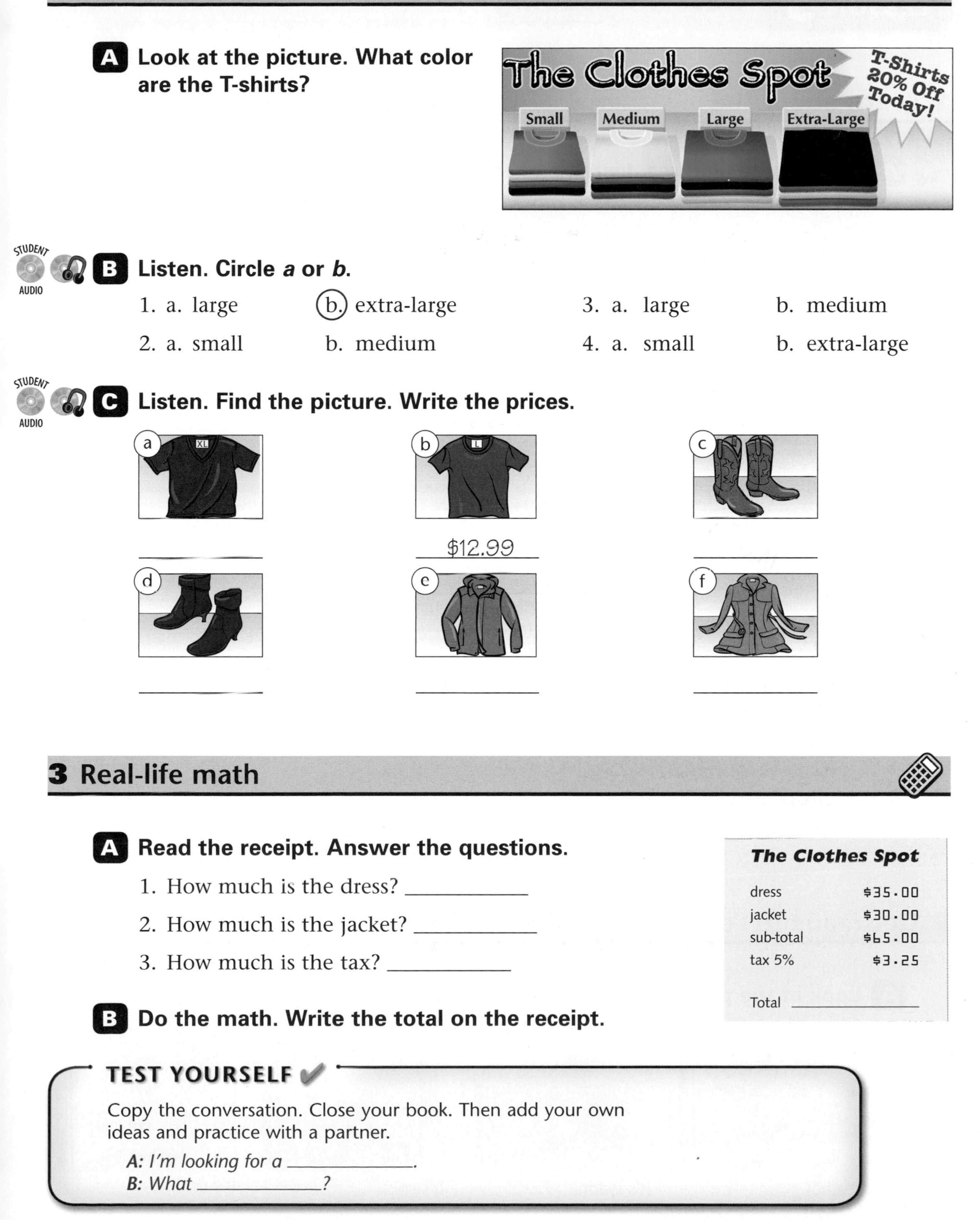

2 Listen for sizes

A **Look at the picture. What color are the T-shirts?**

STUDENT AUDIO

B **Listen. Circle *a* or *b*.**

1. a. large (b.) extra-large
2. a. small b. medium
3. a. large b. medium
4. a. small b. extra-large

STUDENT AUDIO

C **Listen. Find the picture. Write the prices.**

a ________
b $12.99
c ________
d ________
e ________
f ________

3 Real-life math

A **Read the receipt. Answer the questions.**

1. How much is the dress? ____________
2. How much is the jacket? ____________
3. How much is the tax? ____________

The Clothes Spot

dress	$35.00
jacket	$30.00
sub-total	$65.00
tax 5%	$3.25
Total	________

B **Do the math. Write the total on the receipt.**

TEST YOURSELF

Copy the conversation. Close your book. Then add your own ideas and practice with a partner.

A: I'm looking for a ____________.
B: What ____________?

LESSON 5 Real-life reading

1 Learn about the weather

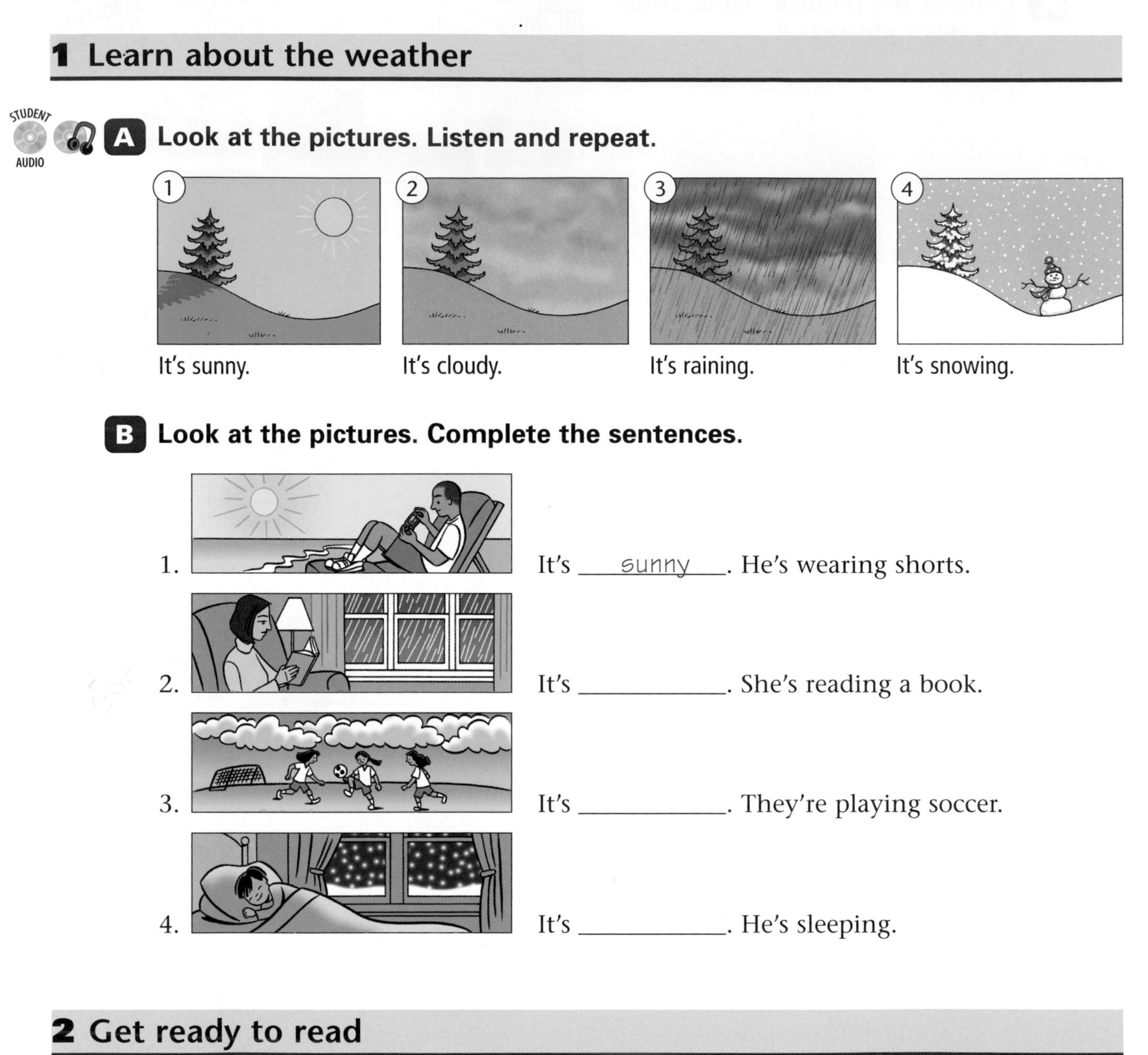

A Look at the pictures. Listen and repeat.

1. It's sunny.
2. It's cloudy.
3. It's raining.
4. It's snowing.

B Look at the pictures. Complete the sentences.

1. It's ___sunny___. He's wearing shorts.
2. It's ___________. She's reading a book.
3. It's ___________. They're playing soccer.
4. It's ___________. He's sleeping.

2 Get ready to read

A Look at the pictures. Read the sentences.

1. It's hot.
2. It's warm.
3. It's cool.
4. It's cold.

B **Check (✓) your favorite weather.**

☐ hot ☐ cool

☐ warm ☐ cold

3 Read a weather website

A **Read the website.**

The Weather This Week

Address: http://www.weatherthisweek.us

Sunday	Monday	Tuesday	Wednesday	Thursday
Sunny and hot	Sunny and warm	Cloudy and cool	Raining and cool	Snowing and cold

B **Match the weather with the days.**

(a) (b) (c) (d) (e)

_c_ 1. Sunday

___ 2. Monday

___ 3. Tuesday

___ 4. Wednesday

___ 5. Thursday

C **Write or draw about the weather for your city this week.**

Sunday	Monday	Tuesday	Wednesday	Thursday

BRING IT TO LIFE

Bring a weather page from the newspaper or the Internet to class. Circle one new word.

UNIT 9 Review and expand

1 Grammar

A Match the questions with the answers.

c 1. Are you looking for a T-shirt?		a. Yes, she is.
___ 2. Is it raining?		b. No, he's not.
___ 3. Is she sleeping?		c. Yes, I am.
___ 4. Is he wearing a coat?		d. No, they're not.
___ 5. Are they wearing boots?		e. Yes, it is.

B Complete the questions and sentences. Circle *a* or *b*.

1. ___ looking for a T-shirt?
   (a.) Are you   b. You are
2. ___ wearing jackets?
   a. They are   b. Are they
3. ___ snowing?
   a. Is it   b. It is
4. ___ wearing a coat.
   a. He is   b. Is he
5. ___ raining.
   a. Is it   b. It is
6. ___ wearing a brown belt.
   a. You are   b. Are you

2 Group work

A Work with 2–3 classmates. Look at the pictures. Say what you see.

B **Work with your group. Look at the pictures in 2A again. Write what you see. Check your spelling in a dictionary.**

1. boots
2. ______
3. ______
4. ______
5. ______
6. ______

C **Work with your classmates. Make a list of the words from 2B.**

PROBLEM SOLVING

A **Listen. Look at the pictures.**

Ethan's Problem

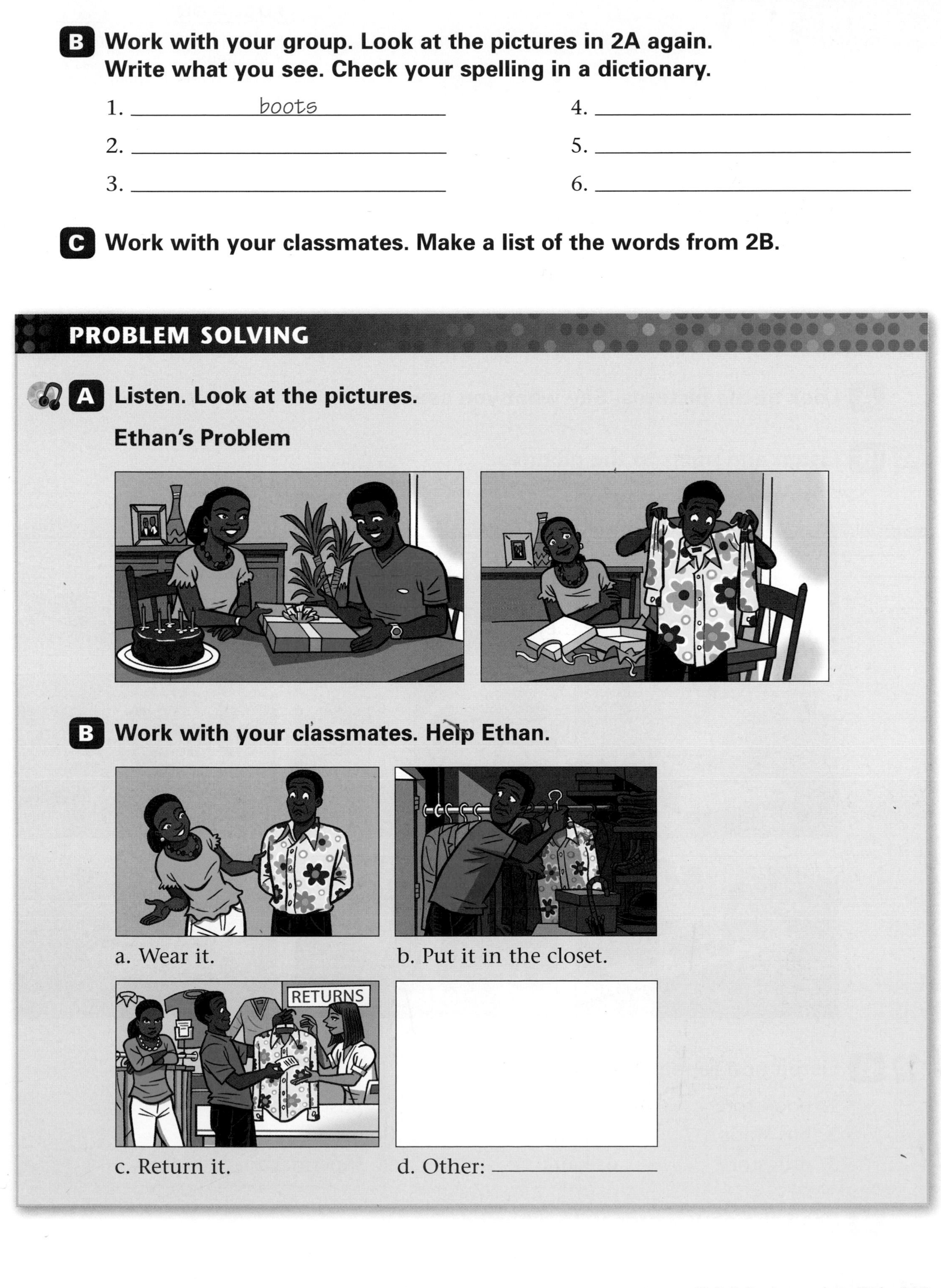

B **Work with your classmates. Help Ethan.**

a. Wear it.

b. Put it in the closet.

c. Return it.

d. Other: ______

UNIT 10

Where's the bank?

FOCUS ON

- places in the community
- locations
- *There is* and *There are*
- asking for and giving locations
- community services

LESSON 1 Vocabulary

1 Learn places in the community

A **Look at the pictures. Say what you see.**

B **Listen and point to the pictures.**

C **Listen and repeat the words.**

1. bookstore	4. laundromat	7. post office
2. bus station	5. park	8. restaurant
3. drugstore	6. bank	9. supermarket

D **Read the new words with a partner.**

 ✔ Identify places in the community

2 Talk about places in the community

 **Look at the picture. Complete the words.**

1. __p__ o s t   o __f__ __f__ i c e
2. b ____ n ____
3. s u ____ e r m a ____ k e t
4. p ____ r ____
5. l ____ ____ n d ____ o m a t
6. b ____ o k s ____ o ____ e
7. r e s ____ ____ u r a n ____
8. ____ r ____ g s t o ____ e
9. b u s   s ____ a t ____ ____ n

STUDENT AUDIO

B Listen and repeat.

1. **A:** Is this the bus station?
   B: No, it's the post office.
2. **A:** Is this the drugstore?
   B: Yes, it is.

C Work with a partner. Point to the places in 2A. Practice the conversations.

1. **A:** Is this the ____________?
   B: No, it's the ____________.
2. **A:** Is this the ____________?
   B: Yes, it is.

TEST YOURSELF ✓

Close your book. Write 4 places in the community.
Check your spelling in a dictionary.

LESSON 2 Life stories

1 Read about locations in the community

A **Look at the picture. Point to the park.**

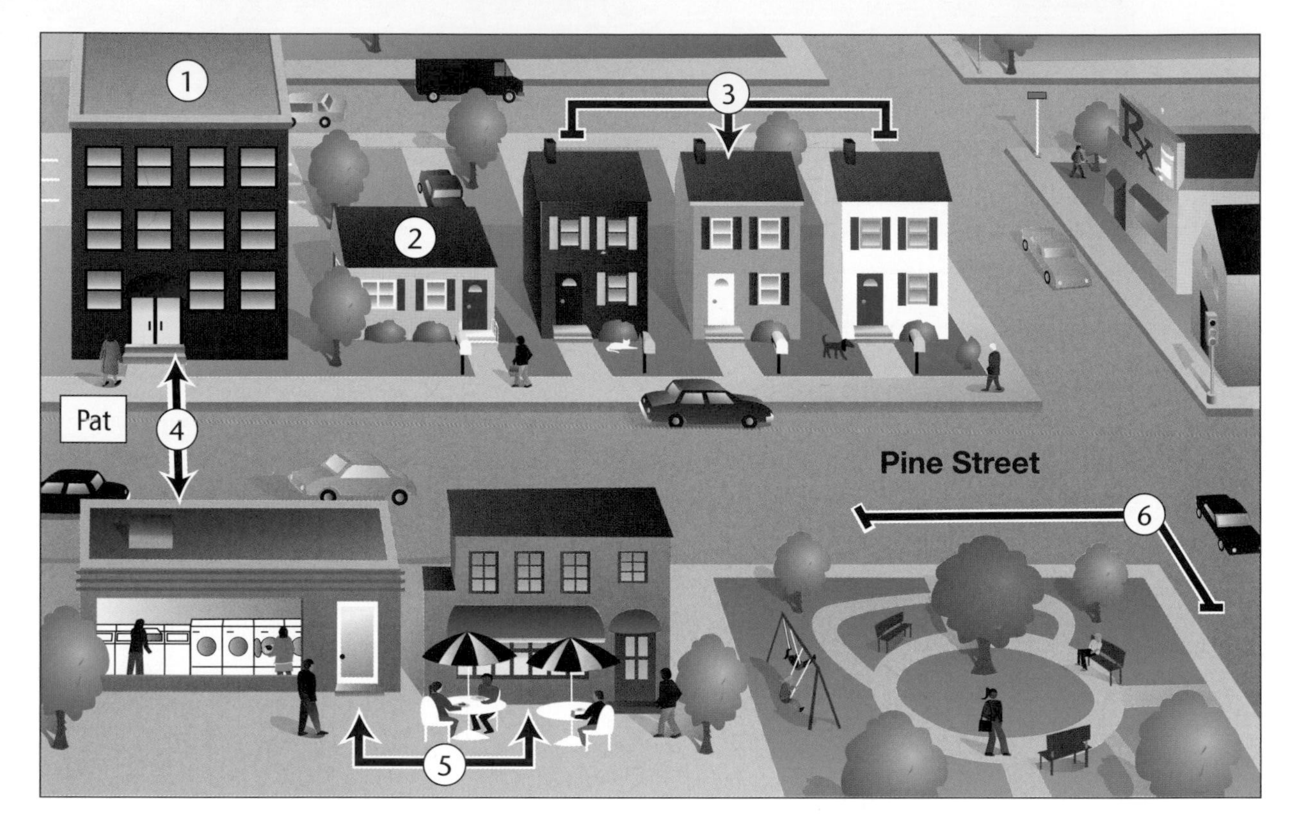

B **Listen and repeat the words.**

1. apartment building
2. house
3. between
4. across from
5. next to
6. on the corner

C **Listen and read Pat's story.**

1. My apartment building is on Pine Street.
2. There is a laundromat across from the apartment building.
3. There is a restaurant next to the laundromat.
4. There is a park on the corner.
5. I go to the park on Saturdays.

D **Listen to Rob's story. Circle the correct word.**

1. My house is ____ Third Street.	(on)	in
2. There is a park ____ the house.	across from	next to
3. There is a post office ____ the park.	across from	next to
4. There is a bank ____ the corner.	on	in
5. I go to the ____ on Sundays.	bookstore	drugstore

Rob

2 Write about a street

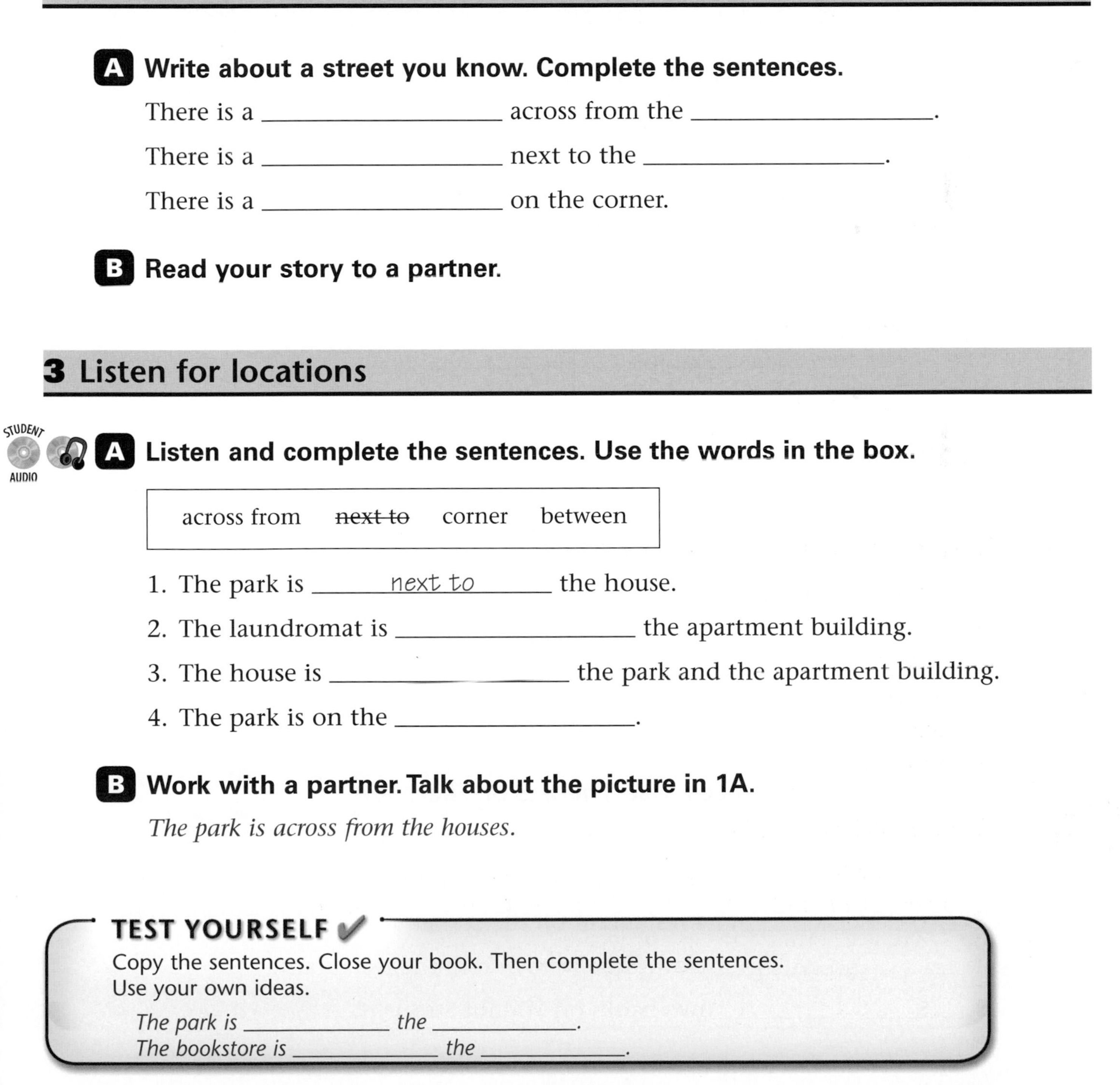

A **Write about a street you know. Complete the sentences.**

There is a ________________ across from the ________________.

There is a ________________ next to the ________________.

There is a ________________ on the corner.

B **Read your story to a partner.**

3 Listen for locations

A **Listen and complete the sentences. Use the words in the box.**

across from	~~next to~~	corner	between

1. The park is ____next to____ the house.
2. The laundromat is ________________ the apartment building.
3. The house is ________________ the park and the apartment building.
4. The park is on the ________________.

B **Work with a partner. Talk about the picture in 1A.**

The park is across from the houses.

TEST YOURSELF ✓

Copy the sentences. Close your book. Then complete the sentences.
Use your own ideas.

The park is ____________ the ____________.
The bookstore is ____________ the ____________.

LESSON 3 Grammar

1 Learn statements with *There is* and *There are*

A Look at the pictures. Read the sentences.

1 There is a supermarket next to the restaurant.

2 There are two schools on Ash Street.

 **B Study the chart. Listen and repeat.**

There is	a supermarket a post office	on Green Street.
There are	two banks three restaurants	

C Complete the sentences. Use *is* or *are*.

1. There ___is___ a supermarket on Green Street.
2. There ______ a post office on Green Street.
3. There ______ two banks on Green Street.
4. There ______ three restaurants on Green Street.

D Complete the sentences. Use *There is* or *There are*.

1. ___There is___ a bank next to the restaurant.
2. ______ two restaurants between the bank and the bookstore.
3. ______ a restaurant on the corner.
4. ______ a drugstore across from the restaurant.
5. ______ two banks on Walnut Street.

2 Learn *Yes/No* questions with *Is there*

A Listen and look at the pictures. Read the conversations.

Salima: Is there a post office nearby?
Mateo: Yes, there is.

Jia: Is there a supermarket nearby?
Dolores: No, there isn't.

B Look at the pictures in 2A. Circle *a* or *b*.

1. Is there a post office nearby?
   (a.) Yes, there is. b. Yes, it is.
2. Is there a supermarket nearby?
   a. No, it isn't. b. No, there isn't.
3. Is there a bookstore nearby?
   a. Yes, there is. b. No, there isn't.
4. Is there a drugstore nearby?
   a. Yes, there is. b. No, there isn't.

C Complete the questions.

1. ___Is there___ a park nearby?
2. ______________ a laundromat nearby?
3. ______________ a bus station nearby?
4. ______________ a library nearby?

D Work with a partner. Talk about your community.

1. **A:** Is there a __________ nearby?
   B: Yes, there is.
2. **A:** Is there a __________ nearby?
   B: No, there isn't.

TEST YOURSELF ✓

Write questions and answers about your community.
Compare your sentences with a partner.

Is there a bus station nearby? Yes, there is.

LESSON 4 Everyday conversation

1 Learn to talk about locations

A **Look at the pictures. Read the conversation.**

B **Listen and read.**

Mario: Excuse me. Where is the drugstore?

Phu: It's next to the bookstore.

Mario: Thank you.

Phu: You're welcome.

C **Listen again and repeat.**

D **Work with a partner. Practice the conversation. Use your own ideas.**

A: Excuse me. Where is the ____________?

B: It's ____________.

A: Thank you.

B: You're welcome.

2 Listen for locations

STUDENT AUDIO

A **Look at the map. Listen and point to the places.**

B **Listen again. Write the places on the map. Use the words in the box.**

~~drugstore~~ bookstore restaurant park

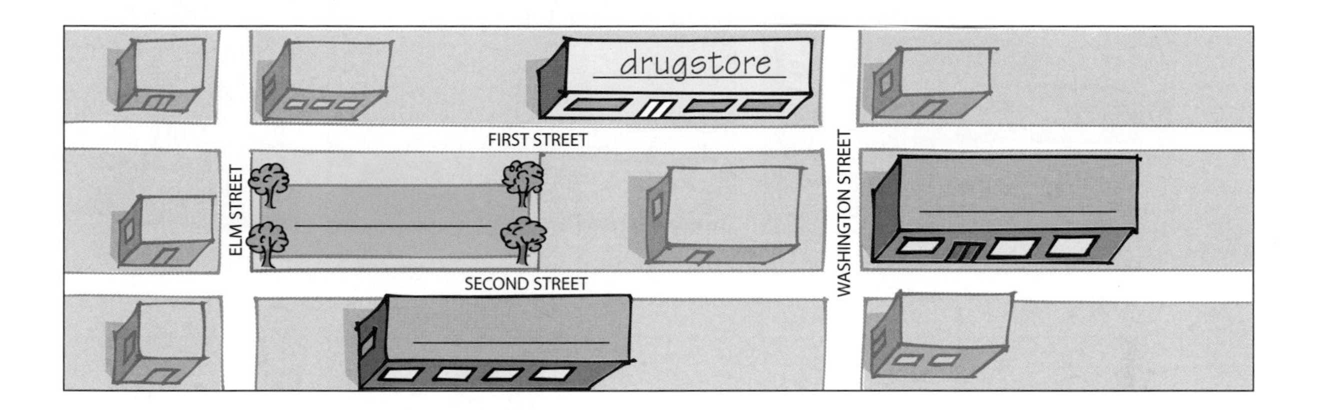

3 Real-life math

A **Look at the map. Read the sentences.**

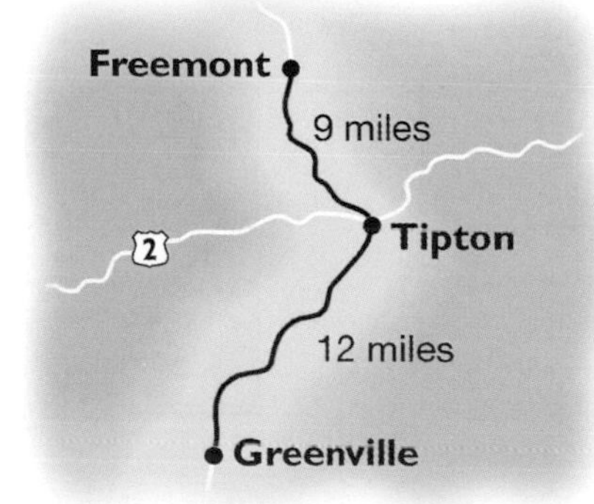

1. Freemont is 9 miles from Tipton.
2. Tipton is 12 miles from Greenville.

B **Look at the map in 3A. Do the math. Complete the sentence.**

9 + 12 = ____ Freemont is ____ miles from Greenville.

TEST YOURSELF ✔

Copy the conversation. Close your book. Then add your own ideas and practice with a partner.

A: Excuse me. Where is the ____________?
B: ____________.

LESSON 5 Real-life reading

1 Learn about community services

A Look at the pictures. Listen and repeat.

1 Department of Motor Vehicles (DMV)

2 police station

3 fire station

4 hospital

5 ambulance

6 courthouse

B Listen. Circle *a* or *b*.

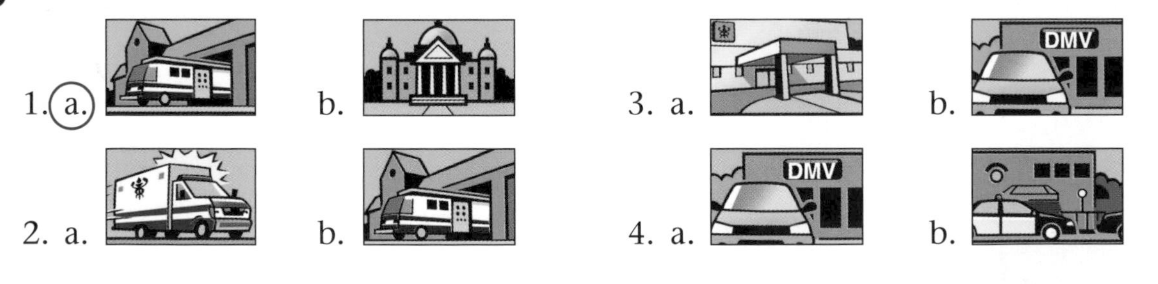

1. (a.) b.
2. a. b.
3. a. b.
4. a. b.

2 Get ready to read

A Look at the pictures. Read the words.

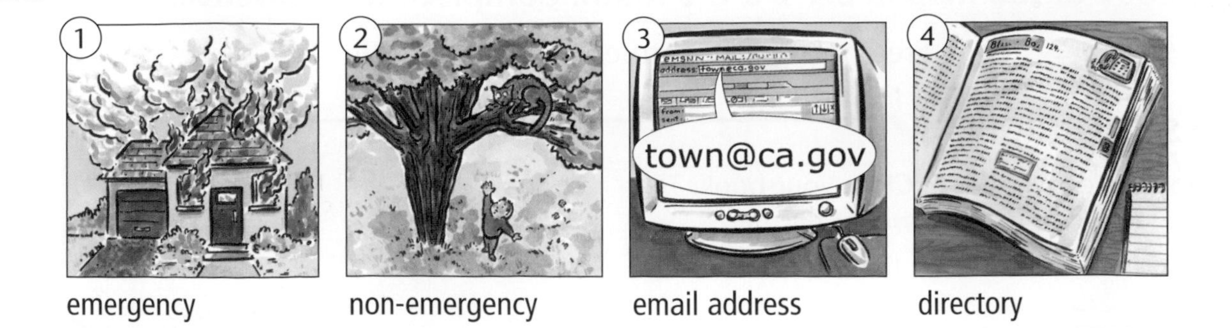

1 emergency
2 non-emergency
3 email address
4 directory

B **Work with your classmates. Look at the pictures. Circle *emergency* or *non-emergency.***

1

emergency non-emergency

2

emergency non-emergency

3 Read a city-services directory

A **Read the city-services directory.**

Lakewood City Directory

Police
Fire
Ambulance and Hospital

EMERGENCY NUMBER
911

Non-emergency numbers

Hospital	311 First Street	(505) 555-9111	
Police Station	1324 Adams Street	(505) 555-1010	
Fire Station	831 Third Street	(505) 555-0985	
DMV	389 Second Street	(505) 555-3421	email address: dmv@lakewood.us
Courthouse	3251 Third Street	(505) 555-1900	email address: court@lakewood.us

B **Look at the directory. Circle *a* or *b*.**

1. For a police emergency, call ____.
   (a.) 911 b. (505) 555-1010
2. The hospital is on ____.
   a. Adams Street b. First Street
3. The fire station is on ____.
   a. First Street b. Third Street
4. The non-emergency number for the hospital is ____.
   a. (505) 555-9111 b. 911

BRING IT TO LIFE

Find the phone number for your police station. Bring it to class.

Midtown Police
(677) 555-9889

UNIT 10 Review and expand

1 Grammar

A Complete the sentences. Use *There is* or *There are*.

1. There is a park on Second Street.
2. ____________ two banks nearby.
3. ____________ a post office on the corner.
4. ____________ two restaurants next to the hospital.
5. ____________ a library next to the DMV.

B Complete the questions and answers.

1. **A:** Is there a police station nearby?
   B: Yes, there is.
2. **A:** ____________ a fire station on the corner?
   B: No, there isn't.
3. **A:** ____________ a park next to the school?
   B: Yes, ____________.
4. **A:** ____________ a restaurant nearby?
   B: No, ____________.

2 Group work

A Work with 2–3 classmates. Look at the picture. Say what you see.

B **Work with your group. Look at the picture in 2A again. Write what you see. Check your spelling in a dictionary.**

1. restaurant
2. ______
3. ______
4. ______
5. ______
6. ______

C **Work with your classmates. Make a list of the words from 2B.**

PROBLEM SOLVING

A **Listen. Look at the picture.**

Elena's Problem

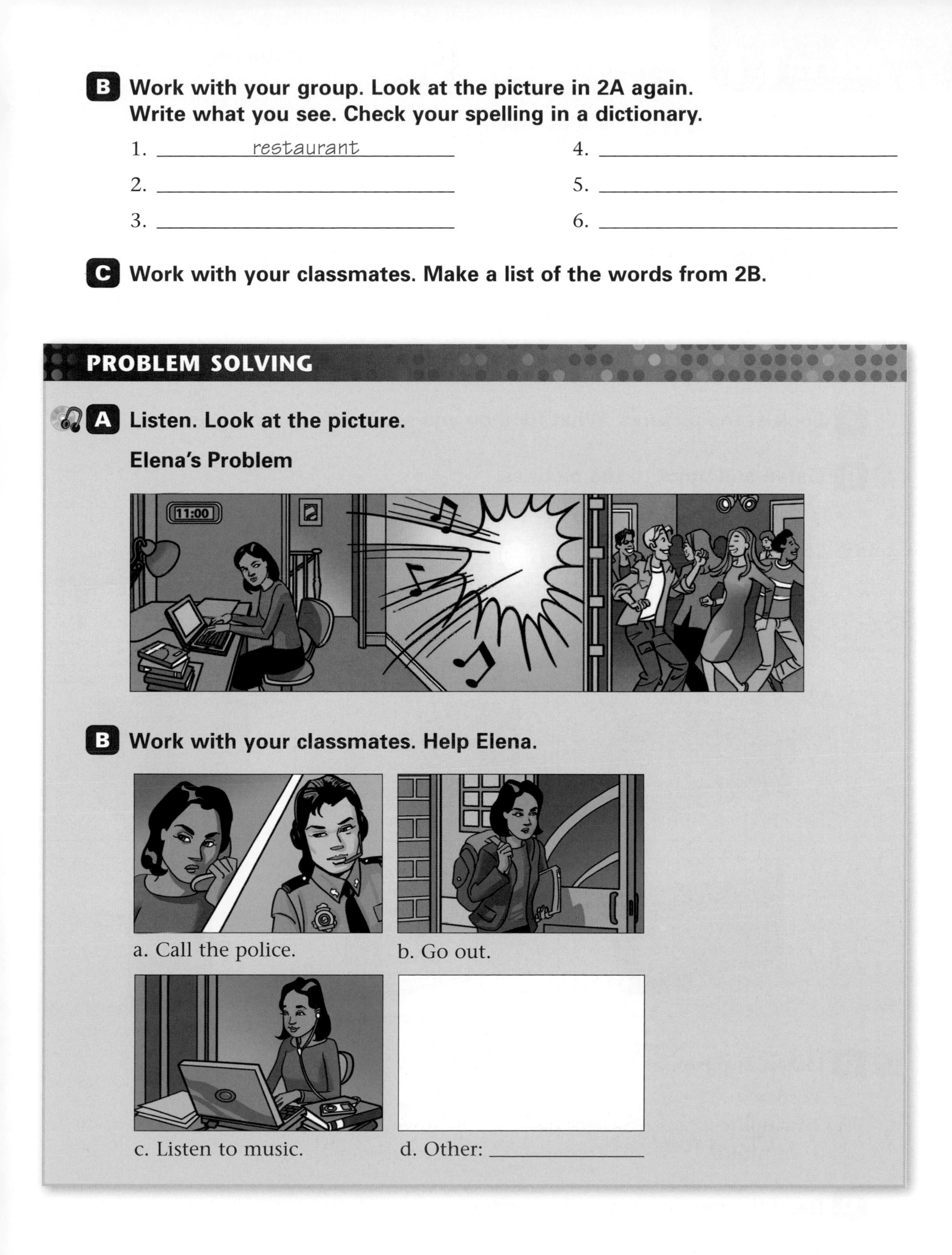

B **Work with your classmates. Help Elena.**

a. Call the police.

b. Go out.

c. Listen to music.

d. Other: ______

UNIT 11
This Is My Home

FOCUS ON
- things in the home
- rooms in a home
- possessive *'s*
- asking about a home for rent
- reading a classified ad

LESSON 1 Vocabulary

1 Learn words for things in the home

A **Look at the pictures. What food do you see?**

STUDENT AUDIO **B** **Listen and point to the pictures.**

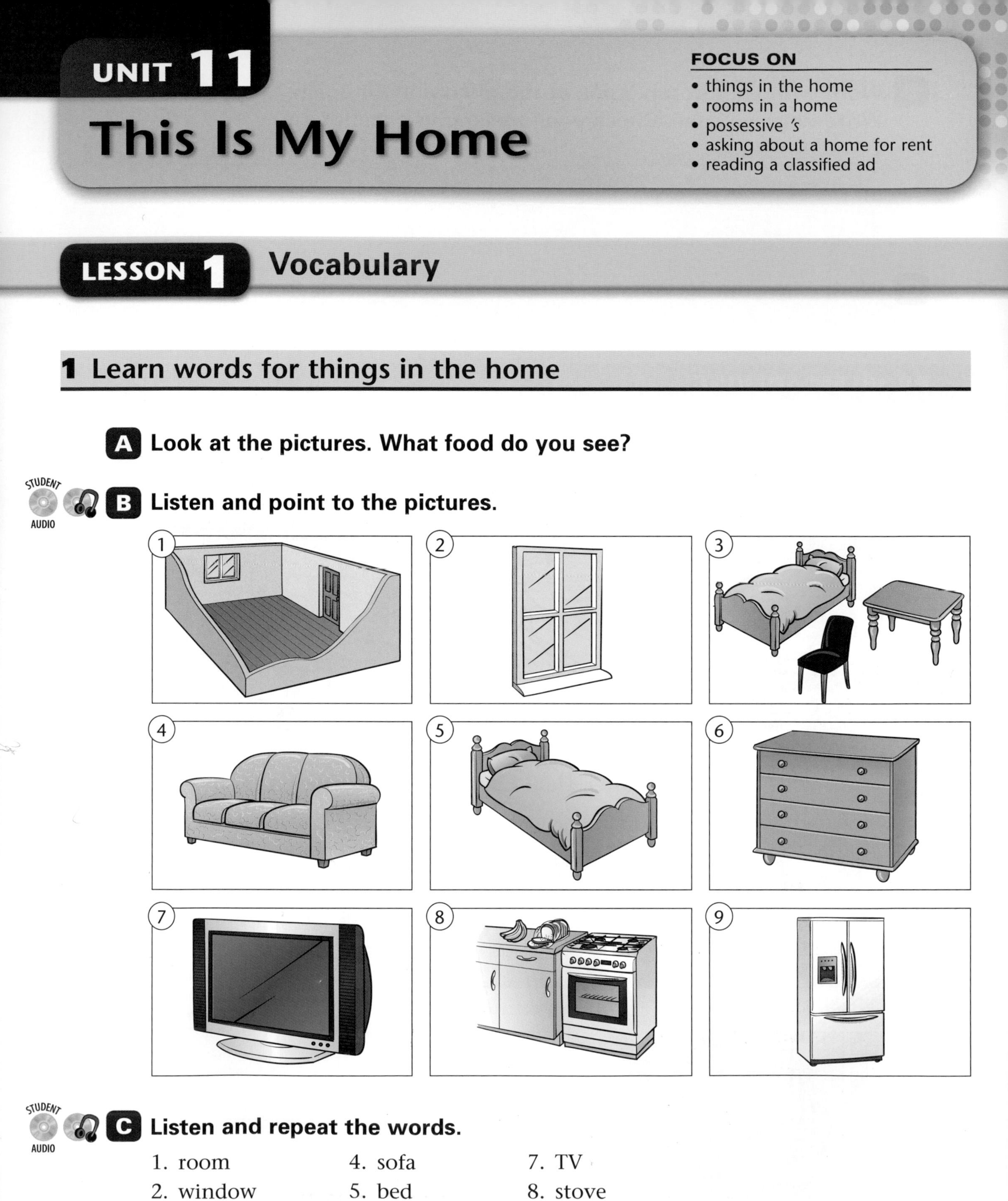

STUDENT AUDIO **C** **Listen and repeat the words.**

1. room	4. sofa	7. TV
2. window	5. bed	8. stove
3. furniture	6. dresser	9. refrigerator

D **Read the new words with a partner.**

2 Talk about your home

A **Look at the pictures. Complete the words.**

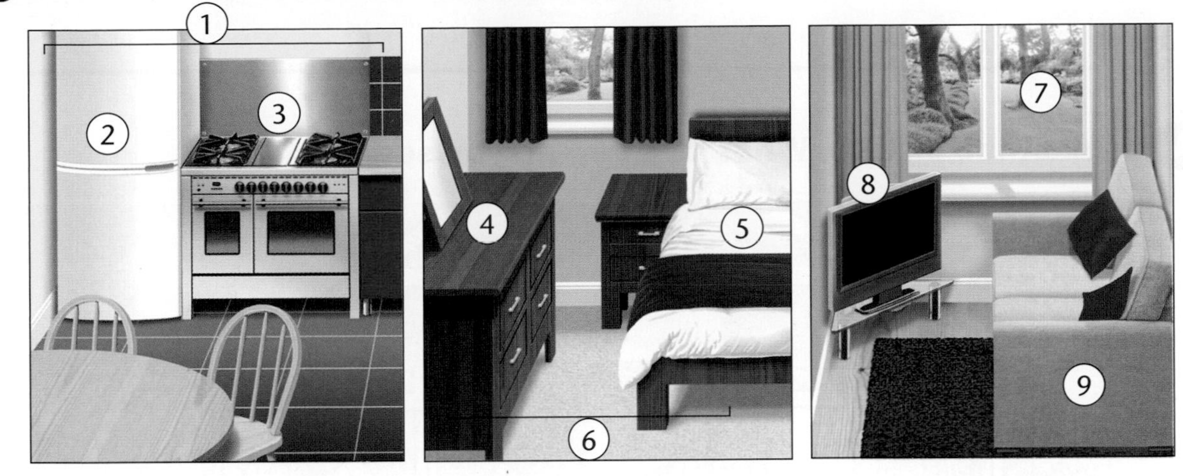

1. r o o m
2. r e f ___ ___ g e r a ___ ___ r
3. ___ t o ___ e
4. d r ___ s ___ e r
5. ___ e d
6. f u r ___ i ___ ___ r e
7. w ___ n ___ ___ w
8. T ___
9. s ___ ___ a

B **Listen and repeat.**

1. **A:** Where's the stove?
   B: It's next to the refrigerator.

2. **A:** Where's the TV?
   B: It's across from the sofa.

C **Work with a partner. Point to the pictures in 2A. Practice the conversation.**

A: Where's the __________?

B: It's __________.

TEST YOURSELF ✔

Close your book. Write 3 furniture words and 3 things in the home.
Check your spelling in a dictionary.

LESSON 2 Life stories

1 Read about a home

A **Look at the picture. What furniture do you see?**

B **Listen and repeat the words.**

1. on
2. in
3. bedroom
4. bathroom
5. living room
6. above
7. below
8. kitchen
9. garage

C **Listen and read Peter's story.**

1. This is my home.
2. There is one bedroom and one bathroom.
3. There is a blue sofa in the living room.
4. There are two windows above the sofa.
5. I like my home.

D Listen to Meg's story. Circle the correct word.

1. ____ is my home.	(This)	There
2. There are three ____.	bathrooms	bedrooms
3. There is a table in the ____.	kitchen	garage
4. There is a window ____ the table.	below	above
5. I like my ____.	living room	bedroom

Meg

2 Write about your home

A Write about your home. Complete the sentences. Draw a picture.

This is my home.

There ____________________.

There is a ____________________ in the ____________________.

There is a ____________________ above the ____________________.

B Read your story to a partner.

3 Listen for locations in the home

A Listen and draw the furniture in the room.

B Work with a partner. Talk about the picture in 3A.

The bed is next to the dresser.

TEST YOURSELF ✔

Copy the sentences. Close your book. Then complete the sentences.
Use your own ideas.

There is a ____________ in the ____________.
There is a ____________ above the ____________.

LESSON 3 Grammar

1 Learn possessive 's

A Look at the pictures. Listen and read the sentences.

1 Teng's house is white.

2 Gloria's home is small.

3 Mr. and Mrs. Smith's home is big.

4 Karen's bedroom is green.

B Match the sentences.

c 1. His house is white.
e 2. Her home is small.
d 3. Their home is big.
b 4. Her bedroom is green.
d 5. His living room is big.

a. Lionel's living room is big.
b. Karen's bedroom is green.
c. Teng's house is white.
d. Mr. and Mrs. Smith's home is big.
e. Gloria's home is small.

C Look at the pictures. Complete the sentences. Write about the pictures.

Min

Alba

Taylor

Mr. and Mrs. Brown

1. Min's kitchen is small.
2. Alba's sofa is purple.
3. Taylor's living room is black and white.
4. Mr. and Mrs Brown TV is in the kitchen.

2 Learn questions with *How many*

 **Read the conversation.**

A: How many chairs are there in the living room?
B: One.

B Study the chart. Listen and repeat.

How many	chairs windows	are there	in the living room?

C Complete the questions. Circle *a* or *b*. Then read the questions with a partner.

1. How many ____ are there in the living room?
   a. chair   (b.) chairs
2. How many ____ are there in the living room?
   a. windows   b. window
3. How many ____ are there?
   a. bedroom   b. bedrooms
4. How many ____ are there?
   a. beds   b. bed
5. How many ____ are there in Sally's home?
   a. bathroom   b. bathrooms
6. How many ____ are there in Flora's house?
   a. TVs   b. TV

D Work with a partner. Look at the pictures in 1A and 1C. Ask and answer questions.

How many __________ are there __________?

TEST YOURSELF ✓

Write questions and answers about the pictures in 1A or 1C. Compare your sentences with your partner.

How many sofas are there in Alba's home? One.

LESSON 4 Everyday conversation

1 Learn to ask about a home for rent

A **Look at the pictures. Read the conversation.**

Is there an apartment for rent?
Yes, there is.
FOR RENT
Oak Apartment
FOR RENT
Diana
Manager
How many bedrooms are there?
Two.
FOR RENT
BR?
Oak Apartment
FOR RENT

B **Listen and read.**

Diana: Is there an apartment for rent?
Manager: Yes, there is.
Diana: How many bedrooms are there?
Manager: Two.

C **Listen again and repeat.**

D **Work with a partner. Practice the conversation. Use your own ideas.**

A: Is there ____________ for rent?
B: Yes, there is.
A: How many ____________ are there?
B: ____________.

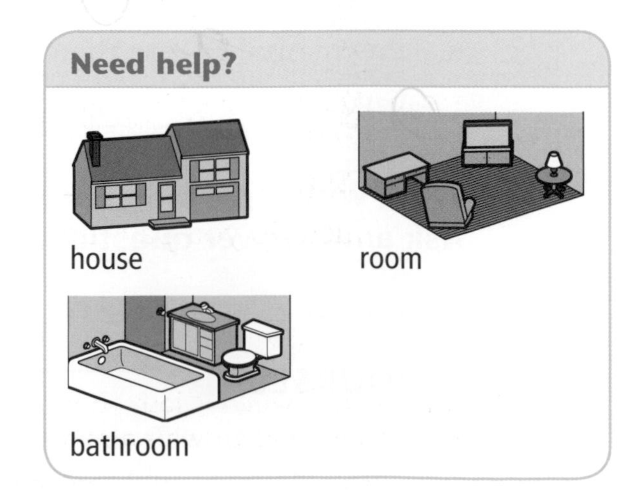

2 Listen for housing information

A **Listen and point to the rooms.**

B **Listen again. Number the homes.**

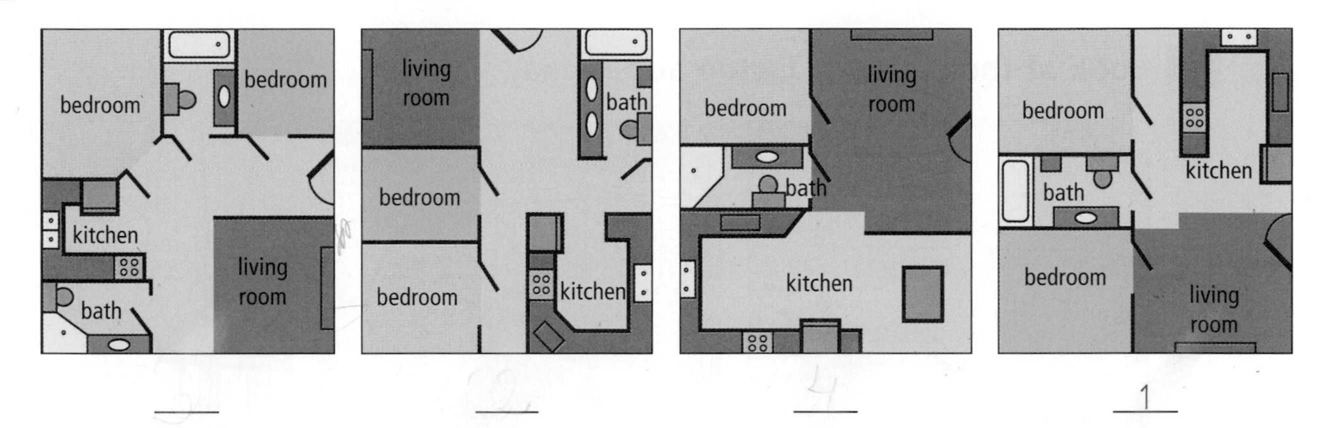

____ ____ ____ 1

3 Real-life math

A **Look at the picture. Read the words. Is the apartment cheap or expensive?**

B **Read the information. Do the math. Answer the question.**

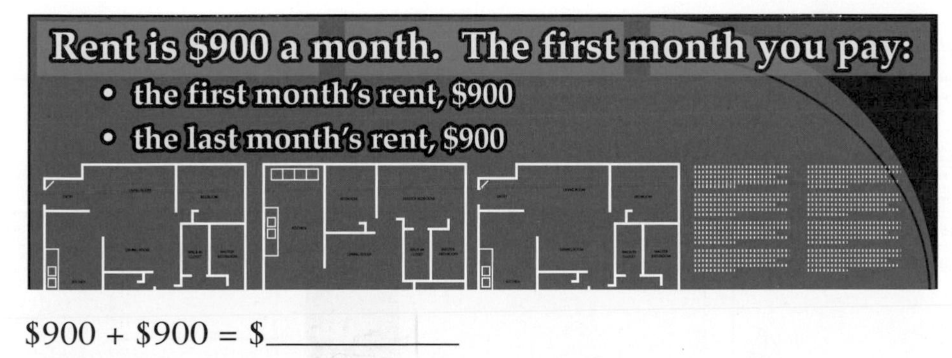

Rent is $900 a month. The first month you pay:
• the first month's rent, $900
• the last month's rent, $900

\$900 + \$900 = \$__________

How much do you pay the first month for this apartment?

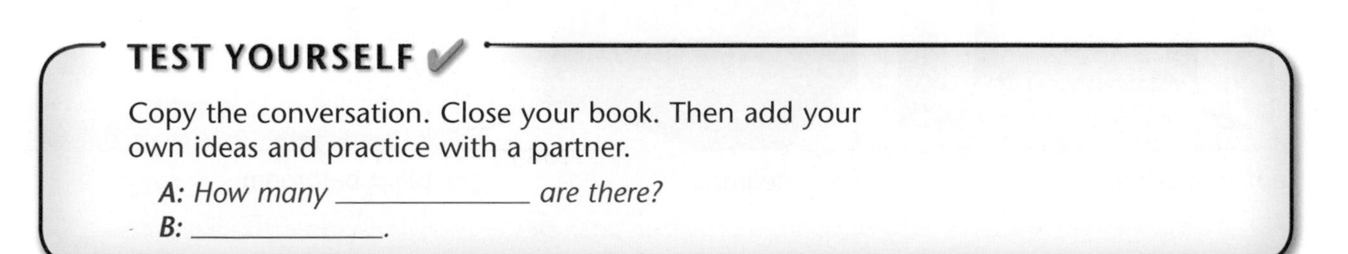

TEST YOURSELF

Copy the conversation. Close your book. Then add your own ideas and practice with a partner.

A: How many __________ are there?

B: __________.

LESSON 5 Real-life reading

1 Learn about types of housing

A Look at the pictures. Listen and repeat.

1 duplex

2 mobile home

3 rented room

B Listen. Circle *a* or *b*.

1. a. duplex (b.) apartment
2. a. rented room b. mobile home
3. a. house b. mobile home
4. a. duplex b. rented room
5. a. house b. apartment

2 Get ready to read

A Look at the pictures. Read the abbreviations and the words.

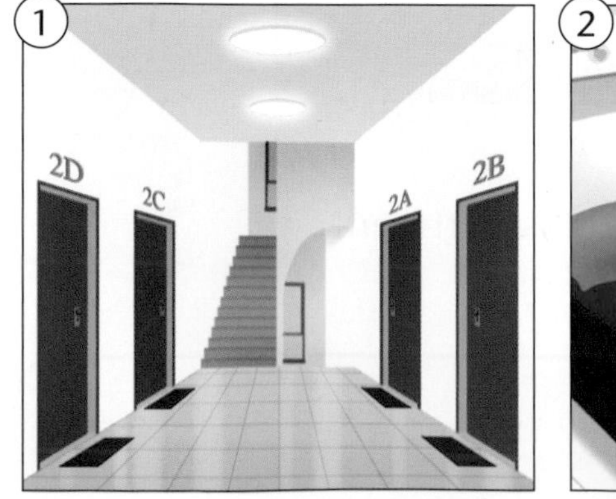

1 apt = apartment

2 BR = bedroom

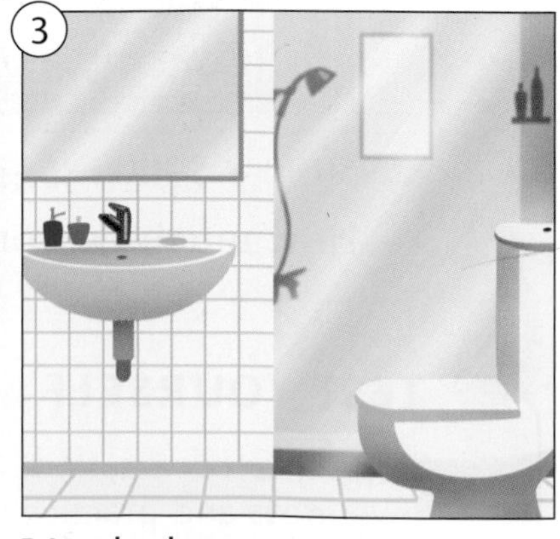

3 BA = bathroom

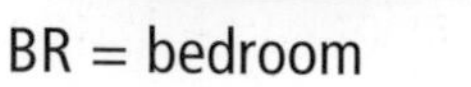

B **Check (✓) the sentence about your home.**

☐ I live in a one-bedroom home.

☐ I live in a two-bedroom home.

☐ I live in a three-bedroom home.

3 Read housing ads

A **Read the housing ads.**

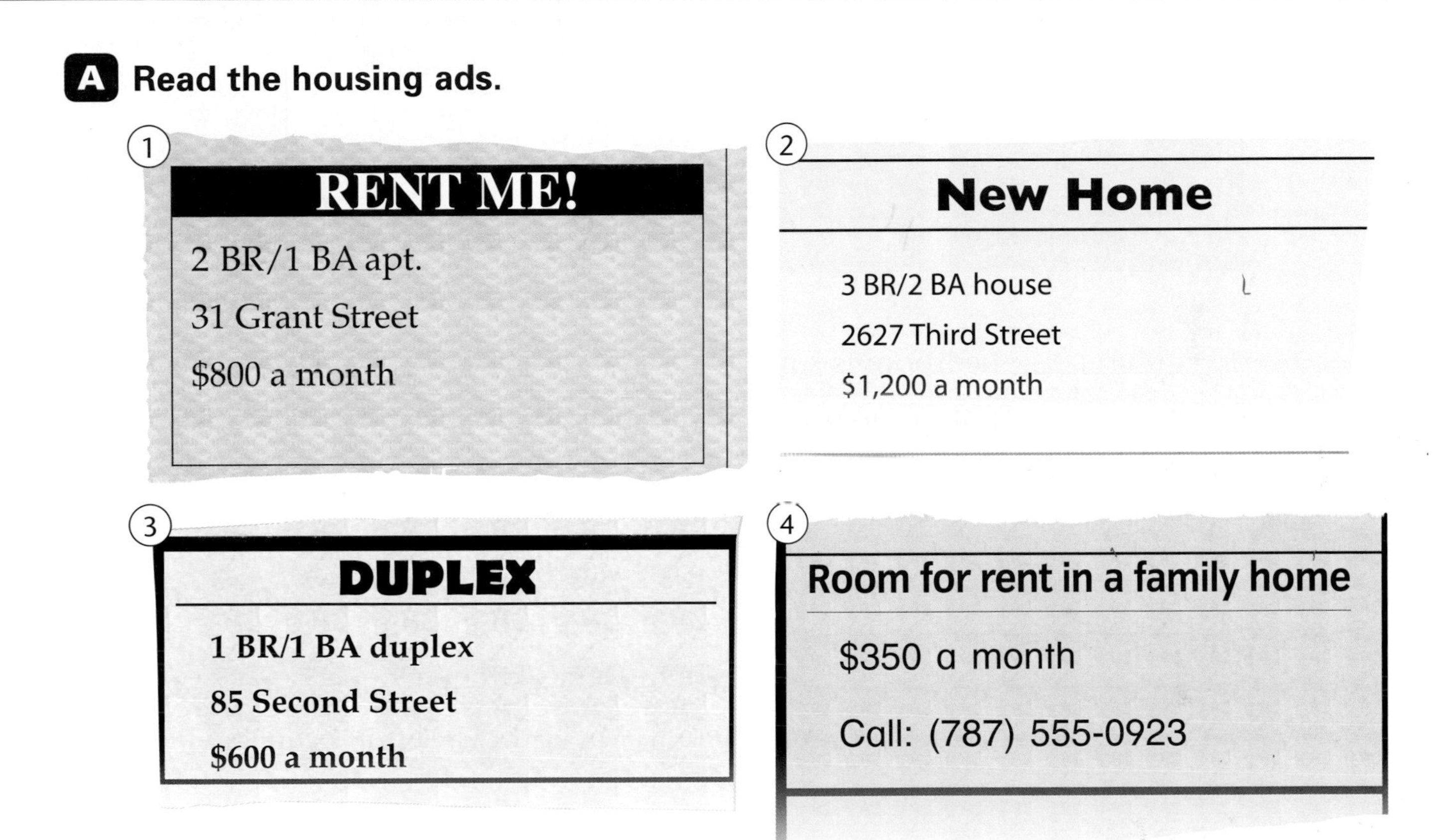

1
RENT ME!
2 BR/1 BA apt.
31 Grant Street
$800 a month
2
New Home
3 BR/2 BA house
2627 Third Street
$1,200 a month
3
DUPLEX
1 BR/1 BA duplex
85 Second Street
$600 a month
4
Room for rent in a family home
$350 a month
Call: (787) 555-0923

B **Look at the housing ads. Circle *yes* or *no*.**

1. The house is on Grant Street. yes (no)
2. The apartment has two bedrooms. yes no
3. The duplex has two bathrooms. yes no
4. The apartment rent is $800 a month. yes no
5. The room for rent is $800 a month. yes no
6. The duplex is on Third Street. yes no

BRING IT TO LIFE

Bring in a housing ad from a newspaper or the Internet.
Circle 2 abbreviations.

UNIT 11 Review and expand

1 Grammar

A Look at the pictures. Complete the sentences. Use the possessive.

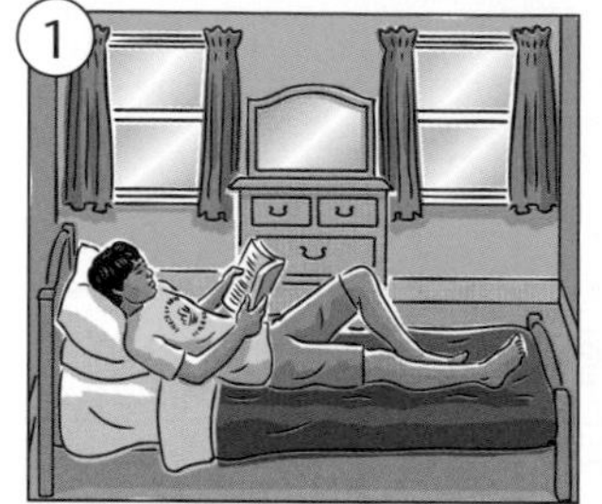

Marco

Lee

Dara

Mr. and Mrs. Luna

1. Marco's bedroom is small.
2. ____________ living room is big.
3. ____________ refrigerator is yellow.
4. ____________ car is blue.

B Look at the pictures in 1A. Complete the questions.

1. How many windows are there in Marco's bedroom?
2. ____________________ are there in Lee's living room?
3. ____________________ are there in Dara's kitchen?
4. ____________________ are there in Mr. and Mrs. Luna's garage?

2 Group work

A Work with 2–3 classmates. Look at the picture. Say what you see.

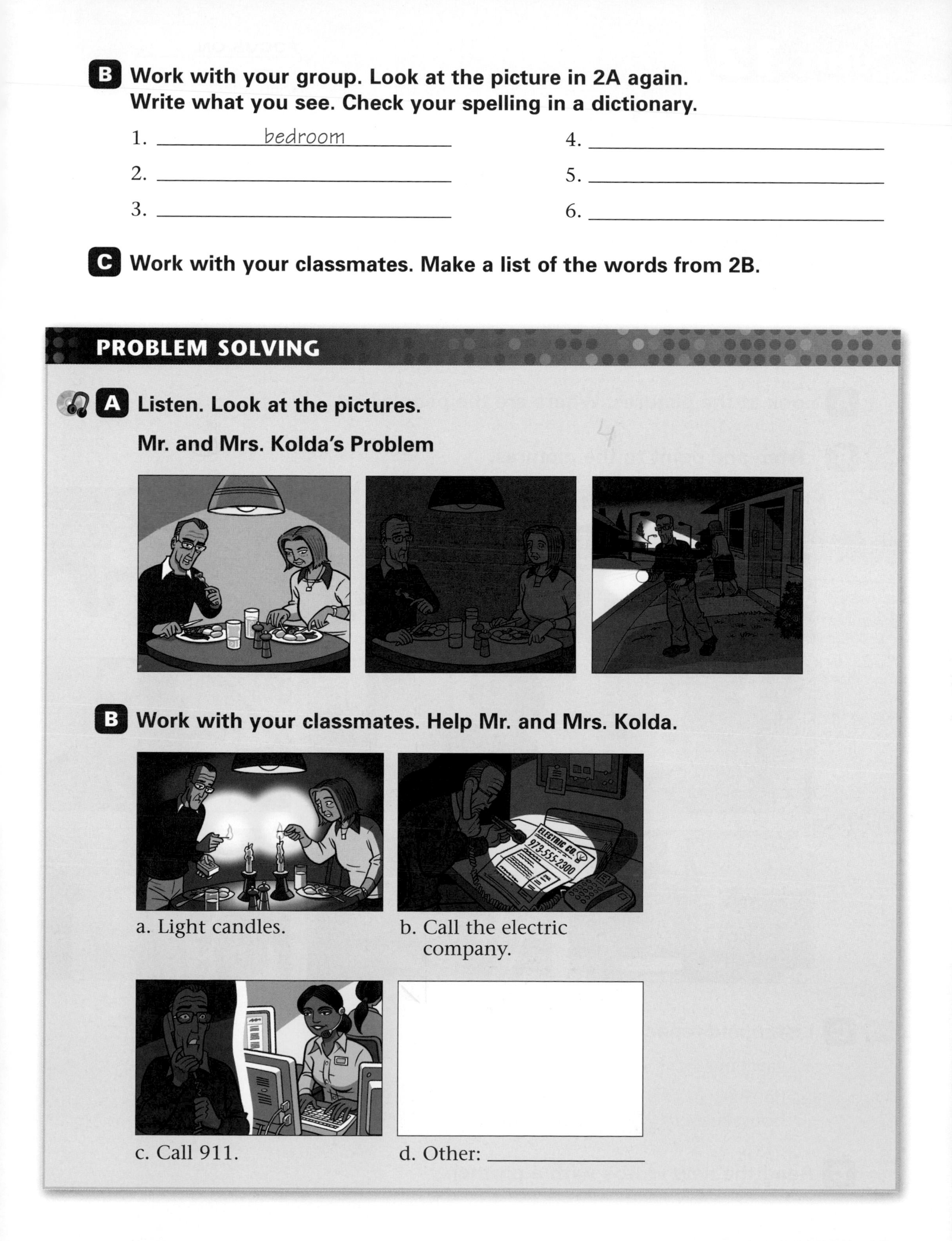

B Work with your group. Look at the picture in 2A again. Write what you see. Check your spelling in a dictionary.

1. bedroom
2. ______
3. ______
4. ______
5. ______
6. ______

C Work with your classmates. Make a list of the words from 2B.

PROBLEM SOLVING

A Listen. Look at the pictures.

Mr. and Mrs. Kolda's Problem

B Work with your classmates. Help Mr. and Mrs. Kolda.

a. Light candles.

b. Call the electric company.

c. Call 911.

d. Other: ______

UNIT 12 Yes, I can!

FOCUS ON
- jobs
- job skills
- *can* and *can't*
- job interviews
- reading a job ad

LESSON 1 Vocabulary

1 Learn the names of jobs

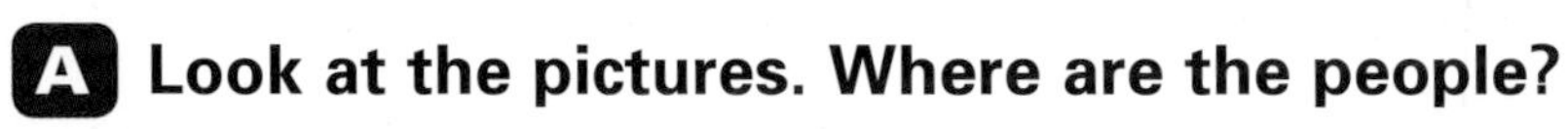

A Look at the pictures. Where are the people?

B Listen and point to the pictures.

C Listen and repeat the words.

1. gardener
2. painter
3. housekeeper
4. cashier
5. hairdresser
6. mechanic
7. truck driver
8. secretary
9. salesperson

D Read the new words with a partner.

2 Talk about jobs

A Look at the picture. Complete the words.

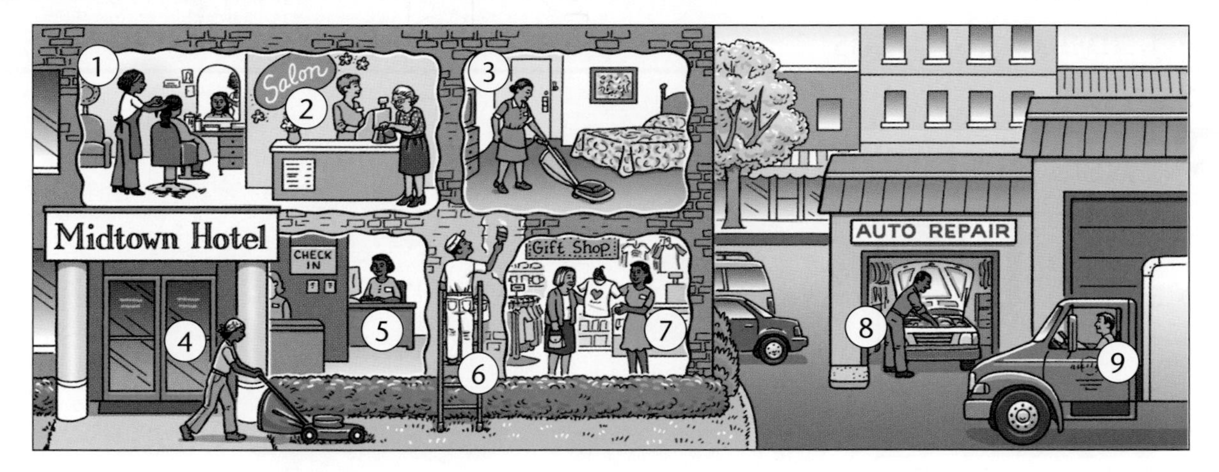

1. h a __i__ __r__ d r __e__ s __s__ e r
2. ___ a s h i ___ r
3. h ___ u s e ___ ___ e p e r
4. g a r ___ ___ n ___ r
5. s ___ ___ r e t ___ ___ y
6. p ___ ___ n t e ___
7. s a ___ e s p ___ ___ s o n
8. m ___ c ___ a ___ i c
9. t r ___ c k d r ___ ___ e r

STUDENT AUDIO

B Listen and repeat.

1. **A:** Is she a salesperson?
   B: Yes, she is.

2. **A:** Is he a housekeeper?
   B: No, he isn't. He's a painter.

C Work with a partner. Point to the picture in 2A. Practice the conversation.

A: Is ___________ a ___________?

B: ___________.

TEST YOURSELF ✓

Close your book. Write 6 jobs. Check your spelling in a dictionary.

LESSON 2 Life stories

1 Read about job skills

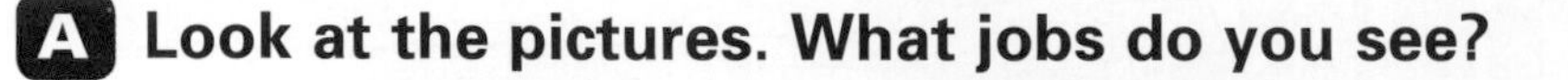

A **Look at the pictures. What jobs do you see?**

B **Listen and repeat the words.**

1. cut hair
2. fix cars
3. drive a truck
4. paint houses
5. clean
6. sell clothes
7. take care of plants
8. use a computer

STUDENT AUDIO **C** **Listen and read Nick's story.**

1. My brother is a mechanic.
2. He can fix cars.
3. My friend is a truck driver.
4. She can drive a truck.
5. I want a job.

D **Listen to Nora's story. Circle the correct word.**

Nora

1. My friend is a ____.	(painter)	gardener
2. He can ____ houses.	clean	paint
3. My sister is a ____.	salesperson	secretary
4. She can ____ a computer.	fix	use
5. I ____ a job.	want	what

2 Write about job skills

A **Write about job skills. Complete the sentences. Use your own ideas.**

My ____________ is a ____________.

He can ____________.

My ____________ is a ____________.

She can ____________.

B **Read your story to a partner.**

3 Listen for job skills

A **Listen and check the skills on the job applications.**

1 **Job Application**
Name: *Lily Ng*
Current job: *secretary*
Job skills:
- ☐ drive a car
- ☑ use a computer
- ☐ speak English
- ☐ other: ____________

2 **Job Application**
Name: Gabriela Valdez
Current job: hairdresser
Job skills:
- ☐ drive a car
- ☐ use a computer
- ☐ speak English
- ☐ other: ____________

3 **Job Application**
Name: *Paul Fields*
Current job: *truck driver*
Job skills:
- ☐ drive a car
- ☐ use a computer
- ☐ speak English
- ☐ other: *drive a truck*

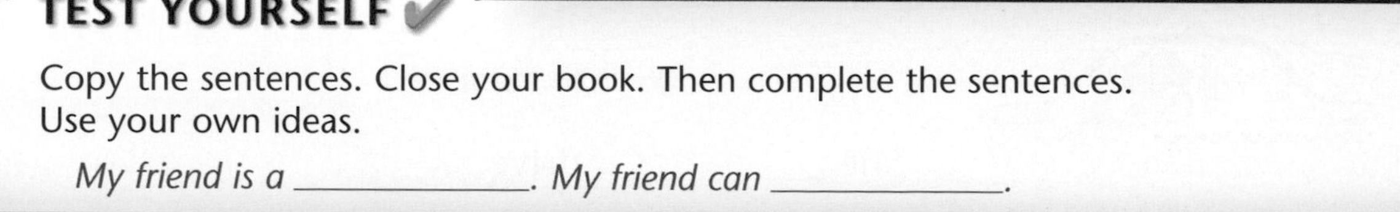
TEST YOURSELF

Copy the sentences. Close your book. Then complete the sentences.
Use your own ideas.

My friend is a ____________. My friend can ____________.

LESSON 3 Grammar

1 Learn statements with *can* and *can't*

A Look at the pictures. Read the sentences.

She can cut hair.

He can sell clothes.

He can't drive.

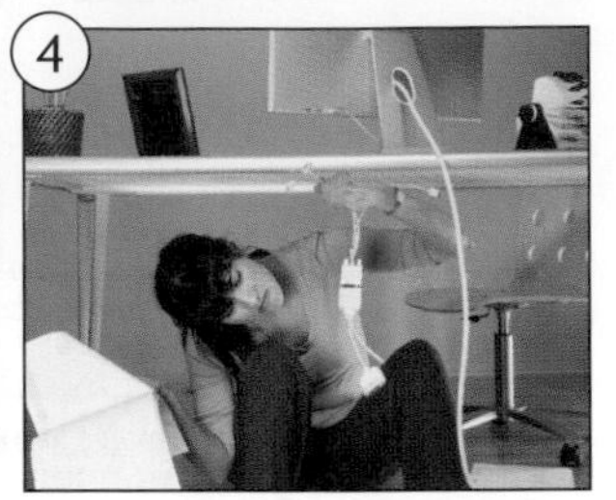

She can't fix computers.

B Study the charts. Listen and repeat.

I You He She It We They	can	cut hair.

I You He She It We They	can't	drive.

C Complete the sentences. Use *can* or *can't*. Then read the sentences with a partner.

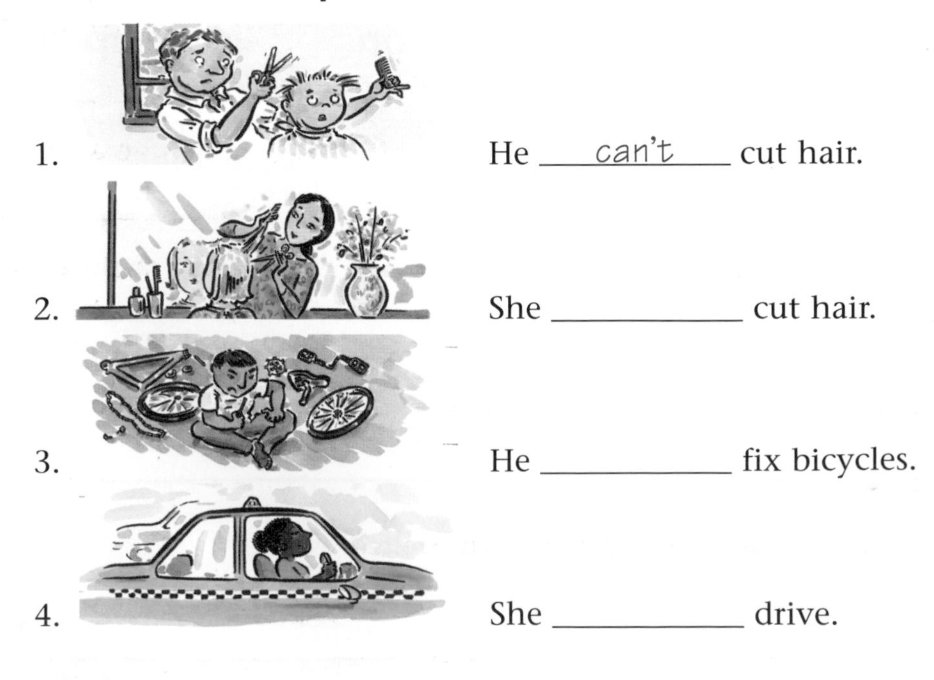

1. He ___can't___ cut hair.
2. She ____________ cut hair.
3. He ____________ fix bicycles.
4. She ____________ drive.

2 Learn *Yes/No* questions and answers with *can* and *can't*

A Look at the pictures. Read the conversations.

1

A: Can you write in English?
B: Yes, I can.

2

A: Can you use a computer?
B: No, I can't.

B Study the charts. Listen and repeat.

Can	you he she they	use a computer?

Yes,	I he she they	can.

No,	I he she they	can't.

C Complete the questions and answers. Use *can* or *can't*.

1. A: Can she use a computer?
   B: Yes, she can.
2. A: ____________ write in English?
   B: No, he can't.
3. A: ____________ fix computers?
   B: Yes, they can.
4. A: Can you sell clothes?
   B: No, I ____________.
5. A: Can he drive a truck?
   B: Yes, he ____________.
6. A: Can she paint houses?
   B: No, she ____________.

D Work with a partner. Read the conversations in 2C.

TEST YOURSELF ✓

Write sentences with *can* and sentences with *can't*. Compare your sentences with a partner.

Jordan can sell clothes. Drew can't cut hair.

LESSON 4 Everyday conversation

1 Learn to answer job-interview questions

A **Look at the pictures. Read the conversation.**

Can you use a computer?
Yes, I can.
Silvia
Patrick

Can you work evenings?
Yes, I can.

STUDENT
AUDIO

B **Listen and read.**

Patrick: Can you use a computer?
Silvia: Yes, I can.
Patrick: Can you work evenings?
Silvia: Yes, I can.

C **Listen again and repeat.**

D **Work with a partner. Practice the conversation. Use your own ideas.**

A: Can you ___________?

B: Yes, I can.

A: Can you ___________?

B: Yes, I can.

2 Listen for a work schedule

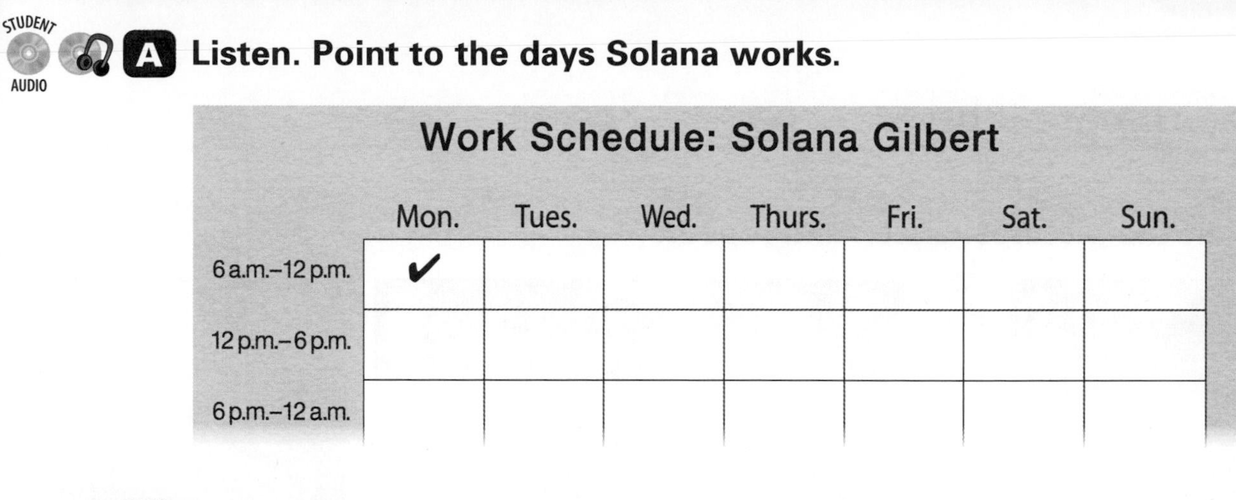

A Listen. Point to the days Solana works.

Work Schedule: Solana Gilbert

	Mon.	Tues.	Wed.	Thurs.	Fri.	Sat.	Sun.
6 a.m.–12 p.m.	✔						
12 p.m.–6 p.m.							
6 p.m.–12 a.m.							

B Listen again. Check (✔) when Solana works.

3 Practice your pronunciation

A Listen for *can* and *can't*.

can	can't
I **can** drive.	I **can't** drive.
I **can** work.	I **can't** work.

B Listen and check (✔) *can* or *can't*.

	can	can't
1.	✔	
2.		
3.		
4.		
5.		
6.		

TEST YOURSELF ✔

Copy the conversation. Close your book. Then add your own ideas and practice with a partner.

A: Can you ____________?
B: ____________.

1 Learn about more jobs

A Look at the pictures. Listen and repeat.

classroom aide
A classroom aide helps students.

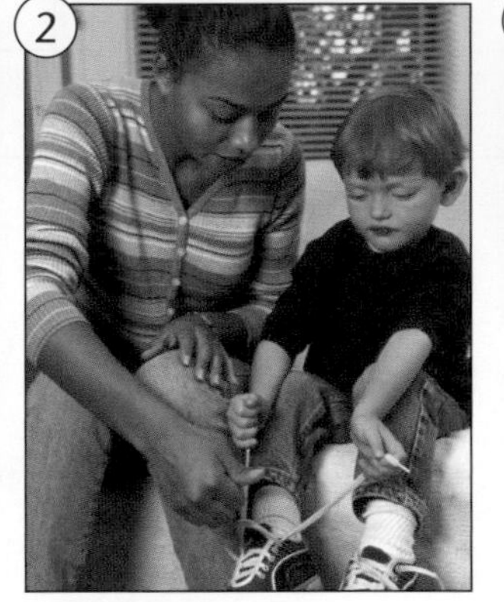

babysitter
A babysitter takes care of children.

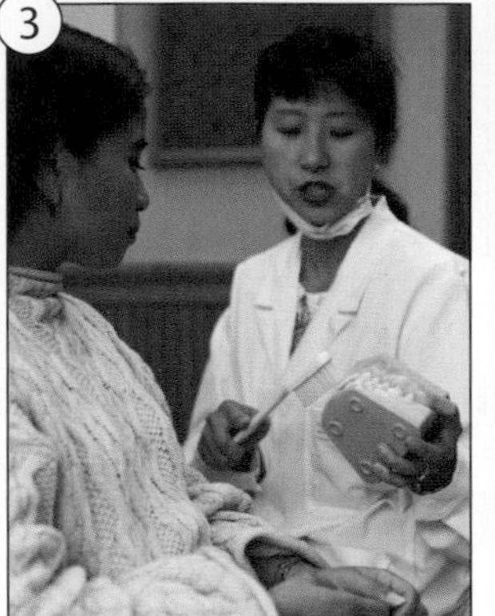

dental assistant
A dental assistant helps a dentist.

construction worker
A construction worker builds houses.

B Match.

_d_ 1. He builds houses.
____ 2. She takes care of children.
____ 3. He helps students.
____ 4. She helps a dentist.

a. babysitter
b. dental assistant
c. classroom aide
d. construction worker

2 Get ready to read

A Look at the pictures. Read the words.

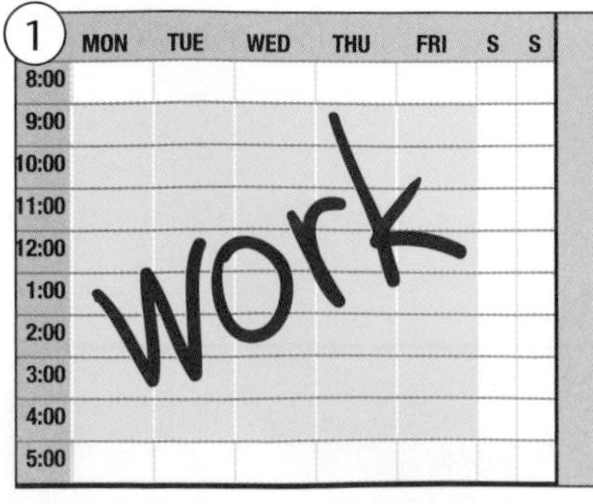

FT = full time = 40 hours per week

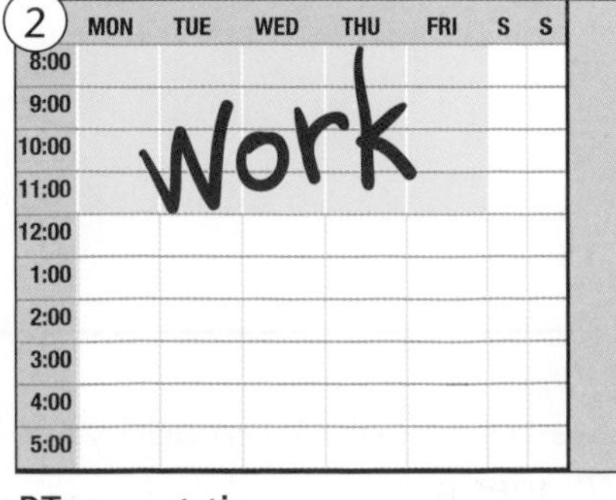

PT = part time

driver's license

B **Circle *yes* or *no*. Use your own information.**

Can you work full time?	yes	no
Can you work part time?	yes	no
Do you have a driver's license?	yes	no

3 Read job ads

A **Read the job ads.**

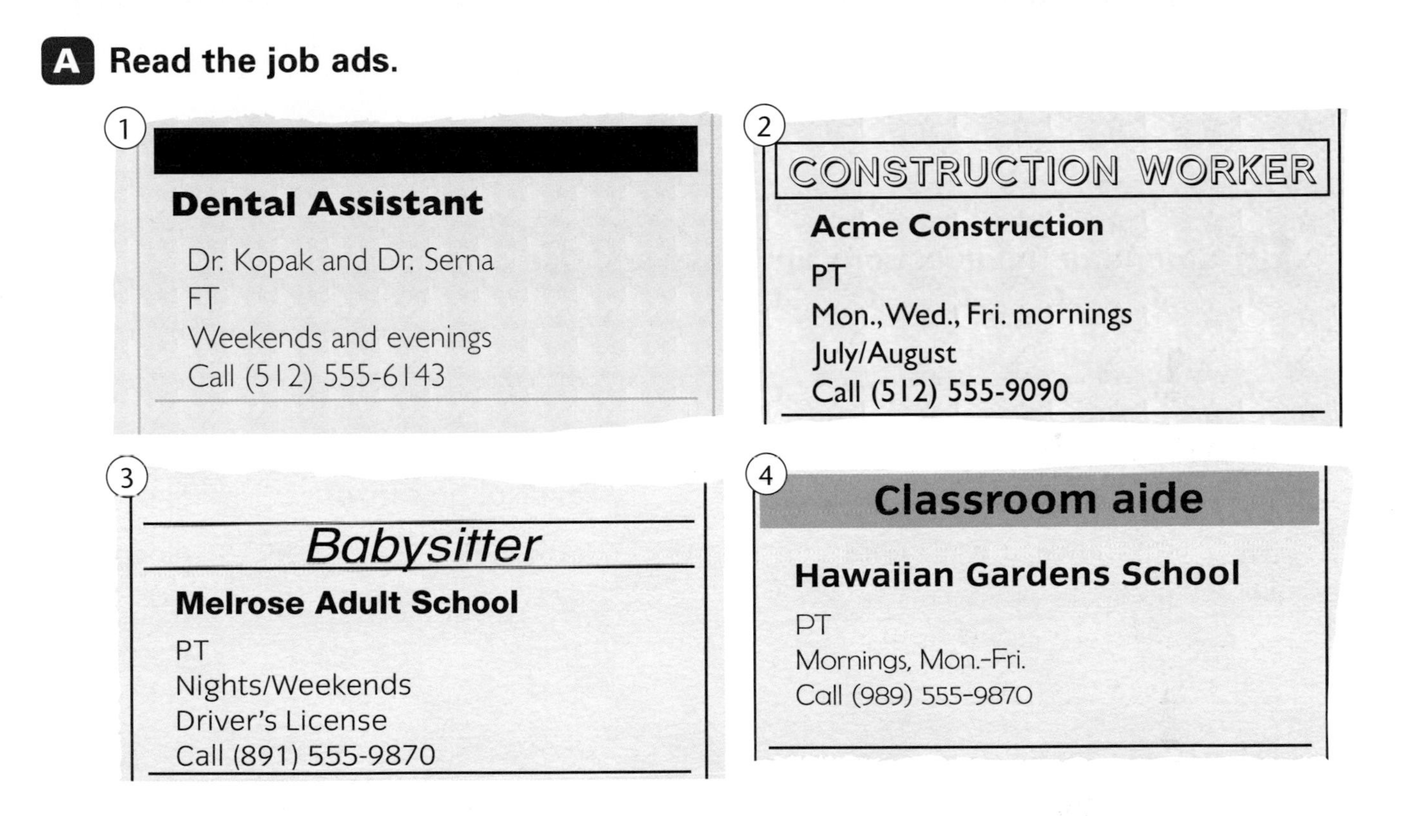

1
Dental Assistant
Dr. Kopak and Dr. Serna
FT
Weekends and evenings
Call (512) 555-6143
2
CONSTRUCTION WORKER
Acme Construction
PT
Mon., Wed., Fri. mornings
July/August
Call (512) 555-9090
3
Babysitter
Melrose Adult School
PT
Nights/Weekends
Driver's License
Call (891) 555-9870
4
Classroom aide
Hawaiian Gardens School
PT
Mornings, Mon.-Fri.
Call (989) 555-9870

B **Look at the job ads. Check [✔] the correct ads.**

	Ad 1	Ad 2	Ad 3	Ad 4
1. work on Saturdays	✔		✔	
2. work full time				
3. work July and August				
4. work in the morning				
5. have a driver's license				
6. work in the evening				

BRING IT TO LIFE

Bring a job ad from a newspaper or the Internet to class.
Circle 3 words you know.

New Jersey Transit
PT
Afternoons, Tues.-Fri.
Driver's License
Call (978) 555-8568

UNIT 12 Review and expand

1 Grammar

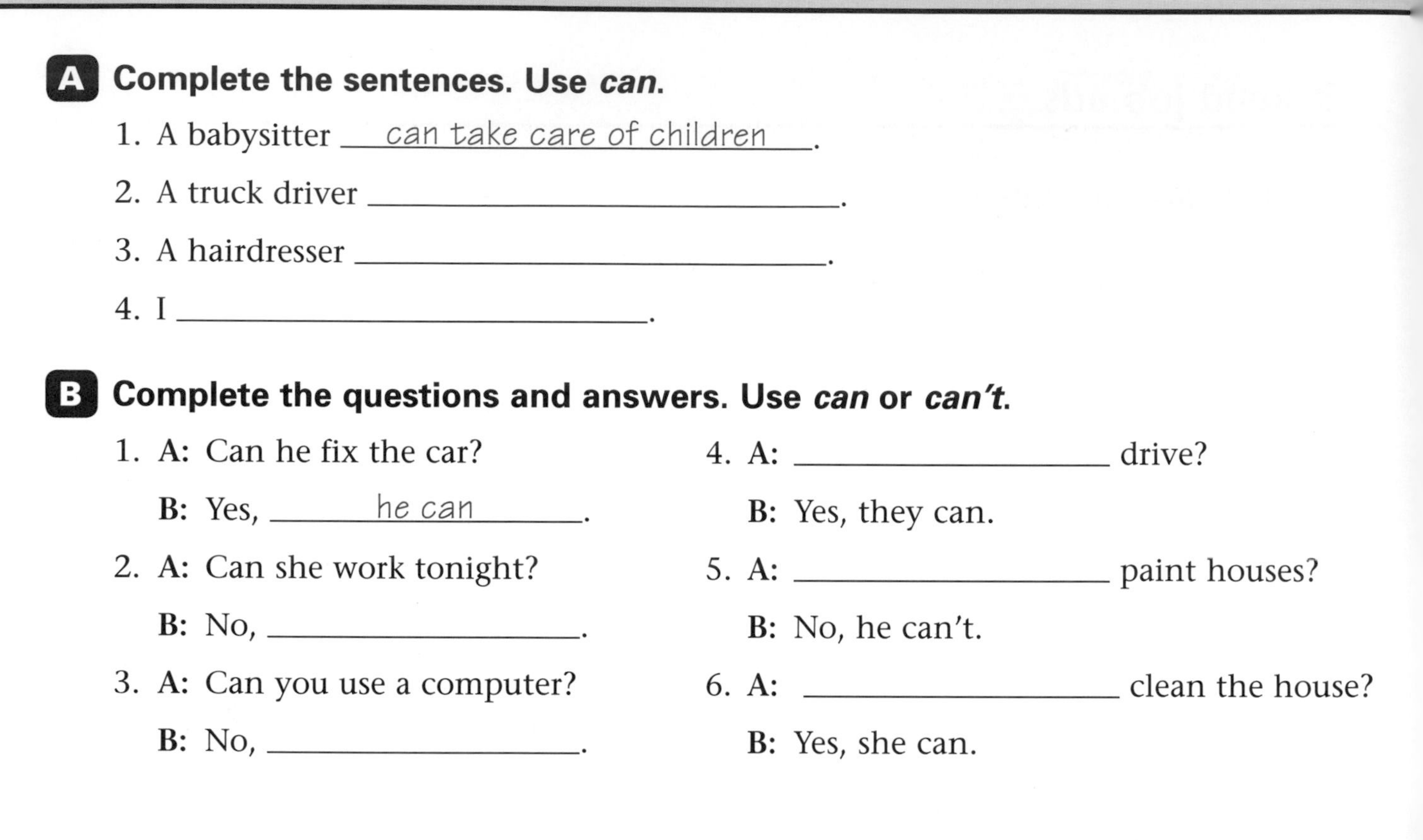

A Complete the sentences. Use *can*.

1. A babysitter ___can take care of children___.
2. A truck driver ______________________________.
3. A hairdresser ______________________________.
4. I ____________________________.

B Complete the questions and answers. Use *can* or *can't*.

1. **A:** Can he fix the car?
   B: Yes, ___he can___.
2. **A:** Can she work tonight?
   B: No, ____________________.
3. **A:** Can you use a computer?
   B: No, ____________________.
4. **A:** ____________________ drive?
   B: Yes, they can.
5. **A:** ____________________ paint houses?
   B: No, he can't.
6. **A:** ____________________ clean the house?
   B: Yes, she can.

2 Group work

A Work with 2–3 classmates. Look at the picture. Say what you see.

B Work with your group. Look at the picture in 2A again. Write what you see. Check your spelling in a dictionary.

1. construction worker
2. ______
3. ______
4. ______
5. ______
6. ______

C Work with your classmates. Make a list of the words from 2B.

PROBLEM SOLVING

A Listen. Look at the pictures.

Adriana's Problem

B Work with your classmates. Help Adriana.

a. Say, "I can't work Saturday. It's my friend's wedding."

b. Call in sick.

c. Go to work. Don't go to the wedding.

d. Other: ______

PRE-UNIT The First Step

Pg. 3 Lesson 1—Exercise 1D

M = Man, W = Woman
1. M: a
2. W: i
3. M: j
4. W: h
5. M: p
6. W: n
7. M: y
8. W: f

Pg. 3 Lesson 1—Exercise 2A

W = Woman, M = Man
1. W: Book. B-O-O-K. Book.
2. M: Pen. P-E-N. Pen.
3. W: Pencil. P-E-N-C-I-L. Pencil.
4. M: Student. S-T-U-D-E-N-T. Student.
5. W: Teacher. T-E-A-C-H-E-R. Teacher.
6. M: Paper. P-A-P-E-R. Paper.

Pg. 4 Lesson 2—Exercise 1E

W = Woman, M = Man
1. W: (212) 555-4261
2. M: (629) 555-7583
3. W: (748) 555-6932
4. M: (256) 555-1407
5. W: (387) 555-6340
6. M: (512) 555-7928
7. W: (936) 555-4821
8. M: (481) 555-6017

UNIT 1 Nice to Meet You

Pg. 8 Lesson 1—Exercise 1B

W = Woman, M = Man
1. M: open
2. W: close
3. M: circle
4. W: say
5. M: check
6. W: sign

Pg. 9 Lesson 1—Exercise 2B

W = Woman, M = Man
1. W: Close your book.
2. M: Say *pencil*.
3. W: Sign your name.
4. M: Read number one.
5. W: Circle your name.

Pg. 10 Lesson 2—Exercise 1D

M = Man
M: 1. My first name is Alan.
2. My last name is Woo.
3. I am a student.
4. My teacher is Marsha Lee.

Pg. 11 Lesson 2—Exercise 3A

W = Woman, M = Man
W: What is your first name?
M: John.
W: What is your last name?
M: Wong.

Pg. 15 Lesson 4—Exercise 2A

M1 = Man 1, M2 = Man 2, M3 = Man 3, M4 = Man 4,
W1 = Woman 1, W2 = Woman 2, W3 = Woman 3
1. M1: What's your name?
   W1: Mary. M-A-R-Y. Mary.
2. W1: What's your name?
   W2: Joan. J-O-A-N. Joan.
3. W2: What's your name?
   M2: Mel. M-E-L. Mel.
4. M2: What's your name?
   W3: Sandy. S-A-N-D-Y. Sandy.
5. W3: What's your name?
   M3: Jerry. J-E-R-R-Y. Jerry.
6. M3: What's your name?
   M4: Corvin. C-O-R-V-I-N. Corvin.

Pg. 15 Lesson 4—Exercise 3B

W = Woman, M = Man
1. W: meet
2. M: nice
3. W: write
4. M: read

Pg. 16 Lesson 5—Exercise 1B

W = Woman, M = Man
1. W: a notebook
2. M: an eraser
3. W: a binder
4. M: an English dictionary
5. W: a pen
6. M: an open book
7. W: an English class
8. M: a teacher

Pg. 19 Problem Solving—Exercise A

W = Woman
W: Amaya is in class. She is writing. Uh-oh! Her pencil!

UNIT 2 How are you feeling?

Pg. 20 Lesson 1—Exercise 1B

W = Woman
W: 1. fine
2. happy
3. excited
4. sad
5. hungry
6. thirsty
7. tired
8. sick

Pg. 23 Lesson 2—Exercise 3A

M = Man, W = Woman
M: Where are you from?
W: I am from Vietnam.
M: Where is Lian from?
W: She is from China.

Pg. 24 Lesson 3—Exercise 1B

M = Man, W = Woman
M: I am not tired.
W: You are not tired.
M: He is not tired.
W: She is not tired.
M: It is not tired.
W: We are not tired.
M: They are not tired.

Pg. 27 Lesson 4—Exercise 2A

M = Man, W = Woman
1. M: How are you feeling?
2. W: Where are you from?
3. M: What's your name?

Pg. 27 Lesson 4—Exercise 2B

M = Man, W = Woman
1. M: How are you feeling?
2. W: What's your name?
3. M: How are you feeling?
4. W: Where are you from?

Pg. 31 Problem Solving—Exercise A

M = Man
M: From Gary Prajak. Four-fifty-three Hill Street, Los Angeles, California, 91324.
To Emily Prajak, forty-nine eighty-seven Broad Street, Boston, Massachusetts. 02901? 02109? 02190? What's the zip code?

UNIT 3 What time is it?

Pg. 32 Lesson 1—Exercise 1B

W = Woman, M = Man
1. W: morning
2. M: afternoon
3. W: evening
4. M: night
5. W: 2:00
6. M: 2:15
7. W: 2:30
8. M: 2:45
9. W: noon
10. M: midnight

Pg. 35 Lesson 2—Exercise 1D

M = Man
M: 1. I go to school at 9:00.
2. I go to the library at 1:00.
3. I go to English class at 2:30.
4. I go to work at 6:00.

Pg. 35 Lesson 2—Exercise 3B

M = Man, W = Woman
1. M: It's 7 a.m.
2. W: It's 7 p.m.
3. M: It's 9 p.m.
4. W: It's 10 a.m.

Pg. 36 Lesson 3—Exercise 1B

M = Man, W = Woman
M: Is he at school?
W: Is she at school?
M: Is it 6:00?
W: Are you at home?
M: Are they at home?

Pg. 39 Lesson 4—Exercise 2A

M1 = Man 1, M2 = Man 2, M3 = Man 3, M4 = Man 4, W1 = Woman 1, W2 = Woman 2, W3 = Woman 3, W4 = Woman 4
1. M1: Hi. Is the school open?
W1: Yes, it is. We open at 10 a.m.
2. M2: Hello. Is the clinic open?
W2: No, it's not. We open at 8:00 in the morning.
3. W3: Is the library open at 9 p.m.?
M3: No, I'm sorry. It's closed.
4. W4: Hi. Is the store open at 10 in the evening?
M4: Yes, it is.

Pg. 40 Lesson 5—Exercise 1B

W = Woman, M = Man
1. W: Excuse me, what time is the bus to Salem?
2. M: Where is the train to Springfield?
3. W: My car is at home.
4. M: The plane is here.

Pg. 43 Problem Solving—Exercise A

M = Man
M: Go to the clinic at 10:00 a.m. My English class is from 9 a.m. to 12 p.m. Hmmm...

UNIT 4 What day is it?

Pg. 44 Lesson 1—Exercise 1B

W = Woman
W: 1. Sunday
2. Monday
3. Tuesday
4. Wednesday
5. Thursday
6. Friday
7. Saturday
8. day
9. week
10. today
11. tomorrow
12. weekend

Pg. 47 Lesson 2—Exercise 1D

M = Man
M: 1. It's April.
2. Next month is May.
3. My birthday is in July.

Pg. 47 Lesson 2—Exercise 3B

W = Woman, M = Man
1. W: 1946
2. M: 2008
3. W: 1985
4. M: 1972
5. W: May
6. M: February 1965

Pg. 48 Lesson 3—Exercise 1B

M = Man, W = Woman
M: The birthday party is on Tuesday at 7:00.
W: The class party is on Thursday at 5:00.

Pg. 48 Lesson 3—Exercise 1D

W = Woman, M = Man
1. W: It's on Wednesday.
2. M: It's at 12:30.
3. W: It's at 6:00.
4. M: It's on Tuesday.
5. W: It's at 9:45.
6. M: The class is on Friday morning.
7. W: The party is at 9:00.
8. M: The party is on Saturday.

Pg. 49 Lesson 3—Exercise 2B

A = Abena, G = Gloria
A: When is the birthday party?
G: It's on Tuesday.
A: Where is the party?
G: It's at my house.
A: What time is the party?
G: It's at 6:00.

Pg. 51 Lesson 4—Exercise 2B

W = Woman, M = Man
1. W: four-six-1999
2. M: seven-twelve-1960
3. W: nine-eleven-1982
4. M: ten-eight-2009
5. W: two-one-2007
6. M: five-three-1951
7. W: five-eleven-1974
8. M: eight-one-2008

Pg. 51 Lesson 4—Exercise 3C

W = Woman, M = Man
1. W: Tuesday
2. M: Thursday
3. W: twenty
4. M: thirteen
5. W: teacher
6. M: three

Pg. 55 Problem Solving—Exercise A

W = Woman
W: English class registration is on Tuesday, September 3rd, from 8 a.m. to 10 a.m.
Today is Tuesday, September 3rd. Oh, no! It's ten o'clock now!

UNIT 5 How much is it?

Pg. 56 Lesson 1—Exercise 1B

M = Man, W = Woman
1. M: bills
2. W: dollar
3. M: coins
4. W: cents
5. M: penny
6. W: nickel
7. M: dime
8. W: quarter

Pg. 57 Lesson 1—Exercise 2C

M = Man, W = Woman
1. M: seventy-five cents
2. W: two dollars
3. M: thirty-five cents
4. W: sixteen dollars
5. M: seven dollars
6. W: eighty cents

Pg. 59 Lesson 2—Exercise 1D

M = Man
M: 1. Shoe World is a good store.
2. The shoes are good.
3. The socks are cheap.

Pg. 59 Lesson 2—Exercise 3B

M = Man, W = Woman
1. M: Three dollars and twenty-five cents
2. W: Four dollars and fifty-two cents
3. M: Eight dollars and ninety-one cents
4. W: Six dollars and thirty-seven cents
5. M: Five dollars and forty-nine cents
6. W: Two dollars and seventy-four cents

Pg. 63 Lesson 4—Exercise 2B

W = Woman, M = Man
1. W: Your change is thirty-five cents.
2. M: That's seven cents change.
3. W: Your change is twenty-five cents.
4. M: That's sixteen cents change.
5. W: That's one dollar and ten cents change.
6. M: That's seven dollars change.

Pg. 64 Lesson 5—Exercise 1B

M = Man, W = Woman
1. M: a check
2. W: a money order
3. M: a debit card
4. W: cash

Pg. 67 Problem Solving—Exercise A

M = Man
M: Twenty dollars and fifteen cents. These shoes are cheap! Twenty dollars and five cents. Uh oh!

UNIT 6 That's My Son

Pg. 68 Lesson 1—Exercise 1B

W = Woman, M = Man
1. W: parents
2. M: mother
3. W: father
4. M: baby
5. W: girl
6. M: boy
7. W: friend
8. M: husband
9. W: wife

Pg. 71 Lesson 2—Exercise 1D

M = Man
M: 1. These are my children.
2. This is my daughter.
3. She's twenty years old.
4. This is my son.
5. He's fifteen years old.

Pg. 71 Lesson 2—Exercise 3B

M1 = Man 1, M2 = Man 2, W1 = Woman 1, W2 = Woman 2
1. M1: I'm divorced.
2. W1: I'm married.
3. M2: I'm single.
4. W2: I'm divorced.

Pg. 73 Lesson 3—Exercise 2B

M = Man, W = Woman
M: I live in New York.
W: You live in New York.
M: He lives in New York.
W: She lives in New York.
M: We live in New York.
W: They live in New York.

Pg. 75 Lesson 4—Exercise 2B

M = Man, W1 = Woman 1, W2 = Woman 2, W3 = Woman 3
1. M: I'm Mr. Jones.
2. W1: I'm Miss Wong.
3. W2: I'm Ms. Park.
4. W3: I'm Mrs. Chavez.

Pg. 79 Problem Solving—Exercise A

M = Man
M: Rosa's son is in fourth grade. He is not a good student. He plays baseball every day. He is very good at baseball.

UNIT 7 Do we need apples?

Pg. 80 Lesson 1—Exercise 1B

M = Man, W = Woman
1. M: fruit
2. W: bananas
3. M: apples
4. W: grapes
5. M: oranges
6. W: vegetables
7. M: broccoli
8. W: cabbage
9. M: corn

Pg. 83 Lesson 2—Exercise 1D

M = Man
M: 1. I like meat.
2. I don't like cheese.
3. My wife likes lamb.
4. My son likes eggs.
5. We all like bread.

Pg. 83 Lesson 2—Exercise 3A

M = Man, W = Woman
1. M: Pork is meat.
2. W: Grapes are fruit.
3. M: Cabbage is a vegetable.

Pg. 83 Lesson 2—Exercise 3B

W = Woman, M = Man
1. W: It's a vegetable.
2. M: It's meat.
3. W: It's fruit.
4. M: It's a vegetable.
5. W: It's fruit.
6. M: It's a vegetable.

Pg. 84 Lesson 3—Exercise 1B

M = Man, W = Woman
M: I don't like cabbage.
W: You don't like cabbage.
M: He doesn't like cabbage.
W: She doesn't like cabbage.
M: We don't like cabbage.
W: They don't like cabbage.

Pg. 87 Lesson 4—Exercise 2A

W = Woman
W: United Supermarket Sale!
Bananas are twenty-nine cents a pound.
Oranges are one dollar and fifty cents a pound.
Grapes are one dollar and ten cents a pound.
Apples are three dollars and eighty-seven cents a pound.

Pg. 88 Lesson 5—Exercise 1B

M = Man, W = Woman
1. M: a can of soup
2. W: a box of cereal
3. M: a bottle of juice
4. W: a can of coffee
5. M: a bottle of water
6. W: a box of tea

Pg. 91 Problem Solving—Exercise A

W = Woman
W: Duncan eats breakfast at six o'clock in the morning. He has donuts and coffee. Duncan eats lunch at the office. He eats pizza. Duncan eats a hamburger at night.

UNIT 8 Take Two Tablets

Pg. 92 Lesson 1—Exercise 1B

M = Man, W = Woman
1. M: head
2. W: eye
3. M: ear
4. W: nose
5. M: arm
6. W: stomach
7. M: hand
8. W: leg
9. M: foot

Pg. 95 Lesson 2—Exercise 1D

M = Man
M: 1. My family is sick.
2. My brother has a fever.
3. My sister has a stomachache.
4. My mother has a cough.
5. I have a cold.

Pg. 95 Lesson 2—Exercise 3A

D = Doctor, W = Woman, M = Man
1. D: What's the matter today, Mrs. Lopez?
W: Oh, I have a cough, a fever, and a sore throat.
D: Anything else?
W: Yes, I have a stomachache, too!
2. D: What's the matter today, Mr. Foss?
M: Oh, I have a headache and an earache.
D: Anything else?
M: Yes, I have a sore throat, too.

Pg. 96 Lesson 3—Exercise 1B

M = Man, W = Woman
M: I have the flu.
W: You have the flu.
M: He has the flu.
W: She has the flu.
M: We have the flu.
W: They have the flu.

Pg. 99 Lesson 4—Exercise 2A

WR = Woman Receptionist, W1 = Woman 1,
W2 = Woman 2, M1 = Man 1, M2 = Man 2
1. W1: Hi. This is Berta Sanchez. I need to see the doctor. I have a stomachache.
WR: Is Wednesday at eight o'clock OK?
W1: Wednesday at eight o'clock? Yes, that's fine. Thank you.
2. M1: Hi. This is Vincent Wu. I need to see the doctor. I have a sore throat.
WR: Is Wednesday at 8:30 OK?
M1: Wednesday at 8:30? Yes, thank you.
3. M2: Hi. This is Mr. Cabrera. My son needs to see the doctor. He has a cough.
WR: Is Thursday at 9:00 OK?
M2: OK. See you Thursday at 9:00.
4. W2: Hi. This is Tan Nguyen. I need to see the doctor. I have a headache.
WR: How about Friday at 9:30?
W2: Friday at 9:30? Well, OK.

Pg. 103 Problem Solving—Exercise A

W = Woman
W: Time for work. Oh, no! I have a cold. 98.6 degrees. Well, I don't have a fever. That's good.

UNIT 9 What size?

Pg. 104 Lesson 1—Exercise 1B

M = Man, W = Woman
1. M: black
2. W: white
3. M: red
4. W: blue
5. M: yellow
6. W: green
7. M: brown
8. W: orange
9. M: purple

Pg. 107 Lesson 2—Exercise 1D

M = Man
M: 1. It's January.
2. I'm wearing a blue coat.
3. I'm wearing brown boots.
4. I'm wearing a brown belt.

Pg. 107 Lesson 2—Exercise 3A

W = Woman, M = Man
1. W: She's wearing a red dress.
2. M: She's wearing an orange jacket.
3. W: He's wearing a black coat.
4. M: He's wearing blue shorts.

Pg. 108 Lesson 3—Exercise 1B

M = Man, W = Woman
M: I am wearing shoes.
W: You are wearing shoes.
M: He is wearing shoes.
W: She is wearing shoes.
M: It is wearing shoes.
W: We are wearing shoes.
M: They are wearing shoes.

Pg. 111 Lesson 4—Exercise 2B

M = Man, W = Woman
1. M: I'm looking for a blue T-shirt, size extra-large.
2. W: I'm looking for a yellow T-shirt, size medium.
3. M: I'm looking for a green T-shirt, size large.
4. W: I'm looking for a purple T-shirt, size extra-large.

Pg. 111 Lesson 4—Exercise 2C

WC = Woman Customer, MS = Man Salesclerk
1. WC: How much is the blue T-shirt?
   MS: It's twelve dollars and ninety-nine cents.
2. WC: How much are the black boots?
   MS: They're forty dollars.
3. WC: How much is the orange jacket?
   MS: It's twenty-five dollars.
4. WC: How much is the extra-large T-shirt?
   MS: It's fourteen dollars and ninety-nine cents.
5. WC: How much is the orange coat?
   MS: It's fifty-three dollars.
6. WC: How much are the brown boots?
   MS: They're eighty-seven dollars.

Pg. 115 Problem Solving—Exercise A

M = Man
M: Today is Ethan's birthday. Ethan's wife is giving him a present. It's a shirt. It's green, yellow, and red. Uh oh.

UNIT 10 Where's the bank?

Pg. 116 Lesson 1—Exercise 1B

W = Woman, M = Man
1. W: bookstore
2. M: bus station
3. W: drugstore
4. M: laundromat
5. W: park
6. M: bank
7. W: post office
8. M: restaurant
9: W: supermarket

Pg. 119 Lesson 2—Exercise 1D

M = Man
M: 1. My house is on Third Street.
2. There is a park next to the house.
3. There is a post office across from the park.
4. There is a bank on the corner.
5. I go to the bookstore on Sundays.

Pg. 119 Lesson 2—Exercise 3A

W = Woman, M = Man
1. W: The park is next to the house.
2. M: The laundromat is across from the apartment building.
3. W: The house is between the park and the apartment building.
4. M: The park is on the corner.

Pg. 120 Lesson 3—Exercise 1B

W = Woman, M = Man
W: There is a supermarket on Green Street.
M: There is a post office on Green Street.
W: There are two banks on Green Street.
M: There are three restaurants on Green Street.

Pg. 123 Lesson 4—Exercise 2A

W = Woman, M = Man
1. M: The drugstore is on the corner of First Street and Washington Street.
2. W: The restaurant is on the corner of Second Street and Washington Street.
3. M: The park is on Elm Street between First Street and Second Street.
4. W: The bookstore is on Second Street between Elm Street and Washington Street.

Pg. 124 Lesson 5—Exercise 1B

W = Woman, M = Man
1. M: Go to the fire station.
2. W: Get an ambulance!
3. M: Go to the DMV.
4. W: Call the police station.

Pg. 127 Problem Solving—Exercise A

M = Man
M: Elena is a student. It's 11 p.m. She is studying. She is not happy about the music.

UNIT 11 This Is My Home

Pg. 128 Lesson 1—Exercise 1B

M = Man, W = Woman
1. M: room
2. W: window
3. M: furniture
4. W: sofa
5. M: bed
6. W: dresser
7. M: TV
8. W: stove
9. M: refrigerator

Pg. 131 Lesson 2—Exercise 1D

W = Woman
W: 1. This is my home.
2. There are three bedrooms.
3. There is a table in the kitchen.
4. There is a window above the table.
5. I like my living room.

Pg. 131 Lesson 2—Exercise 3A

W = Woman
W: There is a desk below the window. There is a dresser next to the desk. There is a bed next to the dresser. There is a clock above the bed. There are two books on the desk.

Pg. 133 Lesson 3—Exercise 2B

M = Man, W = Woman
M: How many chairs are there in the living room?
W: How many windows are there in the living room?

Pg. 135 Lesson 4—Exercise 2A

M = Man, W = Woman
1. M: There are two bedrooms and one bathroom. The bathroom is between the bedrooms.
2. W: There are two bedrooms and one bathroom. The bathroom is next to the living room.
3. M: There is one bedroom and one bathroom. The bathroom is next to the bedroom.
4. W: There are two bedrooms and two bathrooms. One bathroom is next to the kitchen. One bathroom is between the bedrooms.

Pg. 136 Lesson 5—Exercise 1B

W1 = Woman 1, W2 = Woman 2, W3 = Woman 3, M1 = Man 1, M2 = Man 2
1. W1: I live in an apartment.
2. M1: I live in a rented room.
3. W2: I live in a mobile home.
4. M2: I live in a duplex.
5. W3: I live in a house.

Pg. 139 Problem Solving—Exercise A

W = Woman
W: Mr. and Mrs. Kolda are eating dinner. Oh, no! The lights are off. The lights are off in their house. The lights are off on their street.

UNIT 12 Yes, I can!

Pg. 140 Lesson 1—Exercise 1B

M = Man, W = Woman
1. M: gardener
2. W: painter
3. M: housekeeper
4. W: cashier
5. M: hairdresser
6. W: mechanic
7. M: truck driver
8. W: secretary
9. M: salesperson

Pg. 143 Lesson 2—Exercise 1D

W = Woman
W: 1. My friend is a painter.
2. He can paint houses.
3. My sister is a secretary.
4. She can use a computer.
5. I want a job.

Pg. 143 Lesson 2—Exercise 3A

W1 = Woman 1, W2 = Woman 2, M = Man
1. W1: My name is Lily Ng. I'm a secretary. I can use a computer and speak English.
2. W2: I'm Gabriela Valdez. I am a hairdresser. I can cut hair.
3. M: My name is Paul Fields. I am a truck driver. I can drive a car or a truck. I can also speak English.

Pg. 144 Lesson 3—Exercise 1B

W = Woman, M = Man
W: I can cut hair.
M: You can cut hair.
W: He can cut hair.
M: She can cut hair.
W: It can cut hair.
M: We can cut hair.
W: They can cut hair.

W: I can't drive.
M: You can't drive.
W: He can't drive.
M: She can't drive.
W: It can't drive.
M: We can't drive.
W: They can't drive.

Pg. 145 Lesson 3—Exercise 2B

M = Man, W = Woman
M: Can you use a computer?
W: Can he use a computer?
M: Can she use a computer?
W: Can they use a computer?

M: Yes, I can.
W: Yes, he can.
M: Yes, she can.
W: Yes, they can.

M: No, I can't.
W: No, he can't.
M: No, she can't.
W: No, they can't.

Pg. 147 Lesson 4—Exercise 2A

W = Woman
W: Solana works Monday, Tuesday, Wednesday, Saturday, and Sunday.
On Monday she works from 6 a.m. to 12 p.m.
On Tuesday she works from 6 a.m. to 12 p.m.
On Wednesday she works from 12 p.m. to 6 p.m.
On Saturday she works from 12 p.m. to 6 p.m.
On Sunday she works from 12 p.m. to 6 p.m.
She doesn't work on Thursday or Friday.

Pg. 147 Lesson 4—Exercise 3B

M1 = Man 1, M2 = Man 2, M3 = Man 3, W1 = Woman 1, W2 = Woman 2, W3 = Woman 3

1. W1: I can drive.
2. M1: I can't drive.
3. W2: I can work.
4. M2: I can't work.
5. W3: I can't fix cars.
6. M3: I can fix cars.

Pg. 151 Problem Solving—Exercise A

W = Woman
W: Adriana's friend is getting married on Saturday. Adriana works in an office. Her boss says, "See you on Saturday at 9:00."

THE SIMPLE PRESENT WITH *BE*

Statements		
I	am	a student.
You	are	
He She	is	
It	is	a book.
We You They	are	students.

Negative statements		
I	am not	a student.
You	are not	
He She	is not	
It	is not	a book.
We You They	are not	students.

Contractions	
I am = I'm you are = you're he is = he's she is = she's it is = it's we are = we're they are = they're	I am not = I'm not you are not = you're not he is not = he's not she is not = she's not it is not = it's not we are not = we're not they are not = they're not

Yes/No questions		
Am	I	at school?
Are	you	
Is	he she it	
Are	we you they	

Answers					
Yes,	I	am.	No,	I	'm not.
	you	are.		you	're not.
	he she it	is.		he she it	's not.
	we you they	are.		we you they	're not.

Information questions		
Where	am	I?
How	are	you?
How Where Who	is	he? she?
How long How much What What time When Where Who	is	it?
Where	are	we? you? they?

THE PRESENT CONTINUOUS

Statements		
I	am	sleeping.
You	are	
He She It	is	
We You They	are	

Negative statements		
I	am not	sleeping.
You	are not	
He She It	is not	
We You They	are not	

Yes/No questions		
Am	I	sleeping?
Are	you	
Is	he she it	
Are	we you they	

Answers					
Yes,	I	am.	No,	I	'm not.
	you	are.		you	're not.
	he she it	is.		he she it	's not.
	we you they	are.		we you they	're not.

THE SIMPLE PRESENT

Statements		
I You	like	rice.
He She It	likes	
We You They	like	

Negative Statements			
I You	don't	like	rice.
He She It	doesn't		
We You They	don't		

Contractions
do not = don't does not = doesn't

Yes/No questions			
Do	I you	like	rice?
Does	he she it		
Do	we you they		

Answers					
Yes,	I you	do.	No,	I you	don't.
	he she it	does.		he she it	doesn't.
	we you they	do.		we you they	don't.

CAN

Statements		
I You He She It We You They	can	work.

Negative Statements		
I You He She It We You They	can't	work.

Contraction
cannot = can't

Yes/No questions		
Can	I you he she it we you they	work?

Answers					
Yes,	I you he she it we you they	can.	No,	I you he she it we you they	can't.

THERE IS/THERE ARE

Statements			
There	is	a supermarket a drugstore	on First Street.
	are	two banks three restaurants	

Yes/No questions		
Is	there	a post office nearby? a laundromat nearby?

Questions with *How many*			
How many	bedrooms bathrooms	are	there?

THIS, THAT, THESE, AND *THOSE*

Singular Statements		Notes
This That	shirt is $35.	Use *this* and *that* when the people or things are near.

Plural Statements		Notes
These Those	pants are $14.	Use *these* and *those* when the people or things are far.

A AND *AN*

Articles	
a	pencil binder
an	eraser open book

PLURAL NOUNS

To make plural nouns	Examples	
For most nouns, add *-s*.	student—students	orange—oranges
If nouns end in *-s*, *-sh*, *-ch*, *-x*, add *-es*.	bus—buses	box—boxes
If nouns end in consonant + *y*, change *–y* to *–ies*.	family—families	country—countries
If nouns end in vowel + *y*, keep *–y* and add *-s*.	boy—boys	day—days
Some plural nouns do not end in *-s*, *-es*, or *-ies*. They are irregular plurals.	child—children man—men	person—people woman—women

SUBJECT PRONOUNS

Subject pronouns
I
you
he
she
it
we
you
they

POSSESSIVE ADJECTIVES

Possessive Adjectives
my
your
his
her
its
our
your
their

POSSESSIVES

Nouns		Notes
Gloria's Mr. and Mrs. Smith's	home is big.	For two or more nouns together, add -*'s* after the last noun.

PREPOSITIONS

Times and dates		Notes
The party is	on Tuesday. on Thursday.	Use *on* for days and dates. Use *at* for times.
	at 6:00. at 7:00.	

Locations			
The school	is	on	Pine Street.
		across from next to	the bus station.
		between	the post office and the park.
		on the corner.	
The sofa	is	in	the living room.
		below	the window.
The window		above	the sofa.

FREQUENCY AND TIME EXPRESSIONS

Frequency expressions		
Take two tablets	every twice a three times a	day.
	every four hours. every six hours.	

INDEX

ACADEMIC SKILLS

Pronunciation

Reading

Speaking

Writing

CIVICS

LIFE SKILLS

Consumer Education

Environment and the World

Family and Parenting

Government and Community Resources

Health and Nutrition

Interpersonal Communication

Safety and Security

Telephone

Time and Money

Transportation and Travel

TOPICS

WORKFORCE SKILLS

Obtaining Employment

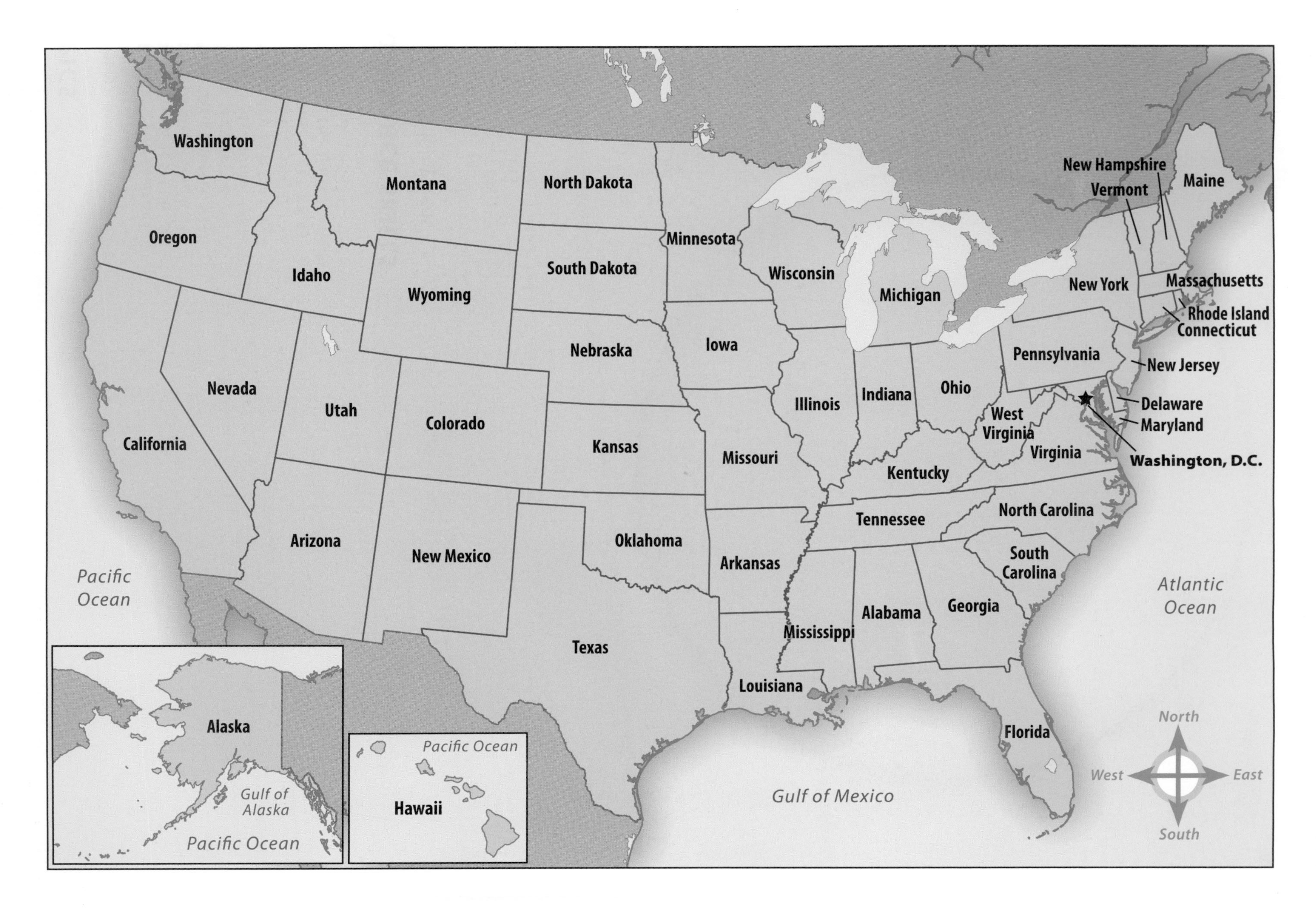
Washington
Montana
North Dakota
Minnesota
Oregon
Idaho
South Dakota
Wisconsin
Michigan
Wyoming
New Hampshire
Vermont
Maine
New York
Massachusetts
Rhode Island
Connecticut
Nebraska
Iowa
Pennsylvania
New Jersey
Nevada
Utah
Colorado
Illinois
Indiana
Ohio
West Virginia
Delaware
Maryland
California
Kansas
Missouri
Kentucky
Virginia
Washington, D.C.
Tennessee
North Carolina
Arizona
New Mexico
Oklahoma
Arkansas
South Carolina
Pacific Ocean
Atlantic Ocean
Alabama
Georgia
Mississippi
Texas
Louisiana
Alaska
Gulf of Alaska
Pacific Ocean
Pacific Ocean
Hawaii
Florida
Gulf of Mexico
North
West
East
South